ADDICTION—
THEORY AND
TREATMENT

Other volumes in the Adelphi University Postdoctoral Program in Psychotherapy Conference Series are:

ADDICTION— THEORY AND TREATMENT

New Approaches to an Old Problem

Compiled and Edited by

George D. Goldman, Ph.D.

Clinical Professor of Psychology,
Supervisor of Psychotherapy and
Director of Clinical Services,
Postdoctoral Psychotherapy Center,
Institute of Advanced Psychological
Studies, Adelphi University;
Private Practice, New York, N.Y.

Donald S. Milman, Ph.D.

Professor of Psychology and
Co-Director, Postdoctoral Program
in Psychotherapy, Institute of
Advanced Psychological Studies,
Adelphi University;
Private Practice, East Norwich, N.Y.

KENDALL/HUNT PUBLISHING COMPANY
Dubuque, Iowa, USA • Toronto, Ontario, Canada

We dedicate this book to two of our children, Deberah S. Goldman and Douglas Milman, who are following in their fathers' footsteps and are presently graduate students in Clinical Psychology. We hope that all of their dreams and all of their plans for their futures become realities.

CONTENTS

Addictive behavior is a disease entity related to man's existential, psychological and physiological dilemmas in relation to cultural demands. Psychodynamic issues are related to the compulsive characterological aspects in the individual's personality organization.

In this article drug addiction is seen as representing a failure of the early internalization of the mother's regulatory and drive soothing influences. Consequently, the drug abuser is viewed as having profound ego insufficiencies which interfere with their evolving ability to regulate tension, tame drives, or postpone immediate gratification. This lack of internalized regulations makes them turn to chemical regulators in order to simulate some temporary psychic equilibrium. Problems relating to the addict's self esteem, separation, anxiety, short comings of parental intrajects and a psychodynamic rationale for the selection of specific drug entities are also discussed.

Recurrent psychodynamic themes, such as the denial and acting-out of dependency and hostility, can be used as a focus in treatment of alcoholic patients. Individual variations of the themes are identified through a detailed history.

Addiction is seen as an expression of exaggerated self-reliance and reluctance to turn to others for help. Feelings of emptiness are decreased by filling up with self-provided substances. Treatment must foster a true sense of competence and self-control as well as provide the basis for developing involvement with others.

The summaries of the chapters have been submitted by each of the authors themselves and are being given to you unedited.

Milton S. Gurvitz, Ph.D.
Selection is essential for office treatment of alcoholics, eliminating the 'essential'. Reactive and neurotic alcoholics need to "hit bottom" first and this is to be expected. Reactive alcoholics need brief treatment with avoidance of dependency. Neurotic alcoholics require longer term therapy. Prognosis on this basis is good with analytic therapy with objectives of ego growth and analysis of resistance.

Richard L. Vickers, Ph.D. and Dolores Etrog, C.S.W.
Early memories of drug abusers reflect characteristic ego deficiency. The authors explore use of early memories obtained from the entire family of the abuser as a diagnostic and facilitative technique.

Lawrence Hatterer, M.D.
In order to understand and treat addictions one must go beyond the specific agent and practice. The word addicted has become generalized. No single addictive personality (addict) exists. People become addictive because specific etiological and constitutional factors contribute to their vulnerability to the addictive process. This process can be defined and diagnosed. It involves common inter-intra personal psychodynamics. One must look for the addictive complement and trigger mechanisms which can initiate and perpetuate the process. The process has a life history and stages, which can be cyclicic, periodic, or sporadic. The individual can shift from one addiction to another or sustain multiple addictions at different times. Understanding the above factors is essential to making an accurate diagnosis and to treatment.

Jay Livingston, Ph.D.
Traditional theories of compulsive gambling (1) take definitions for granted; (2) see compulsive gambling as irrational behavior; (3) seek its sources in internal pathology. In contrast, I argue that the act of definition is problematic; that each bet is rational; and that even abnormal gambling proceeds from normal motives. Instead of looking for unconscious motives and abnormalities, we can explain compulsive gambling by understanding the gambler's cognitions in their social context.

ACKNOWLEDGMENTS

This book, and the conference on which it was based, could never have come about without the help of certain people here at Adelphi and at Kendall/Hunt Publishing Company.

For their work on the conference which was tireless, innovative and conscientious, we wish to thank our secretaries, Mrs. Marge Burgard and Mrs. Sally Jones. They certainly made our lives at Adelphi much simpler and more pleasant by their efficiency, effectiveness, graciousness, and charm in doing their jobs. For their being there when we needed them and for their help in organizing many things, we wish to thank Ms. Bernardette Clark, Ms. Mary E. Gentile and Ms. Barbara Wilckens.

We are particularly appreciative of the tireless and devoted editing done by Ms. Shira Dentz. Her high level professional work has helped to make this book more readable and cohesive. She came through when we needed her despite monumental handicaps. Shira Dentz was ably assisted in her editing by Ms. Maureen Kennedy to whom both Shira and the Editors give a great deal of thanks and appreciation.

The working relationship with members of the Kendall/Hunt staff made a hard job easier by their pleasant and effective cooperation.

And, of course, we thank the Milman family, Marilyn, Douglas, and Lise, and the Goldman family, Belle, Ira, Carol and Debbie, for their patience and tolerance when we were so busy with so many things.

G.D.G.
D.S.M.

INTRODUCTION

To put into perspective some facts and figures on addiction can give us some idea of the enormity of addiction as a problem to the people of the United States and the need for a book such as this. For to understand addiction can also possibly help us control it.

One way of feeling some of the impact of this phenomenon on our economy, for example, is to examine incidence estimates. There are upwards of 200,000 narcotic addicts in the country at this time with probably anywhere from 7 to 10 million alcoholics. The loss of productive lives as well as the economic and societal losses are staggeringly high. An October, 1978, estimate by Secretary of HEW Califano indicated a possible 43 billion dollar loss to our economy this year alone because of alcoholism, and this does not take into account the loss through other addictions. Addiction is a problem of monumental importance to our country. Mental Health professionals can help through their understanding, treatment and cure of their addicted patients.

In this book descriptions and the psychodynamics of all addiction and their treatment are spelled out in detail. One immediately sees that there are different theoretical approaches to understanding the source of addictive behavior. The chapters of this book contain both theoretics and actual case experiences with addicts to illustrate and help us understand the theoretics in each instance.

Addiction is the dependency upon a substance or behavior to provide gratification and/or relief from tension. To resolve the addiction, the original need for it must be understood and resolved. The purpose of addiction as a substitution for the actual fulfillment of a need is but a temporary compromise as more of the addictive substance is needed to maintain the equilibrium the addict is seeking. The addiction itself then becomes a problem, interfering with the addict obtaining gratification from any other source as his addiction becomes a less and less pleasurable activity and more and more compulsive in nature. The resulting physiological and psychological dependence on his addictive substance assumes more and more control in his life, leaving the addict with few other activities other than those that center around and feed his addiction.

The underlying conflicts that may be manifested in addictive behavior are discussed in this book. Let us hypothesize that in a human's developing his personality, he or she is flooded with both inner and outer threatening stimuli without having, as yet, an adequate defensive structure. If there is an adequate mothering one and the correct amount of nurturing is present, the ego grows and matures appropriately. Then, for example, the child can tolerate and develop a tolerance for non-immediate gratification. If something interferes with this benign mothering process, this capacity to delay gratification will be somewhat impaired with a resultant predisposition to addiction.

One of the more important phases of development is during the weaning process. If there are traumas and disturbances, oral stimulation will play a more important role in the person's life. Also, certain traumas can tap into this developmental period and the person can regress back to it.

It is suggested that in the adult addicts's unconscious alcohol, drugs, smoking and certain behavioral excesses such as hypersexuality have a symbolic value comparable to being given to by the mother figure. Loneliness is appeased and nutrient needs met through the intake of these substances. Crucial then are these unresolved dependency needs when they are translated into the symptoms of addiction.

The addict needs a constant and continuing supply of whatever he is taking or doing to ward off the psychic pain and emptiness which is often felt as depression. The stimulation dispels the tension and has the same psychic effect as food and warmth did in infancy. Like the infant the addict is interpersonally a taker rather than a giver. Object relations are characteristically difficult, short-lived ones, where one object is readily exchanged for another, more gratifying object.

In this book, besides the two main addictions, drug and alcoholism, which are the most overtly destructive addictions, other addictions including behavioral ones are studied: these are specifically food, smoking, money, sexual practices and interpersonal dependencies. The addict's tendency towards masochism, as a coping mechanism, is seen to be acted out in his addictive behavior. The term "addiction" conjurs stereotyped images of "the addict," however, it is used here in this volume for description, without evaluative or pejorative connotations.

The book explores the enormity of damage caused by a chemical addiction which may include serious physiological injury, in addition to the psychic pain to the user and those in his family and environment. It shows how, when the addiction involves illegal narcotics, antisocial as well as criminal behavior may result, as the addict is sometimes forced to steal, prostitute himself or enter the illegal trade himself, in order to feed his habit.

The addictive personality is viewed to be as much a result of as a cause of the addictive process. It is a more defensive personality that serves the process that perpetuates the addiction. This process is referred to and further detailed in this book as a close understanding of it is essential to the elimination of the addictive pattern. Because of unique personal histories, family backgrounds, and particular socio-economic factors, no specific "addictive personality" can be categorized. Ensuing, however, in many of the chapters, are descriptions of several addictive personalities, as there are many common traits and characteristics in their behavior. Characteristically, an extremely low self-image and self-esteem is compensated for by a grandiose sense of self. This sense is fostered by the addict's belief that he is impervious to the consequences of his behavior, and is symbolized by his mastery over the addictive substance. To acknowledge that his addictive pattern is self-perpetuating and that he is no longer in control is to the addict ultimate surrender. Often, he will recognize his problem and seek help only after it has resulted in much destruction to himself and his environment, i.e., losing his job, spouse, alienation from his family, immediate danger to his health, etc. Whether it be self-inflicted pain or drugs, the addictive substance is used to suppress awareness of a conflict that cannot be dealt within the already existing character structure of the individual. As addiction becomes the central core activity of his life, the identity of the addict becomes synonymous with his addiction.

Addiction is presently a growing social problem, in many forms it is a common response to external pressures in our shifting society. The persistency of the problem necessitates innovative methods of treatment. Such programs are the focus in the final section of this book. Treatment attempts to relieve an addiction, and aims at reintegration of new behaviors to reduce the anxiety that has triggered the need for the addictive substance.

Thus, the book ably and clearly takes us from understanding the dynamics of addiction, clarifies the addictive process and finally gives attempts at alleviating the addiction. It is divided into these three sections, each with a unity and consistency that aids in the clarification of addiction in our country today.

Part I

Addiction as a Replacement for Other Ego Gratifications

The underlying motivations in an individual to seek substances that alter his state of consciousness are described in this section as arising from an inability to gratify his needs and as an attempt to replace the ensuing frustration with synthetic stimulation. The more intense the persons' limitations the more deeply felt are the mounting frustrations and the more desperate the drive becomes to eliminate the pain through the intake of pleasure inducing substances. The pleasure is temporary and his inability unresolved although accentuated as the relief afforded by the substance fades. The contrast between his former ecstacy and present dissatisfaction emphasizes the deficiency that initially caused him to turn to the substance and he turns to it again. Survival is at stake as this rhythm becomes fixed and dependency on an external substance is established. The self-destructiveness of this cycle, and the sources of the patient's inability to cope with life is elaborated upon in the following six chapters.

Addiction is prompted by feelings of helplessness and yet an adamant belief in self-sufficiency. It is this unrealistic stance that contributes to the feeling of helplessness, as the denial of dependency needs initiates and secures the addiction. The liberation to be found in the understanding and love of others is thus shunned while the absence of the fulfillment of this need is intrinsic in the despairing helplessness. As the addict cannot function without his substance his world centers on this activity. The resulting perspective and physiological effects of his addiction produce further symptoms that affectively alienate him from society. Other substances may be used to compensate for the decreasing gratification obtained in the original stimulant. The problems exacerbate as withdrawal is symptomatic and the addict is exposed to danger to his health and isolated within an impersonal world: that of his substance dependency.

The keynote chapter of this section is the one by Dr. Leon Salzman which is an overview of the material covered in this section. His focus is on the psychodynamic meaning, to the individual, of the particular compromise of addiction to other ego gratifications.

1

Drs. Sternberg and Cohen, in *Drug Dependency: The Substitution of Substance Nutrients For Love,* present an in-depth study of what they suggest is the original dynamic of the addiction. They suggest that addiction is the result of a faulty internalization of the early mothering role to alternately provide gratification of the infant's needs and to allow frustration. The maintenance of a consistent rhythm is necessary to enable the successful separation between mother and child which is essential for the ego-development of the child. If this process is unsuccessful, dependency problems persist. No learned coping mechanism is established. This early process correlates with the hunger/satiety pattern in drug addiction. As the person begins coming "down," his discomfort warrants another dose. As early dependency needs were not fulfilled the conflict develops into a neurotic compromise where gratification remains of immediate importance. In this article, the compromise theorized is drug addiction and its ramifications. Through this observation, neurosis is understood as a symbolic replacement for the deprivation of ego-gratification during this internalization process.

Dr. William Browne, in his article, *Defense Mechanisms Expressed In Alcoholism,* and Dr. Richard Vickers and Dolores Etrog, C.S.W., in their article, *The Extension of Early Dependency Problems in the Development of Drug Addiction,* impress the significance of family history in their observations that substance dependency is a working out of childhood conflicts; resulting from the resignation to what is perceived as a hopeless situation, that is, the harboring of needs that can neither be expressed nor fulfilled. A perception at the base of which is the experience of repeated disappointment in relationships, is a focus in the chapter by Dr. Jacobs, *Characteristic Motivations In Addictive Behavior,* where he analyzes the use of alcohol as substitute food and warmth. The expression of strong dependency is studied in the pattern of alcoholism as well as in the treatment of neurotic alcoholics by Dr. Gurvitz in his article, *Understanding the Neurosis in Alcoholism.*

Chapter 1

THE NEUROTIC COMPROMISE OF ADDICTION

Leon Salzman, M.D.

Leon Salzman, M.D.

Dr. Salzman is Professor of Clinical Psychiatry at Georgetown University Medical School. He is Professor of Clinical Psychiatry at Albert Einstein Medical College; Past President, American Academy of Psychoanalysis; is a member of the American Psychoanalytic Association. He is the author of DEVELOPMENTS IN PSYCHOANALYSIS, THE OBSESSIVE PERSONALITY, and THE TREATMENT OF THE OBSESSIVE PERSONALITY.

3

Addiction of various kinds, particularly drugs and alcohol, has created sociological, theological and moral problems from the time of the discovery that grapes, roots and flowers had virtues which went beyond their nutritional values and visual satisfactions. When mystical and dissociated states were honored and manic frenzies and cortical disorganizations dignified as divinely inspired, the toxic effects of these substances inspired awe and reverence. With increasing sophistication and a growing need for stability, responsibility and cerebral clarity, and a more rational and less primitive concept of God and religious practice, excessive use of these same exhilarant and intoxicant plants was viewed as destructive and was criticized, restrained or punished by the authorities. Addictions as such were unknown to the early pagan and judaic theologies since these substances were an intrinsic part of the ritual and dogma of these religious systems. Only in later Christian teachings against gluttony and licentiousness was such unrestrained behavior condemned as immoral and sinful. Until recently and even now, among large segments of our population, rich, and poor, intelligent or ignorant, sophisticated or backwards, the view still persists that the excessive and undisciplined involvement in certain activities, namely the intake of food, drugs or the abandonment in excessive pleasures in sex, gambling or the like, is a moral defect or a degenerative human development related to sinful, ungodly and inhuman causes. Uncontrolled behavior in every form is looked upon with scorn, contempt and disdain so that the goal of cultured and mature living is to restrain and control one's appetite, interests, emotions and activity.

Consequently, it is not surprising that the cultural attitude toward the addictions, which are in essence uncontrolled and undisciplined involvement in certain drugs or activities, are strongly condemned in moral terms rather than viewed as disease processes requiring the medical as well as non-medical resources of the community. Until very recently the approach to these individuals and the social catastrophies which resulted from their behavior was directed at spiritual value systems and moral exhortation, theological sermonizing and humanistic appeals to the use of will power was stressed. If these failed, then the use of restraint, imprisonment and punishment followed. Whether such prescriptions can be useful is not the issue at this moment. What should be noted is that such attitudes derive from a view of the phenomenon that does not take into account the centuries of growth of understanding of how man functions, and what devices and techniques he utilizes to minimize his discomforts and anxieties. Neither does it sufficiently acknowledge the human propensity to evade insuperable difficulties by escapist techniques and to take recourse into blissful and fantastic solutions which avoid confronting the real problems. Such tendencies characterize all men and not only depraved, degenerate, sinful, and diabolical humans. These moralizing attitudes fail to comprehend the advances in our understanding of human behavior which have revealed that there are activities in man that go on beyond his control and outside of his awareness and regardless of his desires and wishes to alter or terminate such behavior, he cannot do so until he comprehends the sources and motive power that maintain the compulsive activity. More significantly, such attitudes do not take into account the enormous knowledge of the physiology of man and the effect of these toxic agents which, producing physiological or psychological addiction or a combination of both, render the individual incapable of determined and willful behavior even if all the prior considerations are understood and overcome.

It is only in very recent years that we have been able to study such behavior in psychological terms of what motivates or drives man to it in spite of his intellectual, spiritual and humanistic desires to avoid such action. The emphasis on causative factors, such as degeneracy or hereditary taint or neuropathic predisposition, implied a psychopathic tendency that overlooked the individual or the influence of the culture. As a reaction to the previous neglect of individual or characterological factors, psychodynamic theories tended toward formulations of the opposite extreme and overlooked the chemical characteristics of the addicting agent or the social conditions encouraging escapist defenses, focusing exclusively on the inner dynamics which were held responsible for the addiction.

Taking a historical view, we can spotlight the deficiencies in these formulations as well as limit the endless controversies regarding the social value of some of the drugs, namely the hallucinogens and other stimulants, by clearly defining the addictions as socially and individually destructive, and the concern of the community as well as the individual. The addictions therefore require a therapeutic program that acknowledges and encompasses these factors. Such a view might reduce the inclination to be drawn to the extraordinary range of prescriptions and nostrums, each drawing on a single or combination of features and claiming sole virtue in eliminating these profound social and individual disasters.

More and more, addictive behavior is being viewed as a disease related to man's existential, psychological and physiological limitations which develops in an interaction with the cultural situation, both past and present. At this point of history we know more about the external forces, pressures, denials and determinants of such behavior than the inner psychodynamic issues. I shall attempt to present some thoughts that may add to our knowledge of the aetiology of the addictive disorders from a psychodynamic point of view.

Psychodynamic explanations of addictive behavior were first offered by Freud and his colleagues who viewed the behavior in the category of characterological disorders generally involving notions about orality and the overwhelming needs for reassurance and security that comes from a weak ego. Addiction being defined as an insatiable craving for certain substances or activities which eliminates unpleasure or induces a state of euphoria, acknowledged excessive dependency and immaturity. Dr. R.A. Savitt's formulation represents the range of psychodynamic thinking on the addictions. He said, "Object relationships are on an archaic level and the addict is unable to experience love and gratification through the usual channels of incorporation and introjection. Because of the inability to tolerate delay, he seeks an emergency measure which bypasses the oral route of incorporation in favor of a more primitive one, the intraveneous channel." This formulation, sometimes includes notions of infantile omnipotence or narcissistic mortification, defective superego, oral deprivation, repressed homosexual tendencies, and has had a widespread influence in the development of therapeutic programs to date even though their application was limited and their value highly doubtful. The formulations of S. Freud, F. Alexander and S. Rado attempted to identify specific characterological traits that related directly to the particular addiction, whether it was alcohol or drugs. The early psychoanalytic theorists viewed the addictions as distortions of the developing libido involving oral incorporative drives and representing repressed oral-dependencies and latent passive homosexual striving. In general, whatever the mode of entry, it was assumed that addictions were desires to escape from stressful situations and regressive gratifications of repressed or inhibited impulses.

Initially Freud believed that addictions were substitutes for sexual satisfaction and he said in 1893 (Vol. 3, Page 276), "Not everyone who has occasion to take morphine, cocaine, chloral hydrate and so on, for a period acquires in this way an addiction to them. Closer inquiry usually shows that the narcotics are meant to serve directly or indirectly as a substitute for a lack of sexual satisfaction."

In 1897 (from Schur, page 61) in a letter to Fleiss, he attributed all addictions to this single source and said, "I have gained the insight that masturbation is a primary addiction," and that the other addictions, alcohol, morphine, tobacco, etc., enter into life only as a substitute for a withdrawal (symptom) from it. This addiction plays an enormous role in hysteria, and my great unsurmounted obstacle is wholly, or in part, to be found in it. The doubt of course arises whether such an addiction is curable, or whether analysis and therapy must stop short at this point and remain content with transforming a hysteria into a neurasthenia." S. Rado postulated a quasi-orgasm that involved the whole alimentary canal which he called an alimentary orgasm that accounted for alcoholic addictions and he extended this notion to all addictions regardless of the route of entry of the addicting substance. At a later date, he de-emphasized these factors and reformulated his theory of addiction relating it to depressions and elations and the attempt to deal with painful tension in individuals with a high degree of intolerance to pain. These notions were still tied to the instinct theories although Rado placed great emphasis on the vicious circle which developed around the feelings of invulnerability that permitted an individual to deal with his feelings of low esteem by drugs which produced elation and gave him an illusory feeling of power and invulnerability. The post drug effect with its depression required the drug to again reinstate the fleeting elation. This cycle was tied to the libidinal deficiencies of the individual even though external situations might be supporting factors.

Everybody involved in studying and treating the addictions has emphasized the escapist function of drugs and alcohol and the need to deny reality. The early psychoanalytic theorists emphasized the sexual issues, involving either an unwillingness to recognize a developing impotence or a repressed homosexual striving. In this connection Freud said, "The alcoholic will never admit to himself that he has become impotent through drink. However much alcohol he can tolerate, he cannot tolerate this piece of knowledge." (Vol. 1, Page 210) In recent years, the need to escape reality is viewed in much larger terms than sexual capacity and is not necessarily considered to be part of a psychopathic tendency or some issue of homosexuality.

Addictions are probably not limited to specific character types, nor do certain characterological traits or characteristics predispose an individual to addictive potentialities. Thus they should not be classified under character disorders but viewed as universal responses to internal and external pressures which the community looks upon as a disease, a disorder, or an anti-social act. This implies that certain defense mechanisms may be so disruptive to the individual's functioning and so disorganizing to the individual's social role that they stimulate repressive or primitive responses from the community. In the addictions the techniques of defense, namely denial, rationalization, projection and many others, are responses to the human propensity for easy magical solutions and for man's inability and unwillingness to endure discomforts or tolerate anxiety over any period of time. Some psychiatrists see addiction not as an escape, but a search for a better life in the face of insuperable, realistic obstacles and this view is extremely helpful in understanding the phenomenon of drug dependence and drug addiction. The methods employed in this humanistic striving for more productive living may have disastrous consequences; nevertheless the intent is to move towards a higher, more satisfactory mode of living. This was its principal role in religious rituals and, even though it provides an escape from the realistic burdens of living, it promotes creative and humanistic fantasies. This view of drug use helps us to understand the futility of sermonizing or using moral injunctions to uplift the "lost souls" rather than recognizing their misdirected efforts at fuller and more productive living. This issue is not universally present in drug abuse, particularly of the narcotic variety, but is extremely common in alcoholism and addictions utilizing stimulants and marijuanas. With the narcotizing drugs, kleptomania and obesity, it is more difficult to identify the positive strivings in the addictive process. Thus our understanding of psychodynamics of addiction will need to comprehend their use for transcendence as well as escape.

Our therapeutic program will be significantly influenced by the way the community looks upon addictions to food, drugs, and to alcohol as well as towards stealing or gambling. Whatever the agent, or the psychodynamic motivations for addiction, the ultimate physiological and psychological cycle is similar and we then are dealing with a single disorder, even though properties of the addicting substances and the cost of obtaining them have secondary consequences which dramatically influence the clinical picture and therapeutic program. In order to develop a comprehensive psychodynamic understanding of addictions, they must be examined from three frameworks:

1. Physiological—The toxic effect of the substance and its influence on cellular metabolism produces a physiological craving in spite of any desire to terminate its use. Prolonged use of the drug results in organ dysfunction which requires treatment with other drugs to overcome the deficits, thereby producing a vicious cycle. This is particularly true with those substances which impair sexual potency and creative potentiality when the drug may have been taken in the first instance to deal with concerns. Drug, alcohol and food addictions cause the most physiological damage.

2. Psychological—This includes an understanding of the character structure of the individual and the underlying needs that are being dealt with in the particular addiction. Here the factors of dependence, orality, masochism and passivity play a large role but the use of obsessional devices to control and manipulate oneself and the environment are even more important. The type of addiction, whether it be drug, food, gambling, stealing or masturbation, can be related to specific factors in the individual's psychology to account for the choice of one type of defense over another and one variety of compulsion in contrast to another. It is in this area that psychotherapy has its greatest potential in the overall therapeutic programs.

3. Cultural—In this category we must not only include the cultural pressures that tend to initiate, promote and sustain certain escapist maneuvers, be they drugs or food, but also the attitudes toward the particular addiction. Some addictions are almost inevitably involved with criminal and punishable activities, while others are viewed as aesthetically or morally reprehensible. Both types of community response produces severe psychological distress to the user which tends to increase the addictive process rather than support the individual's effort to abandon it. The community includes not only the influence of the immediate family and one's idiosyncratic life history within it, but

also the broader social units including the politics, religion, economic and historical forces that impinge on the individual.

Surpassing the significance of addictions is the even greater medical and social disruption caused by drug independence. This includes the widespread use of nicotine, alcohol and the fantastic assortment of pills, nostrums, dietary fads, psycho-philosophical prescriptions including meditation, transcendental and transactional experiences with gurus, gestaltist leaders, prophets and teachers. We must distinguish between drug dependence and drug abuse. Drug dependence speaks loudly and emphatically about the ills of our technological culture overburdened by Vietnam, racism, hypocrisy, economic recession and depression. But dependence is not yet compulsion. Dependence on drugs or devices may arise for many reasons and serve many purposes which can be generalized under two headings (a) analgesic, (b) stimulants. In either case, drugs are taken to alleviate painful feelings or to stimulate and enhance pleasurable affects, and the individual does not suffer from this behavior, but enjoys it. This seems to be the case in most instances with the use of marijuana and alcohol.

The transition from drug dependence to addiction is not simply a matter of character structure or interpersonal or social disturbances; it is related to the pleasant effects of the drug combined with a capacity to deny the deleterious effects. This latter factor, I believe, accounts for the development and persistence of drug addictions in contrast to occasional drug abuse, and is the key issue in other addictive disorders, such as obesity, gambling, and masturbation as well as the drugs, and "The more potent a dependence-producing substance and the more pleasant the psychopharmacological effects, the quicker and stronger is the development of the addiction," says Bejerot.(3)

Drug abusers can also be categorized as (a) the experimenter or explorer of the range of human potentialities who dabbles for a while with drugs as with other activities, and (b) the compulsive or addicted user where the combination of psychological and physiological factors serve to maintain the compulsion.

Any individual can develop an addiction if certain drugs are taken over a period of time. Bejerot in his excellent article, "Theory of Addictions as Artificially Induced Drives," indicates that "Probably everyone after only a week's continual use of cocaine would long for the drug for the rest of his life, so strong and pleasurable are its effects during the first phase of abuse."(3)

In this connection, Freud, who discovered cocaine and advocated and used it quite extensively for a while, was responsible for producing an addiction in his highly regarded teacher Ernest Fleischl von Marxow, a famous physiologist in the Bruche Laboratories where Freud worked. Fleischl, known to most of us for the Fleischl stain, developed a morphine addiction because of severe pain in an amputation neuromata. Max Schur, in *"Freud:* Living and Dying," describes Freud's harrowing nightly vigils with Fleischl who developed a cocaine addiction following Freud's attempt to cure the morphine addiction. The symptoms of the cocaine addiction were even more disastrous than morphine resulting in physical and mental deterioration. His friend Fleiss also used it extensively in his ENT practice and Freud himself used it occasionally for its stimulating effect, as well as prescribing it for his fiancee Martha and his sister. Schur says, "However, neither they nor he had developed an addiction to cocaine. We can only speculate why Freud, who was addicted to nicotine, did not develop an addiction to cocaine."(10)

Some addictions, namely drugs and alcohol, have physiological accompaniments that require continued use because of the biochemical changes they produce, while other addictions, namely gambling or compulsive stealing or kleptomania, are maintained exclusively by psychological imperatives and compulsions, bolstered by a defense structure which prevents a realistic confrontation with the consequences of the behavior. Drug addiction therefore does differ essentially from other addictions in this significant regard, even though the underlying psychological factors may operate in both as major supports for their maintenance.

There are certain characteristics of the addictive process, which are universally manifested, such as the element of compulsion and the capacity of the addicting substance to relieve the immediate anxiety even if it produces greater anxiety over the long range. The addict's inability to tolerate discomfort or to postpone gratification even for a brief period of time makes him appear infantile and immature and sparks the demand for the immediate use of a drug whatever the future consequences might be. This is often described by observers as a gluttonous urge for fulfillment which in alcoholism, obesity or drug addiction has been called orality.

The compulsive aspects of addictive behavior involves pharmacological agents or other behavior patterns which are pursued in a typically ritualistic fashion in order to deal with the addict's intolerable anxieties. The initial phases of such a compulsion is the abuse of drugs or the success of the behavioral patterns which reflect social and psychological conflicts, but when the addiction develops we are dealing with a different dimension of behavior. Now choice is eliminated and a compulsion supervenes and the dynamics and patterns of behavior can be viewed as a syndrome in its own right. (3) Freud acknowledged the compulsive nature of addictive processes in dealing with a case of alcoholism when he said, "The compulsions transferred from brooding to motor impulses, namely, drinking."(6, Vol. 7)

Davidson noticed the marked similarity of addiction to the compulsive neuroses. He was referring to the mounting tension in addicts—which seems to be relieved only by taking the addictive medication. He said, "Psychologically, it seems strikingly similar to a compulsive (neurotic) reaction. The kleptomaniac or pyromaniac will tell you, 'I get no pleasure out of stealing (or setting fires) but I have a mounting unendurable tension (or anxiety) which can be relieved in this way.' "

To justify the continued use of a drug that one has no control over, the user frequently denies the physiological danger involved or else insists on his ability to terminate its use whenever he makes up his mind to do so. At times the addict must convince himself of the safety and value of the drug, either by being unaware of the consequences of its use or immediately denying them when they are evident. He invariably insists that he is really exempt from the effect of the drugs and can control the intake if he wishes to. This is a grandiose pretension invariably present in the obsessive-compulsive neurosis and is a crucial factor in maintaining the addiction. Such individuals insist that they are significantly different from other people, and that they can control or modify the effects and the consequences of the drug on them.

Grandiosity is the assumption of an exalted superior state which is beyond realistic possibility or actuality. While it is related to a feeling of high esteem and worth, it is qualitatively different. It is an illusory conception of strength, unjustified by actual or potential achievement. It is a defensive and adaptive development which arises out of certain psychological needs. Its characteristic presence in the obsessional neurosis casts some light on its adaptive role in the psychological problems of obesity, alcoholism, narcotic addiction, compulsive gambling, masturbation, and kleptomania.

In all these conditions the common thread of grandiosity is to be found when the individual tends to assume a privileged status. In each instance the grandiose feelings are expressed in terms of being exempt from the consequences of one's behavior, and not being subject to the laws of nature, which accounts for the excesses in the person's activity. It is a short step from a compulsive necessity to be universally capable, never deficient, and all-knowing to feeling super-human. Grandiosity is the negation of real self-esteem; it denies one's real assets and demands impossible, super-human attributes to overcome one's doubts.

It is a commonplace that alcoholics cannot moderate their drinking. It is all or nothing. This is precisely the obsessional problem. After abandoning all controls and getting lost in alcoholic binges, or drug reveries, the illusory superman can be revived in the grandiose fantasies of the intoxicated state. After an alcoholic bout there is great remorse and guilt, which produces the inevitable resolution to abandon the addiction. Since the underlying compulsion is untouched, the resolution has no chance of succeeding. The inability to honor his resolution only reinforces the awareness of his inability—which produces more drinking. The grandiose patterns that ensue not only serve temporarily to reinstate the illusion of superhuman capacity for control but also serve to deceive the person into believing that he can exert the necessary control whenever he decides to do so. This feeling of privilege and exemption from human frailties and natural laws plays a prominent role in the alcoholic addictive state. The alcoholic always insists that he can drink moderately and that he can stop in time. For him it is a grandiose statement—with all the deception and illusion conveyed by such claims. The alcoholic may secretly believe his grandiose claims and his superior capacities and skills. He may even demonstrate it in his contempt for himself and others, before and during his alcoholic bout. He may admire his cleverness in deceiving others and in outwitting them in the never-ending hunt for the bottle. In this way he is emphasizing the grandiose view of himself and his exemption from being human. He cannot understand why others fail to believe or accept his superior claims.

It is characteristic of the obese individual as well, who feels that calories will not affect him or that he can eat what he likes and stop before overindulging. The addicted gambler insists that he can stop while he is winning even though innumerable past experiences prove otherwise. The predominating characteristic of the feeling of grandiose exemption from consequences, is tied very closely to the markedly immature propensity toward the immediate gratification without any regard to the future effects. It is no wonder that there was a tendency to describe a common personality structure which was presumed to predispose one to alcoholism, drugs, obesity or the like. In fact there are a number of common personality traits in all the addictions which are related to the obsessional tendency towards grandiosity, demand for superhuman control and an overriding capacity to replace ritual and compulsive activity for direct confrontation of one's weakness and incapacities. However, these tendencies characterize mankind and the presence of external precipitating and predisposing factors is what initiates the process of abuse and addiction.

Rado noted this matter in his recognition of a necessary additional element in maintaining an addiction in the face of obvious self-destructive dangers. He was referring not only to the relief of anxiety, physiological compliance and the feelings of elation that accompany drug abuse, but to the singular, distinctive use of denial supported by grandiose feelings of a special privileged exemption and immunity from the consequences. He said, "It is impossible for the patient not to perceive what is happening. His friends and relatives deluge him with warnings to 'pull himself together.' At the same time the elation (following use of the drug) diminishes in intensity and the depression becomes more severe. Physical illness, unmistakably due to the use of the poison, afflicts him with pain. Then everything was in favor of the elation, whereas now the hopes set upon it have been revealed as deluding. It might be supposed that the patient would reflect on this and give up the drug—but no; he continues in his way. I must admit for many years I could not grasp the economics of the state of mind until a patient himself gave me the explanation. He said, "I know all the things that people say when they upbraid me, but mark my words, Doctor, *nothing* can happen to me." This then is the patient's position. The elation has reactivated his narcissistic belief in his invulnerability and all of his better insight and all of his sense of guilt are shattered on this bulwark."

The tendency to seek immediate gratifications and to feel immune and superhuman characterizes obsessional thinking and behavior, while it participates in an immature personality, it does not necessarily lead to addiction. Consequently, we must have an additional factor for the addictive processes to take place. This involves the issue of stress, tension, or the social or economic conditions that become intolerable and require some magical release. It is for this reason that we find addictive processes in low socio-economic groups involving pharmacological agents, while food addictions are more prevalent in more affluent groups. Addictions have been characterized as the products of civilization, where coping with the inner and outer complications of a high level of sophisticated technological society becomes too prolonged or too difficult and where the individual is conditioned to rapid, magical, instantaneous benefits from any ameliorative prescription. Consequently, we find that addictions are not necessarily tied to severe neurological disorders or neurotic states but are attributable to socio-economic conditions where the recourse to the easy escape and comfortable release from overbearing oppressiveness can be quickly achieved even in minor oppressive emotional situations. The reports from China, as sparse and uncertain as they are, tend to support the sociological factors as the prime issues in drug addiction since they seem to imply that the drug problem is markedly reduced and perhaps eliminated in China. If this is true, we may be forced to conclude that the addictive disorders, particularly those involving drugs or alcohol, may be social diseases, not psychiatric disorders at all. This does not rule out the role of compulsivity as a characterological prerequisite and a universal factor which may be influenced, reduced, and even ameliorated by a rectification of social and economic conditions as well as through psychotherapy.

In addition to the social, political and economic factors that may encourage and support the use of chemicals to deal with emotional and social dysfunctioning, we must examine, as I indicated earlier, the community's attitude towards the addict in view of the secondary complications of the addiction. Such understanding not only influences our notion of causality but clarifies our efforts to control and treat the addictive disorder. The community reaction to the addict, whether it be his need for money to support his expensive addiction or because of his irresponsible family behavior resulting from the addiction or because of the effect on his physical health and personal esteem or vanity, produces secondary complications over and above the physiological and psychological problems that are present in the first place. These problems are not intended but are consequences of the addiction. The addict, for example, wants to obtain the drug, alcohol or food, but the large sums of money required to support some addictions demands illegal ways of obtaining it since the addiction itself makes a successful professional life impossible. This results in the marked anti-social activity and the variety of illegal behavior beginning with the buyer all the way to the supplier. The anti-social behavior leads the psychiatrist or social scientist to describe the addicts in the categories of anti-social, asocial or psychopathic character disorders. However, the error is in confusing intent with consequence. Anti-social behavior involving the addict in legal as well as moral difficulties is the result of the addiction, not its cause, even when we find addictions prevalent in such antisocial characters to begin with. The secondary consequences of alcoholism have been described at great length in view of the irresponsible behavior of the alcoholic who tends to abandon his profession and family and become a charge on the community. The public reaction towards alcohol has always had a strong overlay of moralistic and punitive attitudes, while the drug addictions for the longest time were viewed with some compassion because the addictions usually occurred in professional groups who had access to the drugs or to individuals who were treated with the drug by a physician. They generally could financially support the addictions. Only when the lower socio-economic groups became the major victims, and their disease became too costly to maintain did the community become outraged and punitive. Today drug addictions have produced social and legal problems throughout the world.

With regard to obesity, the victim is looked upon with some scorn and some contempt, but hardly with the same degree of critical, punitive orientation as the drug or alcoholic addict.

Before suggesting some general approaches to therapy programs based on this view of the psychodymamics, let me summarize what I have said so far. Addictions can be viewed on two levels:

1. Drug dependence—this is widespread and may or may not be a necessary precondition for

2. Drug abuse—which may be (a) casual, transient, exploratory and intermittent, or (b) addictive—where the physiological and psychological factors combine to produce a condition characterized by compulsive behavior in which choice and decision is lacking and, where there is no limit to the lengths the addict will go to fill his needs.

The term habituation, I believe, is a way of labelling minor addictions, such as smoking, etc. Prior attempts to distinguish habituation from addiction by emphasizing the physiological dependence appears to be invalid since all habits are physiologically maintained even if psychologically motivated and initiated.

Addictions have two levels of action:

(a) primary—that effect on the organism itself producing massive physiological changes in all areas of functioning but specifically a need for a chemical substance or some other compulsive action to relieve the intolerable anxiety.

(b) secondary—the consequences of the addiction outside of the organism whether it be the irresponsible behavior towards one family, the illegal actions of kleptomania, or the need for money to secure the chemical, or the community censure on the obese individual. These factors stir up compassion or punition which effects the status of the addict.

Treatment

A valid treatment program for the addictive disorders must therefore approach it from the three points of view, detailed previously, namely:

(a) physiological
(b) psychological, and
(c) socio-economic factors.

While some addictions like drugs, alcohol, and obesity, involve all three factors, others like kleptomania and compulsive masturbation seem to be exclusively tied to psychological elements, none of them can be adequately comprehended as intrinsic and psychodynamic disorders based on some inner distortions which make the individual susceptible to addictive processes. The problem is not a simple psychodynamic one although it is clear that the individual's personal history and development does involve issues of immaturity, and the tendency to cope by utilizing the techniques and resources of magical fulfillment rather than by confronting and attempting to resolve the difficulties by realistic efforts. Since this is a universal tendency we should not be astonished at the widespread prevalence of addictive disorders even though it appears to be more potential in some individuals than in others. The recognition of the role of the psychological factors, however, must transcend and permeate the total program if other measures of control are to succeed, since they are the inner motivational forces that initiate and sustain the addiction and lay the ground work for the substitution of one addiction for another.

Initially, however, treatment must occur on the physiological level if a psychotherapeutic program is to be useful. We must concern ourselves with the addicting agent and view the situation in terms of an acute crisis in which the addicting behavior must be terminated or the drug intake prevented by such techniques as substitution (Methadone), cold turkey, and a host of aversive conditioning techniques designed to shift the pleasure of the addiction into pain. These can be physical, such as electro-shocks, antabuse, or psychological factors, such as humiliation, guilt and the like.

However, such emergency therapeutic measures must be viewed as only one piece of the total program even if economic or political circumstances prevent us from going further. To overlook this fact, results only in widespread dissatisfaction, disappointment and discouragement in the validity of all programs designed to deal with the addictions. The overemphasis on one aspect of the total program, such as the physiological, and a neglect of the other two can only prove to be temporary and ultimately unconstructive. Likewise the overemphasis on the psychological factors without altering the physiological or socio-economic factors results in minimal results with maximum outlays of money. Unless we quickly intercede, the actual physiological damage to the brain and other organ systems may make the addict inaccessible to any psychotherapeutic measures. The chemicals themselves produce character changes and behavioral manifestations which do not necessarily reflect the pre-addictive personality, though they were mistakably viewed as such for a long time.

I do not propose to deal with the variety of recommended approaches for the crisis or physiological aspect of such addiction programs, or discuss the socio-economic issues that must participate in a well rounded program, but will focus on some issues that relate to my view of the psychodynamic factors.

Dr. Leon Wurmser in an interesting article in the *American Scholar* describes the interacting facets of the aetiology of drug addiction by a series of five concentric circles (a) inner problems, (b) family, (c) peer group, (d) culture and its values, (e) philosophical problems.

The five concentric circles relate to the psychosocial factors and confirm the impression that the addictive disorders will never be resolved without the participation of non-physicians, such as teachers, social workers, nurses, psychotherapists and a major overhaul of our philosophical and economic resources to deal with the factors that encourage insecurities, anxieties, tensions, boredom, and unemployment with its dehumanizing effects.

Psychodynamic insight, however, must be brought to bear on the therapy program from the outset, as I indicated earlier. Particularly the addict's sense of invulnerability and his grandiose expectations of exemption from the realistic consequences of his behavior. This is a piece of the compulsive elements in his personality which also involves his false pride and pseudo maturity and his tendency towards easy solution and escapist maneuvers which are covered by grandiose fantasies of superhuman capacities.

As with all compulsions, external force, persuasion, threat and humiliation cannot undo the compulsion which has an inner dynamics that must be exposed and understood. The addict must not only become aware of his grandiosity but must accept some limitations and commitments to his realistic potentials. He needs to develop other techniques for dealing with his feelings of powerlessness and helplessness than through compulsive rituals and illusory feelings of strength and power.

The contradictory nature of compulsions is most evident in drug addicts and alcoholics and emphasizes the utter helplessness of traditional psychotherapeutic methods which by encouraging the individual to undo his compulsion actually strengthens it. This is the dilemma of how to utilize our determination and will to overcome defects when such defects are due to a disorder of the will and where the focus and preoccupation on the goal interferes with its attainment. Dr. Otto Fenichel noted this fact in his authoritative volume of *The Psychoanalytic Theory of Neurosis*.(5) He said, "The situation, therefore in the case of compulsion neurotics, is that they must be healed with the aid of functions that are themselves affected by the illness." A patient made a comparison that fits the case. He said, "it was as if he had fallen into the water with a towel in his hand and someone were trying to dry him with the towel which had become wet along with his body." There is no solution for the dilemma except through an awareness of the limitations of traditional psychotherapeutic techniques and the utilization of the intact aspects of the ego. We must avoid compulsive efforts on the part of the therapist as well as patient to overcome the compulsion. This is precisely the difficulty in the treatment of the obsessional disorders in which the value of the technique of paradoxical intention has been established. With this technique we overcome a destructive behavioral disorder by advising and encouraging its persistence. Paradoxically such an emphasis results in the abandonment of the symptom. While unfortunately this technique cannot be applied to most of the addictive processes because of the physiological complications, the underlying principle is valid. Compulsions or addictions cannot be overcome by direct action, calling upon our will power or our determination and strength. Paradoxical intention is occasionally successful because it removes our focus from overcoming the symptoms to an exaggeration of it. This takes the behavior which was derived from unknown sources and outside of volitional control to one of choice and volition. At such a time, one can then choose to stop or continue such behavior while previously we had no choice in the matter.

In fact the patient generally does not come for treatment in order to terminate his compulsion or addiction but to get help in making it tolerable or successful. In 1920, Dr. Kempf, in his famous textbook on *Psychopathology* (7) was aware of this when he said, "The patient *never* comes for relief from the repressed wish, but desires to be relieved of the exhausting drains necessary to maintain the substitution (symptom)." To abandon compulsive behavior one must acknowledge that one is totally powerless to deal with it and accept the necessity for outside help. It is a matter of finally giving in and recognizing one's weakness and helplessness to deal with the problem. Only then will he be able to deal with the out of awareness forces that maintain the compulsive substitutive activities. By giving up absolute control over his living through his compulsive behavior he can begin to exert reasonable controls without grandiose pretensions of invulnerability. This will result in abandonment of compulsive rituals and other symptomatology without any focus on special effort. They will wither away, rather than being driven out by directed efforts. The recognition of one's powerlessness cannot be simply verbal but must go much deeper since it is the compulsive's verbal capacity that allows him to circumvent commitments and maintain his grandiosity, thereby never really accepting his deficiency. This is strikingly clear in the obese or alcoholic individual who is forever making verbal assaults on his behavior saying, "never again," "I now really want to stop," etc., etc.

The achievements of Alcoholics Anonymous illustrates this point even though its success has often been justified by the assumption of spiritual frustrations rather than psychological readjustments. The achievements of A.A. lie, I believe, in the insistence that the alcoholic accept in advance:

(a) the fact of being alcoholic means being helpless to control or alter his compulsive drinking, and

(b) his acceptance of his need for help on more than a verbal acknowledgement.

T. Bateson noted this in his excellent article, *A Theory of Alcoholism,* where he indicates that the process of 'surrender' in A.A. involves the alcoholic's recognition of the compulsive nature of his drinking, his powerlessness in the face of it and his inability to resolve it by will power. The alcoholic also must agree that only a greater power can restore his former state of non-drinking. In this regard Bateson is aware of the grandiosity of the alcoholic which sustains the addiction. This recognition breaks the myth of self-power. According to Bateson, it is not really a surrender by a change of epistemology but a change in how to know about one's personality in the world. He says, "The whole epistemology of self control which his friends urge upon the alcoholic is monstrous. In this reserve the alcoholic is right in rejecting it." He is referring to the tendency to urge the alcoholic, drug addict, or obese individual to use his will power and determination to terminate the addiction. Bateson points out that the technique of paradoxical intention works because a positive feedback loop develops to increase the behavior which preceded the discomfort. As I indicated earlier, paradoxical intention seems to work because the patient against his will and free choice pursues his compulsion even while knowing it is absurd and irrational to do so. He must pursue it because the threat of anxiety is so great. The paradoxical intention technique forces a patient to accept the symptom willingly and deliberately and put it under his voluntary control. This focuses not only on the absurdity of the symptom but it also gives the person the possibility of controlling its manifestations by putting it squarely under his responsibility. While the paradoxical nature of a therapist encouraging his patient to continue his symptom is most evident, the real issue is in terms of putting the action under the patient's choice and control. Once this begins to happen, the positive feedback provides the verification that the individual is not really totally powerless but in rejecting the superhuman pretension, he can actually control some of his living. While the process of paradoxical intention is not applicable to the addictive disorders is such, it helps us understand the necessity for total surrender or total awareness of the therapeutic double bind, in which we challenge an individual to attempt some changes or do some controlled drinking or eating or drug taking so that the addict can at first recognize his inability to limit or control his intake while later in the process can experience the possibility of total renunciation through positive controls. The factor of the positive feedback is not included in conventional theories of learning.

The philosophy of Zen portrays the dilemma in a different way and suggest the road toward successful therapy in the addictive and compulsive states. It portrays the paradox of how we can work towards understanding, but are able to achieve it only when we stop working towards it. It validates the cardinal principle in the therapy of the addictions, that is, to encourage patients to examine their behavior and focus on it without trying too hard or becoming too preoccupied with it. It strives to encourage the individual's free choice or free will, rather than his behaving from compulsion or habit. In order to overcome both the inability to act or the compulsion towards action, the element of necessity must be removed and the notion of spontaneity introduced. Yet, when the compulsive recognizes the need to be spontaneous, he makes this also into a compulsion, with the result that a "bigger and better" compulsion ensues. Zen philosophy deals with this problem, by encouraging the individual to "Just be," or to "let go" and not do as a way of doing.

The therapy of the addictions demands that in addition to controlling the intake by forceful measures described earlier, we must make the addict aware of his insecurities, anxieties and his essential powerlessness to deal with his anxieties. Only then can he face the consequences of his behavior and only then can we mobilize his remaining strengths and assets to begin the process of repair. As his esteem grows and the awareness of his strength increases, he can then slowly risk abandoning his addictive patterns and be freed to make a valid choice regarding the addicting agent provided the physiological factors have been dealt with.

Consequently, our efforts to force or encourage the addict to relinquish his compulsion by will power, persuasion, moral injunction, punition, etc., will be of no avail. We cannot extol him to utilize his incapacity to make a free choice or to exercise his will or determination to overcome the incapacity. It only emphasizes his powerlessness and fortifies his addiction. Support for undoing his compulsion must come through the simultaneous recognition of his strength and capacity by the combined utilization of physiological, psychological and socio-economic resources. Under such conditions he may be able to strengthen his capacities for decisive commitment and determined effort to function without the use of chemicals. In this sense the psychodynamics of addiction does constitute the overall umbrella under which all other modalities of treatment must operate in order to get a long time remission rather than a temporary subsidence of the symptoms.

References

1. Alexander, F.: *History of Psychiatry*. New York, Harper and Row, 1966.
2. Bateson, G.: The cybernetics of self—a theory of alcoholism. *Psychiatry, Vol. 34*.
3. Bejerot, N.: Theory of addictions as artificially induced drives. *American Journal of Psychiatry,* 128:7.
4. Davidson, H.A.: Confessions of a goof ball addict. *American Journal of Psychiatry,* 120:8, 1963.
5. Fenichel, O.: *The Psychoanalytic Theory of Neurosis*. New York, Norton, 1945.
6. Freud, S.: *Standard Edition of the Complete Psychological Works of S. Freud*. London, Hogarth Press, Vol. I, III, 1966.
7. Kempf, E.J.: *Psychopathology*. St. Louis, C. V. Mosby Co., 1920.
8. Rado, S.: *Psychoanalysis of Behavior*. New York, Grune and Stratton, 1920.
9. Savitt, R.A.: Psychoanalytic studies on addiction ego structure. *Psya. Quart.,* 32: 43–57, 1963.
10. Schur, M.: *FREUD: Living and Dying*. New York, Int. Univ. Press, 1972.
11. Wurmser, L., Drug abuse—nemesis of psychiatry. *American Scholar,* Summer Issue, 1972.

Chapter 2

DRUG DEPENDENCY: THE SUBSTITUTION OF SUBSTANCE NUTRIENTS FOR LOVE
Genetic and Environmental Factors

David Sternberg, Ph.D. and Abraham Cohen, Ph.D.

David Sternberg, Ph.D.

Abraham Cohen, Ph.D.

Dr. Sternberg is Associate Director of the Psychological Services Clinic, Adelphi University. He is Associate Clinical Professor and Supervisor of Psychotherapy in the Institute for Advanced Psychological Studies, Adelphi University. He is a member of the Nassau County Mental Health Board; Consultant, New York State Alcohol and Drug Abuse Commission and is in private practice.

Dr. Cohen is Director of the Psychological Services Clinic at Adelphi University. He is Associate Professor and Supervisor of Psychotherapy in the Institute of Advanced Psychological Studies and in the Postdoctoral Program of Adelphi University. He is a Clinical Psychologist and Consultant to the Nassau County Drug Abuse Commission; a Consultant Lecturer and Trainer for the New York State Narcotic Addiction Control Commission; Psychological Consultant, Medical and Surgical Specialists Plan and is in private practice of psychoanalysis and psychotherapy.

> Addiction . . .
> To attach oneself personally as
> to a master, leader, or a cause;
> to give oneself up or over to as
> a constant practice; to become
> habituated, consecrated to some
> object.(18)

In this paper the writers intend to suggest that vulnerability to addiction represents a failure of the internalization of regulatory controls; that is, deficiencies in the rhythm of gratification and frustration provided by the early mothering one. A faulty internalization of the maternal role is presumed to lay the developmental groundwork for a predisposition to addiction.

Krystal and Raskin (11) present the general psychoanalytical view that the drug dependent person is invariably seeking relief, modification or avoidance of a painful state. In his drug, he finds a buffer for his intolerable tensions. His own ego functions suffer impairments that inevitably lead to an inability to deal with pain and tension without his drugs. Ostow (14) concurs that the intake of drugs permits a withdrawal into a state of "narcissistic tranquility."

Addicts rarely estimate interpersonal relationships highly. Fixated to a passive-narcissistic aim, they are interested in getting their gratification, not in satisfying their partners or in the specific personalities of their partners. Others are merely "purveyors of supplies." The effect of the drug is experienced as food and warmth. They seize any opportunity for escape. Reality evolves into a rush to secure one's "fix."

This process is rooted in an oral dependency on substitute nutrients. The eventual "amorphous tension" resembles the earliest stage of libidinal development before there was any organization at all; namely, the oral orientation of the infant who signals for gratification without any capacity for giving and without any consideration of reality.

In the final stages of their illness, drug addicts live in alternating states of elation and depression corresponding to the rhythm of hunger and satiety in the psychically undifferentiated infant. In this state, the hypodermic needle is used less for pleasure than as protection against the unbearable tension associated with hunger and guilt feelings.(4) Accordingly, drug abuse seems to be related to a primary ego deficiency.

The users of non-narcotic drugs appear to be involved in more than the avoidance of the pain and conflict. They are evidently seeking some substance to reduce tension that is caused by feelings of inadequacy and/or alienation. In reality, the addict feels an unsatiated longing for meaningful experiences. Frustrated in their efforts to shape their identities, they resort to mind-expanding drugs for liberation from a painful reality.(11)

Hallucinogens seem to absolve the users of their neurotic conflicts. Through perceptual distortion, they feel they have become in reality what they seek or believe they are in fantasy.(12)

Frequently, the hallucinogen (LSD) user is also intrigued by the prospect of blurring his former internal structures. This state is evidently induced by the gradual deterioration of preconditioned behavioral responses that ordinarily facilitate biological and psychological survival of the personality. However, under special conditions of dysfunction as in an LSD state, the pragmatic, ego-controlled systems of automatic selection (e.g., Hartmann's autonomous ego functions) are sublimated or discoordinated in favor of alternate modes of consciousness. Since the stimulus-response process has been interrupted, normative biological functioning becomes deficient. This breakdown tends to distort the internal reality and external reality of experience. His particular neurophysiological and psychological state, as well as the environmental conditions, encourage or discourage a change in the variable functions of motivation.

Users of narcotics try to resolve problems related to low self-esteem. Their feeling of alienation leads them to reject socio-cultural values. The ensuing withdrawal from object relations is a compromising attack on the society for the problems they create for it [ie., "I don't take from society, so why should I give anything to it . . . "].(15)

Neurotic individuals may find that alcohol provides surcease from pain or deadening feelings of inferiority, isolation, anxiety, pain, rage, obsessive rumination, conflicts, depression, sexual problems, etc. Borderline or overt psychotic individuals may also turn to alcohol or other drugs, thereby adding addiction to their already excessive mental and emotional problems.

The psychological testing of three hundred alcoholic patients disclosed markedly similar character traits. Low frustration tolerance and an inability to endure anxiety or tension were invariant. All manifested depression, with withdrawal, a sense of isolation, an extremely low self-esteem, a sensitivity and a self-punitive behavior. Dependency strivings were heightened, the frustration of which led to depression, hostility or rage. Most individuals manifested impulsive, repetitive "acting out" of conflicts with little or no insight. In all cases, marked hostility and rebellion, conscious or unconscious, were evident in their defiance toward authority figures and by their problems with sex.(5)

Blank (1) clarified the developmental antecedents to tension intolerance by pointing out that regulatory processes are in early life the function of the stimulus barrier in the maternal adjunct. After the first few weeks of life, regulation becomes more complex. Not only must the child be protected from excessive external and internal stimuli, such as untempered rages resulting from excessive pain and frustration, but, the rhythm of gratification and frustration must be consistent for homeostasis. The maternal role of drive-tamer, tension-regulator and soother are gradually internalized during the first few years of life.

In this context, Spitz (16, 17) details some infantile mechanisms of coping with the intolerable anxiety of separation. By way of imitation, the precursor to identification, the child begins the long process of internalization. He attempts to provide himself with the gratifications that have previously been provided by the maternal adjunct.

Kohut's (10) theorizes that such internalizations are not substitutions for the mothering persons but are structural adaptations of her functions. This accords with Hartmann's (8) assertion that, as internalization proceeds, so does greater self-regulatory independence from the environment. However, due to inadequate nurturing homeostasis in the child cannot be achieved. When maintenance mechanisms are not balanced, the self-regulatory capacity fails and rapid ego regressions ensue. The function of the mechanism to signal anxiety and defense is faulty.

According to Jacobson (9), it is not until the superego coalesces as a discrete structure, formed during the several years of early acquisition, that the ability to maintain an identity and to regulate a stable structure of defense is assured. This suggests that individuals with deficient inner regulatory controls are particularly vulnerable to addiction.

Concerning narcissism, Kohut (10) focuses on early traumatic disturbances in the initially idealized self-other relationship. Traumatic disappointments may interfere with the development of the psyche to maintain the narcissistic equilibrium of the personality, or the re-establishment of balance after it has been disturbed. Specifically, traumas considered include sudden disappointment in the idealized mother due to her unreliable empathy, depressed moods, physical illness, absence or death. Such, evidently, is the case in personalities who become addicts.

> The trauma which they (the addict) suffer is most frequently the severe disappointment in a mother who, because of her defective empathy with the child's needs (or for other reasons) did not appropriately fulfill the functions (as a stimulus barrier; as an optimal provider of needed stimuli; as a supplier of tension-relieving gratification, etc.) which the mature psychic apparatus should later be able to perform or initiate on its own. . . . Such individuals remain fixated on aspects of the archaic objects and they find them in the form of drugs.(10)

In correlation with Freud's Nirvana Principle, Spitz (17) considers that there are homeostatic regulating principles already functioning at birth. This formulation presupposes that the inherently programmed progression of maturation is synchronous with the progression of development which varies according to environmental factors. According to Spitz, asynchronicities mark the ego levels at which the device for discharging tension becomes inadequate. As agitation mounts some new outlet for discharge must be sought through a process of trial and error. The new arrangement temporarily establishes synchronous progression until the next asynchronicity.

The important function of the maternal object from this point of view is to regulate the frustrations of the critical periods; not to remove frustration but, when necessary, to impose it, for optimal frustration is structure and ego building.

Impaired development which results when severe narcissistic trauma occurs is further elaborated by Kohut (10). If the disappointment is in the admired parent, there results a failure of the idealized self-object to become transformed into an internalized self-regulating aspect of structure. Such developmental failure is fostered largely by the shortcomings of the maternal person. Traumatic disappointments result from her impaired capacity to become attuned to the infant, to act as an auxiliary stimulus barrier, to be a tension-relieving regulator, and to provide the kind of stimulation and gratification that enables the infant to begin to recognize himself as a person. Accordingly, structural weakness results that is unable to maintain basic narcissistic homeostasis.

With this failure in internalization, the individual does not acquire self-soothing mechanisms which aid sleep. To illustrate this, Kohut refers to the psychopathology of drug addiction; he concludes that the psychological facet of the craving for drugs is not object seeking but a distorted attempt at creating a structure in the absence of the partner in the dyad whose role is to provide opportunity for transmuting internalizations.

Distinguishing the archaic, undifferentiated self-object from the internalized structures which take over drive-regulating functions formerly performed by the object, Kohut cites as an illustration of the former, the addicts feeling of "depletion" in the absence of the soothing therapist. It is in this connection that Glover (6) concurs that the "function of the drug serves as a 'cure' for the pathogenic introjects"—i.e., the chemical equivalent of mother.

Perhaps the most poignant clinical evidence of desperate measures to neutralize tension and restore some semblance of inner homeostatic regulatory control is illustrated by the amphetamine abuser. As is well known, amphetamine abuse is often half of the vicious cycle. The abuser, finding that he is constantly agitated and anxious ingests large amounts of barbituates to calm himself. But these drugs induce feelings of weariness and listlessness.

To counter this state, he again takes amphetamines, then back to sedatives and so on and on frequently culminating a decompensating "crash" into suicidal depression or amphetamine psychosis.

Viewed from this vantage point, the danger of our pharmacological culture is the illusory promise of an (ego-bypass) avoidance of development—the short-circuiting of frustration with tranquilizers, amphetamines, alcohol, etc. The result is disturbed structure and disorder in ego and superego development.

Bibliography

1. Blanck, G. and Blanck, R. *Ego Psychology, Theory and Practice,* New York, Columbia University Press, 1974
2. Capone, T., Brahen, L., Brahen, R., Psychoanalytic and Behavioral Considerations in Antagonist and Methadone Programs, *Journal of Contemporary Psychotheraphy,* Vol. 9—No. 2, 1978
3. Deikman, A.J. "Deautamization and the Mystic Experience" in *Altered States of Consciousness,* New York, Edited by Tart, C., John Wiley and Sons, Inc., 1969
4. Fenichel, O. *The Psychoanalytic Theory of the Neurosis,* New York, W.W. Norton and Company, Inc., 1945
5. Fox, R. and Lyon, P. *Alcoholism: Its Scope, Cause and Treatment,* New York, Random House, 1955
6. Glover, E. *The Technique of Psychoanalysis,* New York, International Universities Press, Inc., 1958
7. Greenacre, P., The Transitional Object and The Fetish, *International Journal of Psychoanalysis,* 51 (1971) 447–56
8. Hartmann, H. *Ego Psychology and The Problem of Adaptation.* New York, International Universities Press, 1964
9. Jacobson, E. *The Self and the Object World,* New York, International Universities Press, 1964
10. Kohut, H. *The Analysis of the Self: A Systematic Approach to the Psychoanalytic Treatment of Narcissistic Personality Disorders,* New York, International Universities Press, Inc., 1971
11. Krystal, H., and Raskin, H.A., *Drug Dependence: Aspects of Ego Function,* Detroit, Wayne State University Press, 1970
12. Levy, N.J. The Use of Drugs by Teenagers for Sanctuary and Illusion, *The American Journal of Psychoanalysis,* 28:15, 1968
13. Mahler, M.S., *On Human Symbiosis and The Vicissitudes of Individuation,* New York; International Universities Press, 1968
14. Ostow, M. *Drugs in Psychoanalysis and Psychotherapy,* New York, Basic Books, 1962
15. Sharoff, R.L. Character Problems and Their Relationship to Drug Abuse, *The American Journal of Psychoanalysis,* 29:192, 1969
16. Spitz, R.A. Anaclitic Depression: An Inquiry into the Genesis of Psychiatric Conditions in Early Childhood, *The Psychoanalytic Study of the Child,* New York, International Universities Press, 2:313, 1946
17. Spitz, R.A. Anxiety in Infancy: *International Journal of Psychoanalysis* 31:138, 1950
18. Webster, A.M. *International Dictionary of the English Language,* Springfield, G. and C. Merrian Company, 1953

Chapter 3

DEFENSE MECHANISMS EXPRESSED IN ALCOHOLISM

William J. Browne, M.D.

William J. Browne, M.D.

At the time this paper was delivered Dr. Browne was clinical director of Woodville State Hospital, Carnegie, Pa., 15106; and psychiatric consultant to the St. Francis Hospital Clinic for Alcoholism, Pittsburgh, Pa., and the McKeesport Hospital Alcoholism Clinic, McKeesport, Pa. (His current address is VA Hospital, Highland Dr., Pittsburgh, Va. 15206.)

27

Introduction

This paper deals with some defense mechanisms and other psychodynamic themes as expressed in alcoholic patients. The themes are not unique to this group of patients but they can help us toward understanding the disorder of alcoholism. They can also serve as a focus in treatment to help the alcoholic patient understand himself and what drinking means to him. The material for the paper was gathered during the course of individual long-term psychotherapy with over a hundred alcoholic patients, and from the study and evaluation of several thousand additional patients who were seen in both private practice and in alcoholism clinics over the past fifteen years.

The patients comprised all social classes but most of them were white working or middle class married men. In the beginning of our studies the average age of the patients was close to forty, and eighty percent of them were men. In recent years more young persons and more women are seeking help. (Percentages cited are approximate. The emphasis of this paper is on individual dynamics and not statistics.)

Therapy based on psychoanalytic theory is only one of many psychological approaches to the treatment of alcoholism (2). Perhaps less than ten percent of alcoholic persons are amenable to this method, even though some of the themes to be discussed are present in nearly everyone who uses alcohol to excess.(15)

In viewing alcoholism as an emotional disorder, we must not overlook its organic and medical dimensions. For example, there appears to be a physiological component in the loss of control and withdrawal symptoms characteristic of the addictive stage of drinking (13); such that, addiction, once established, is irreversible either through the passage of time or the acquiring of insight. Therefore it is an illusion to expect that psychotherapy will enable an alcoholic person to drink again in a controlled manner. Many patients will assume that if only they knew why they drink, they would be able to stop or control their drinking. The opposite is true—the drinker will not find out why he drinks until he stops drinking. This is because he uses alcohol to evade stress and to drown out psychic problems. Effective psychotherapy requires sobriety. An intoxicated patient will often not recall what was said during a therapy session, or even that a session occurred. The early prescribing of disulfiram (antabuse) will insure sobriety and increase the chances for success in treatment.

Evaluation of the Patient

Alcohol is a toxic substance and can affect nearly every organ of the body. A physical examination and laboratory studies, particularly to detect liver damage, should be a routine part of the evaluation of every patient. Insight is not very helpful to someone who is about to become moribund. It is possible, for example, to have sustained a severe degree of liver dysfunction without being aware of it.

Some of the less serious toxic effects of alcohol, such as anxiety, sleeplessness, and gastro-intestinal symptoms should not be misdiagnosed as neurotic. Nor should tranquilizers be prescribed since they too can be addicting and, if the patient combines them with alcohol, fatal toxicity may occur. Patients with these complaints, and a history of excessive drinking, should be detoxified.

Some type of hospital or medical back-up is necessary whenever one undertakes the treatment of alcoholic patients. At least once in their drinking career most of these patients will require hospitalization. Having provided for this, the therapist can then devote his major efforts to psychotherapy.

The History

An integral part of the evaluation is the taking of a detailed history. The dynamic themes in which we are interested will show different variations in each patient, and these should be precisely identified. Exact dates should be obtained for critical events in the patient's life, such as the deaths of significant persons, his marriages, and the births of his children. These can then be correlated with the times of the onset, exacerbations, and remissions of his drinking problem. Both the usual social history, which should include the drinking habits of parents and relatives, and a separate drinking history are needed. The latter should include the time and circumstances of the first drink, when drinking became a problem, and the current drinking pattern in terms of what is drunk, how often and how much, and whether loss of control, blackouts, or withdrawal symptoms have occurred. Legal difficulties and hospitalizations due to drinking should be noted.

Where and when a patient drinks, as determined by the history, often indicates why he drinks. For example, a patient may proudly state that he never missed a day's work in his life because of drinking, and that he drinks only at home in the evenings and on week-ends. This patient may be telling us that work is not too much of a stress for him, but that he cannot tolerate being with his family unless he is drunk. (This same theme is ritualized in the five o'clock cocktail hour which ostensibly is to provide for relaxation from the cares of the day, but whose real purpose may be to prepare for the stresses one is to meet at the other end of the commuter line.) Further examples of the use of the history to highlight dynamic themes will be given in other sections of the paper.

The history should also include a record of the patient's past treatment experiences and the response to them. Was help sought only in crises? Did the patient discontinue treatment after a few sessions? Did he or she "shop" for treatment, or go to more than one doctor or clinic at the same time? Was he ever helped by taking antabuse or by joining Alcoholics Anonymous?

Patients are quite likely to repeat past treatment patterns with each new therapist. We can be forewarned as to what to expect, if we have secured an adequate history.

In respect to the current request for treatment one should always ask: "Why now?" Why, for instance, should someone whose drinking has obviously been excessive for five to ten years finally ask for help? Usually, it is because of one of the secondary consequences of drinking. There is a threatened loss of a job, or break-up of a marriage; delirium tremens has occurred, or damage to health can no longer be ignored. Patients are more willing to acknowledge that their drinking has caused problems, than they are to admit that they have emotional problems which have led them to drink.

In many cases, however, it is something extraneous to the drinking which determines when help is sought. The drinker may have teen-age children who have started to drink. He then becomes belatedly concerned that his drinking is having a bad effect on them. For many of our men drinkers it was the wife's menopause that triggered their desire to change. The wife became depressed. She was less tolerant of the drinking, attributed her depression to it, and insisted that it be stopped.

Another theme was presented by a woman who came to see me in a panic because her husband, while drunk, had tried to choke her the previous night. I asked her if this had ever happened before. She replied: "Oh, no! Up until now he just chased me with knives and tore my clothes off." I wondered why choking was so much worse. She said that as a child she used to see her drunken father trying to choke her mother. For years she had a repetitive nightmare of her father coming into her room to choke her. It was not clear how she had managed to provoke her husband into changing his method of assault, but it was this reenactment of a childhood trauma that led to her plea for help.

Patients in general may seek help, or have drinking exacerbations, on the anniversaries of traumatic events, such as the death of a mother. Emphasis on precise dating in the history helps us to detect such themes.

Psychodynamic Themes

Proceeding from the history we will consider other themes beginning with those defense mechanisms which are most likely to be encountered at the start of treatment.

Denial

Alcoholic persons will go to absurd lengths to rationalize their drinking or to minimize its significance. They can always give a "reason" for their drinking—"my job demands it"; or, "I was upset about my mother's death";

or, "My wife nags me"; etc. Each drinker attempts to define alcoholism in terms which exclude himself. Thus patients will state: "I'm not alcoholic because . . . I don't drink in the mornings"; or, " . . . I only drink beer"; or, " . . . I can take it or leave it." One man said to me: "I only drink enough to keep my bowels open, Doc." To achieve that end-point he was consuming a fifth of whiskey plus a case of beer a day.(16)

To cut through such rationalizations, it is necessary to get answers to only a few questions related to what happens after alcohol has been consumed. Does loss of control occur; i.e., has the person ever been unable to limit his drinking once it starts? Have there been withdrawal symptoms such as delirium tremens or convulsions? If so, addiction is present regardless of any other details of the drinking pattern. On another level, a drinking problem is present if the drinking has resulted in jeopardizing a job, in domestic strife, or in damage to health.

Often it is necessary to get corroborative information from someone other than the drinker. Usually this is the person, such as spouse or employer, who referred the drinker for help. Alcoholic patients are adept at manipulating the situation so that it appears that they are being pressured to get help. In this way they can point to someone else as the source of the problem, with the implication that on their own they would never have considered coming for treatment. One man was brought to the clinic by his wife. Contrary to our usual procedure, the couple was interviewed together instead of separately. He said: "I just have a few beers after work and go home and lie down." At which point the wife interjected, "Yeah, he lies down!—in his dirty work clothes, on the living room rug, and pisses his pants." The prospective patient then stalked out of the office in a fury, never to return. Sometimes it doesn't pay to confront the patient with the whole truth too soon.

Why, in the case of alcoholism, is there such a strong need to deny? And, what is being denied? Alcoholism is defined as a disease but it does not seem to be accepted as one. Those afflicted with it, unlike patients with heart disease or peptic ulcer, resist treatment. Most often, denial focuses on the issue of control. The drinker is extremely reluctant to admit that he cannot control his drinking, or that he really needs alcohol. In this respect he differs from the narcotic addict who has no difficulty in admitting that he is "hooked."

In part, this is accounted for by the pharmacology of alcohol, which lends itself to denial. It may take eight to ten years for addiction to alcohol to develop, and then only ten percent of the users succumb. With heroin, addiction can occur in a few weeks, and in eighty to ninety percent of its users. Furthermore, in our culture alcohol is *the* legal and acceptable drug. It is unpopular to acknowledge that it can be harmful, let alone addicting. Self-esteem is at stake in how one handles alcohol.

Our studies point to a conflict about dependency as the unconscious source of the denial. This is so, whether the drinker is a man or a woman. Many alcoholic patients will say that they never want to rely on drugs. (Rarely do they put alcohol in this category.) Some will proudly assert: "I won't even take aspirin for a headache." Others will reject antabuse because they want to achieve sobriety "on my own." Alcoholics Anonymous has an appeal for such drinkers even though that organization meets the dependent needs of its members on many levels. Membership in it, however, does not carry the connotation of "sickness" which is implicit in going to a doctor or clinic.

Male drinkers frequently equate dependency with weakness or effeminacy. A concern about potency underlies their battle with the contents of the bottle. They must repetitively try to prove to themselves that they are the masters of alcohol, and unaffected by its toxic properties. Just as repetitively they prove the opposite, as they become intoxicated and have to be taken care of. These men often need the support of alcohol in order to approach women; but, ironically, alcohol diminishes their sexual potency. Thus, their fear of impotency is confirmed and they are trapped in a vicious circle.

Acting Out

"Acting out" denotes the stereotyped re-enactment of a past conflict. Fenichel (6) noted that through this defense, actions in real life become repetitions of childhood situations, or attempts to end infantile conflicts, rather than rational undertakings. Freud (10) stressed that the patient does not *remember* anything of what he has repressed but reproduces it as an *action*. Such action prevents insight or understanding and, therefore, is counter to the goal of psychotherapy.

Alcohol, by reducing superego controls, facilitates action, so that acting out becomes a primary mechanism of defense for alcoholic patients. These patients, when drinking, give direct expression to sexual, dependent, and hostile urges. To the extent that this activity connotes independence or masculinity to the patient, it is an acting out of such strivings. The stuporous stage of drunkenness when the patient needs to be hospitalized or taken care of, is similarly an acting out of passive and dependent urges.

As therapists, we must be aware that this is happening so that we can explain the meaning of the behavior to our patients. Most patients are reluctant to accept their drinking behavior as part of themselves, and frequently develop amnesia for it. They would prefer to believe, for example, that alcohol causes hostility rather than releases it. They also see themselves as utterly independent, and reject the idea that their repetitive use of alcohol is to satisfy dependent needs.

I developed the theme of drinking as a repetition of the nursing situation in an earlier paper (4). The reader is referred to it for an elaboration of these ideas.

Identification

Identification is a defense mechanism of the oral stage, through which one becomes like someone else by devouring or incorporating him. It is prominent in alcoholic patients. By drinking alcohol one absorbs its potency, and its powers become part of oneself (3).

Through drinking, many alcoholic patients identify with an alcoholic parent. More than half of our patients have had this type of parent, usually the father. (About fifteen percent of the patients had abstaining parents, but in these families there was often an alcoholic grandparent—against whom the parents were reacting.) Quite often the patient did not begin to drink, at least not excessively, until after the alcoholic parent had died, left the home, or became sober while still in the home.

An example is a young man who began drinking heavily shortly after his alcoholic father stopped drinking through the help of Alcoholics Anonymous. When the patient was in his teens his mother sent him to the neighborhood bar to bring his father home. When he became our patient, his father was going to the bars to rescue him.

A fifty-year old man came to us for help because his doctor told him he had cirrhosis. This frightened him because his alcoholic father had died of cirrhosis at age fifty-two. Our patient had begun drinking soon after his father's death at twenty-five, and his children were now approaching that age. His drinking behavior was violent like that of his father, and when he was drunk he beat his wife and children just like his father had beaten him and his mother when he was a child.

Most patients are not as aware of their identification as was this man. In fact, they vow that they will never become like the detested alcoholic parent. Nevertheless, this appears to be their fate. In their families it was the only model of masculinity or femininity available. For some men the identification is part of the oedipal conflict, as if they were saying: "I will become a man just like the one mother married."

Alcoholic persons may identify with their children as well as with their parents. For the patients we have studied the event which most frequently triggered problem drinking was the birth of a baby. The wives of our men patients lamented that while they were in the hospital having a baby, the husband was out on a drinking spree. He would often continue heavy drinking the whole first year of the baby's life. One man confirmed this by saying: "I loved getting up in the middle of the night to give the baby its bottle, because then I could have my bottle without my wife bugging me about it."

In the cases of alcoholic women the care of the baby had to be taken over by someone else, such as grandmother, older sibling, or nurse. Rarely were these women able to give adequate mothering to their children. For example, if a child became sick, the mother used this as a reason for drinking. Even after the children were in college, their visits home would be occasions for the mother to be drunk.

In these examples we see both a regression to the oral stage and identification with the baby, and an acting out of dependency. Hostility toward the child as a sibling rival is also evident. (Some wives reported that when they were pregnant their drunken husbands kicked them in the belly, or threw them down stairs.) In counselling alcoholic patients we must be aware of the stresses posed by pregnancy and childbirth.

Alcoholism "Equivalents"

The circumstances under which patients remain sober, and what happens when they do so, provide insight into the meaning of drinking. Many of our patients have had months or years of sobriety interspersed with their drinking. The usual situations in which they are able to stop drinking provide alternate ways of meeting dependent needs. Hospitalization for any reason is an example, as is affiliation with Alcoholics Anonymous. Entering psychotherapy frequently results in a period of sobriety. Some of our married male patients stopped drinking when they had a mistress. On a different level, other patients stop drinking when they can submerge or deny their own dependent needs by taking care of others. Working as an aide in a hospital, or as a bartender or a waitress, are examples. Alcoholics Anonymous offers this outlet also.

Most alcoholic patients who stop drinking do so without developing any serious alternate symptoms, although transient weight gain, increased coffee intake and cigarette smoking, sleeplessness and mild depression are common. In many cases, however, other disorders occur when sobriety is achieved. Those which we have noted most often are discussed below. Their importance lies in the light which they shed on the meaning of drinking. They can be considered at least partial equivalents of alcoholism.

Other Addictions

Alcohol may be directly replaced by other addicting substances. Barbiturates and minor tranquillizers such as librium and meprobamate are examples. Patients may come for treatment with combined addictions to alcohol and other soft drugs already established. Less frequently, narcotics may replace alcohol, although they are in a different pharmacological class. Compulsive eating, with resultant obesity, can become a substitute for alcohol. In all of these cases no real intra-psychic change has occurred. The patient has simply transferred his addiction from one substance to another. The disorders which we will consider next are also alcoholism equivalents but in a more subtle sense, and they involve a change in the patient's usual defense mechanism.

Depression

Depression in alcoholic patients cannot be considered in isolation from its polar affect—elation. Lewin (12) lists intoxication as one of the equivalents of mania. If a person has a repetitive need to get "high" or intoxicated, we can infer that he is attempting to escape from depression. Some drinkers are aware of this; others deny that they ever feel depressed except during the hangover period. (Nearly one third of our patients have attempted suicide, most frequently during a withdrawal period.) It is probable that the latter group of drinkers tries to drown out unpleasant feelings before they even surface. On one level, loss of control signifies the perpetual pursuit of euphoria. As soon as the withdrawal effects of one drink are felt, the drinker must take another.

In many patients a manifest depressive reaction does not occur until after a period of sobriety. It then becomes evident that these patients were using alcohol as an antidepressant. One group in which this is particularly true is menopausal women, whose alcoholism is clearly a depressive equivalent.

Although alcohol is used to counter depression, alcoholism and depression are similar in that both are self-destructive disorders, and both indirectly satisfy dependent needs by enabling the patient to escape from routine responsibilities and thus force others to take care of him. Also, in the psychoanalytic schema, both are oral disorders.(3) These are characterized by a strong need for external supplies or symbols of love.

Important to note is that when an alcoholic patient responds to stress by becoming depressed instead of resorting to drinking, he has changed his typical mode of defense. He is no longer acting out, but is internalizing his conflicts in a neurotic manner. He is then easier to treat.

Peptic Ulcer

Approximately twenty percent of our patients have had a peptic ulcer. This is twice the incidence noted in the general population. Mirsky found blood pepsinogen levels of some 500 of our patients to be uniformly high (*). An elevated blood pepsinogen is a predisposing factor to peptic ulcer.

Of most interest, however, were the patients (approximately ten percent of those who had an ulcer) in which there was alternation of alcoholism and active peptic ulcer. This could occur from either direction. Some patients first developed an ulcer after they stopped drinking. If they resumed drinking the ulcer disappeared. (These patients are the exception to the usual observation that alcohol aggravates an active ulcer.) Other patients, who had undergone

---

*Data to be published.

gastrectomy to remove an ulcer, then became alcoholic, although they had not been heavy drinkers prior to the gastrectomy.

Here again we have an oral disorder, the treatment for which brings about considerable regression. The patient may have to be hospitalized and his diet consists of frequent feeding of milk and baby food.

In the case of the ulcer, the patient is handling his conflicts through somatization rather than acting out. Alexander (1), in outlining the psychosomatic view of peptic ulcer, notes that when the wish to be loved or to depend on others is rejected and denied by the adult ego, then a regressive pathway is used and the wish to be loved is converted into the wish to be fed. This stimulates gastric activity and hypersecretion which may lead to ulcer formation. Self-destructive forces are at work in this process, since the patient is unconsciously producing a potentially fatal lesion.(14) The frequent occurrence of peptic ulcer in our patients suggest that it can be an emotional equivalent of alcoholism.

Phobia and Counterphobia

Over twenty percent of the patients we have studied developed phobic reactions when they became sober. A fear of heights was most frequently noted, but fears of crossing bridges, of closed spaces and crowds, and of going out alone, also appeared. The phobias might persist for months but usually were not seriously disabling. Some of the patients had originally used alcohol to relieve phobias, and then gradually became addicted.

The phobias which respond best to alcohol are those of space and movement. This is probably related to the pharmacological action of alcohol on the cerebellum (11), which is the part of the brain that controls equilibrium, motor coordination and orientation. But the symbolic connotations of alcohol are equally important, particularly the one of the good and giving mother. Some phobic women are able to relieve their fears merely by carrying a bottle of whiskey in their purse. Alcohol then becomes the companion and a substitute for mother.(5)(8)

Difficulty in separating from mother is a key theme in the lives of alcoholic patients. Our patients, whether single, married, or divorced remained emotionally bound to her. Two-thirds of the patients lived in the same house or neighborhood as the mother, with the mother continuing to give them financial support. Some type of regular, ritualistic contact with the mother was the rule. Our interviews with the mothers confirmed that they too had anxiety about activity and separation which began in the patient's childhood, at the time the patient first started to walk. This mutual separation anxiety can be viewed as the pre-oedipal prototype or anlage of the phobias which later developed.

In psychotherapy we must be alert to the symbolic expression of the phobias. For example, the fear of heights may be equated with the fear of success. This is particularly important in alcoholic men because it can affect their whole work career. One man became more and more phobic as he was promoted up the executive ladder of his organization. With each promotion he was moved to a higher floor of the company's building. He developed such a marked fear of heights that he had to pull the draperies across the windows and turn his desk so that he could not look out the window. He became so anxious that he could not eat in the executive dining room, and was not able to urinate in the executive washroom. He had always been a heavy drinker but in order to overcome his fears he increased his drinking to such an extent that he lost his job.

Some men repeat this pattern over and over, working up to the verge of success and then destroying their chances by drinking. Such repetitive attempts to approach or overcome the feared situation is termed counterphobic behavior. The counterphobic attitude (7) is characteristic of alcoholic persons and is expressed in their drinking when they repeatedly challenge the toxic powers of alcohol in an attempt to *control* them.

Insofar as this pattern is a compulsive attempt to resolve childhood conflicts, it meets Freud's definition of repetition-compulsion.(9) Our evidence that this is the case is the observation that many of our men patients start destructive drinking just at the point where they are about to surpass their father in economic or career status. One man who was the son of a famous jazz pianist was becoming a well-known jazz pianist in his own right. As his success increased so did his drinking. He began to have blackouts. Early one morning, after a drinking binge the night before, he found himself in a cemetery at his father's grave. His right arm was bleeding profusely. He had cut himself with a knife, so deeply that he severed the nerves. After that he was no longer able to play the piano.

In summary, alcoholic persons have strong dependent and hostile urges which they tend to deny. They satisfy these urges through a regressive acting out. When intoxicated they give direct expression to hostility, and force others to care for them. Often they are amnesic for this behavior. During sober periods, they frequently develop characteristically oral disorders, such as depression and peptic ulcer, which in part are the emotional equivalent of alcoholism. These psychodynamic themes can be useful as a focus for psychotherapy.

No attempt has been made to cover the complete psychodynamics of alcoholism. Important themes such as compulsivity, and sexual disorders have been merely alluded to. The emphasis has been on a particular approach to therapy.

References

1. Alexander, Franz: *Psychosomatic Medicine.* New York, Norton, 1956, p. 101f.
2. Blum, E.M.; and Blum, R.H.: *Alcoholism: Modern Psychological Approaches to Treatment.* San Francisco, Jossey-Bass, 1967.
3. Brody, M.W.; and Mahoney, V.P.: Introjection, identification, and incorporation. *Int. J. Psycho-Anal., 45*:57, 1964.
4. Browne, W.J.: The alcoholic bout as an acting out. *Psychoanal. Quart., 34*:420, 1965.
5. Deutsch, H.: The genesis of agoraphobia. *Int. J. Psycho-Anal., 10,* 51, 1959.
6. Fenichel, U.: *The Psychoanalytic Theory of Neurosis.* New York, 1953, p. 506.
7. ——: The counter-phobic attitude (1936). In *Collected Papers,* II, New York, Norton, 1954.
8. Frances, A.; and Dunn, P.: The attachment-autonomy conflict in agoraphobia. *Int. J. Psychoanal., 56*:435, 1975.
9. Freud, S.: Beyond the pleasure principle (1920). Standard Edition, *18,* London, Hogarth, 1963.
10. ——: Remembering, repeating, and working through (1914). Standard Edition, *12.*
11. Kissin, B.; and Bergleitz, H.: *The Biology of Alcoholism,* Vol. I, New York, Plenum, 1971. (See references to Browne.)
12. Lewin, B.: *The Psychoanalysis of Elation.* New York, Psychoanalytic Quarterly, 1950.
13. Mendelson, J.: Biochemical mechanisms of alcohol addiction (1971). In Kissin and Bergleitz (see above).
14. Schmidt, W.; and de Lint, J.: Causes of death of alcoholics. *Quart. J. Stud. Alc., 33*:179-180 (with refs. to peptic ulcer), 1972.
15. Tamerin, J. S.; and Newmann, C. A.: A clinical reappraisal of the alcoholic stereotype: implications for treatment. *Am. J. Psychoanal., 34*:315, 1974.
16. Twerski, A.: Alcologia: a "logical" paralogia. *Am. J. Psychoanal., 34*:257, 1974.

Chapter 4

CHARACTERISTIC MOTIVATIONS IN ADDICTIVE BEHAVIOR

Martin A. Jacobs, Ph.D.

Martin A. Jacobs, Ph. D.

Dr. Jacobs is Chief Clinical Psychologist at the
Waltham Hospital Community Mental Health
Services. He is Associate Professor of Psychiatry at the Boston University School of Medicine and Visiting Lecturer in Psychology at
Tufts University and is Psychology Consultant
to the Medical Assistance Program for the
Commonwealth of Massachusetts. He is in the
private practice of psychotherapy.

The aim of this paper is to present a dynamic theory of the addictive personality and to discuss treatment considerations based on this theory. These views were first developed in conjunction with systematic observations of over 600 men and later extended via clinical interviews with patients who presented symptoms of addiction to alcohol and drugs as chief complaints in requesting psychotherapy. In the former instance a range of habituation to cigarette smoking was studied. Features characteristic of the most addicted group (men who smoked at least a pack daily) were compared with those of men who (1) had never smoked, (2) engaged in the habit on a take it or leave it basis, and (3) had broken the habit at least six months before being evaluated. Replicated retrospective investigations were carried out (1, 2, 3, 4) later confirmed by predictive studies (5, 6) using a variety of methods including self-report inventories, projective tests and in-depth clinical interviews. In the case of drug or alcohol abusers patients were seen in long-term treatment in order to help them to understand and to gain control over their symptoms.

In evaluating men who smoke, consistent differences appeared to characterize men who smoked to excess. The addicted smoker dealt with the underlying fear that he was helpless to regulate either his feelings or behavior by becoming exaggeratedly self-sufficient and reluctant to turn to others for help. In many cases the smoker took an action-oriented, counter phobic course while in others he appeared to be inhibited, obsessive and aloof, distancing himself socially. Both of these alternative styles were understood to reflect failure to adequately regulate and discharge impulses. For such people smoking becomes both a cure and a curse in that it helps to deal with out of control affects but becomes in turn another behavior pattern which seems out of control.

Excessive cigarette smoking is the most socially acceptable addiction in that it does not detract from one's appearance (with the minimal exceptions of bad breath and discolored fingers) or ability to perform. Unlike overeating, alcoholism or drug abuse one does not look or act impaired following regular heavy indulgence. Like other abuses of substances, heavy smoking is associated with attempts to supress unpleasant feelings such as tension, irritability, loneliness or boredom. It is a way to take care of oneself without having to rely on others to help deal with these affects. It is an attempt to feel in control when in fact it is another sign that one is out of control. Smoking is legal and to a large extent still encouraged by our society. It represents the low end of a continuum extending to the use of street drugs, especially narcotics, the possession of which constitutes a crime.

Though other addictions are more immediately and clearly seen as leading to near term impairments (such as looking fat and slovenly, being hung over, being unable to drive a car or losing contact with reality), long term health hazards (such as pulmonary, cardio vascular or hepatic disease and brain damage) are common to all, so that prolonged abuse is self-destructive. Heavy drug users often admit that their dependency is a slow suicide. Common to addictive behavior is the feeling that the immediate need is paramount and the consequences seem secondary; in fact, the excitement associated with flirting with danger is a cathartic experience like taking the drug.

Thus, addiction in a general sense is theorized to involve impulse and affect control pathology coupled with an inability or unwillingness to establish interdependence with others. This emotional detachment from others ensues from a feeling that no one cares, everyone is alone and there is no one to turn to when one is in trouble. Underlying in this attitude is a low self image. The person believes he is unattractive, hungry, greedy or bad; someone who has been and will be unwanted, neglected or abused by others. This pattern is least rigid and intense in people who limit their substance abuse to cigarettes and becomes most maladaptive in people with multiple addictions or ones involving anti-social characteristics such as heroin abuse.

A sense of despair and helplessness is disguised by an exaggerated self-reliance and hyperindependence. One aspect of this is exemplified by taking care of oneself through "medication." This technique, however, produces a warding off rather than a resolution of the life situation which produced unpleasant affect. As its extreme self medication produces withdrawal and escape such as in an alcoholic stupor or when nodding off from narcotics. Often the effect is simply to desperately fill the current life void and sense of emptiness without regard to future consequences. It is as though nothing is significant beside one's present enjoyment in the relief from discomfort.

Seeking a substance for pleasure or the reduction of pain is a self deter-mined coping mechanism in the sense that asking for help from others is not. An individual can insure that his particular substance is always there and the relief can be felt immediately. As problems accumulate and tolerance develops, higher doses are needed to perform the same task, and experimentation pro-ceeds with the use of more mind and sensation altering drugs. It is rare to find heavy smokers, for example, who do not drink. Similarly, regular abusers of street drugs try anything in their attempts to ward off unpleasant affects. The epitome of self-destructiveness is evidenced during "accidental" over-doses. This is one outcome if life situations continue to be felt to be unpleasant with no resolution.

The availability of people who are seen as caring is one alternative to the abuse of drugs. As mentioned, however, people are not always there when you need them whereas one can assure that his special substance is. (We are all familiar with the image of the heavy smoker who wakes in the middle of the night to find that he is out of cigarettes and immediately dresses to find an all night store which can resupply him.) Since distrust of closeness is a central issue in addiction changes in perception must be accomplished before the availability of people affectively replaces the reliance on substance. In our studies of characteristics which distinguish the heavy smoker from others we found a pattern which suggested that prior experiences with people were unsatisfying so that emotional detachment or hit and run relationships were more common as the person became older. These in turn proved unfulfilling and propelled a cycle whereby loneliness and emptiness became the major reasons for self-medication. This often led to the feeling, "if no one cares about me, why should I care about myself," a rationalization which justified further abuse.

Dynamics of Addiction

One approach to describing personality is to take into account both the image that the person has of himself and his style of coping with his environment, particularly the way in which he interacts with others. Human interaction has been described along continua of control and closeness. Leary (7), for example, emphasized a dominance and a love axis. Schutz (9), refers to dimensions of affiliation, control and affection. In conceptualizing the personality of the addicted person it was hypothesized that a need to be in control covaries with a need for closeness with others.

The need to be in control may be manifestation of the past experience of having been at the mercy of others and of having been disappointed and hurt. Being involved closely in a dependent fashion with others is of course first experienced as a child with one's parents. If parents abuse a child's sense of vulnerability by providing either too much or too little control and affection then the child's future involvements outside the family may be approached with fear and distrust, on the one hand, or with disdain and resentment on the other.

In our previous studies (1–4) of different classes of smoking behavior, the parental pattern most likely associated with heavy smoking was found to be too much control and too little affection. Parental behavior was described as demanding, cold and harsh. Reactions to such previous experiences within the family constellation take two major forms depending on whether domination or rejection is emphasized. In the former case, being close to others means that you will be smothered or drained. There is a fear that one will become trapped by having to comply with another's demands and be taken advantage of without getting anything of value in return. The fear is that you will be used without being appreciated. The sense is that one gives and doesn't get and that an interactional bargain is a poor one at best. The latter instance emphasizes the experience of rejection; i.e., if one needs another and is not taken care of or cared about, then one goes elsewhere or learns that it is safer not to be vulnerable in the first place. It is better to learn to need no one and just to count on yourself. Then you are in command and can minimize the possibility of being abandoned by someone you needed. If you can keep your distance from others and don't get emotionally involved then no one can hurt you. Thus, high needs for control coexist with low expectations for closeness.

The image that the child develops of himself when subject to parental behavior of domination without affection can range between extremes of lowered self-worth based on incompetence ("they didn't love me because I'm no good") to destructiveness ("I hate them for not wanting me, they're no good"). Whether the person feels there is something wrong with him or with his parents, he is still likely to question his attractiveness and chances of being loved by others, e.g. ("Who could love me? I'm a hateful, greedy person.") Thus, the need to be on one's own is intensified by the fear that one has no real choice. If he seeks out closeness he is likely to be rejected so he doesn't even bother. ("Why put yourself in a vulnerable position when the chances for success are so limited?") The degree and type of addiction is likely to be associated with the intensity of despair which a person feels about his attractiveness and the actual repeated experience of disappointment and failure in interpersonal relationships. A self-fulfilling prophecy is set up whereby defensiveness and distrust turns other people off and drives them away. The more one is alone the more one will turn to means of self-gratification. The more one feels that no one else cares the less one cares about himself and self-destructiveness intensifies. Thus frequency and intensity of addiction to substances increases.

Case Histories

The following case histories are presented to illustrate this theory of the addictive personality.

1. A 27 year old single woman sought treatment following the breakup of a four year relationship with a man several years older than her whom she was later to report she never felt close to and never could really consider marrying. She was troubled by her apparent loss of control with respect to eating, smoking and drinking which seemed to follow the termination of the relationship. She felt out of control and thus ashamed of herself. The most important need she felt was to be in command and she found that she really didn't like to become closely involved with others, as she felt more comfortable when she kept them at a distance. In fact, she had a series of relationships with men whom she could describe in retrospect as unacceptable from the onset. It was as if they were selected as unsuitable and therefore safe. She knew the relationships would go nowhere and therefore she couldn't be disappointed. The men were also seen as unacceptable to her parents whom she

reportedly despised because of their snobbishness and coldness. Both were heavy drinkers and she had seen her father violent towards various family members on several occasions when intoxicated. The basic tone of the family interaction was distance and formality. Feelings were not expressed and a proper social facade was erected which was clearly in contrast to the real but secret emotionally labile pattern. Although primarily concerned about her ability to take care of herself and be in control of her impulses, the patient also reported feeling isolated and unhappy. She described herself as if she were off in the void of space, feeling very cold and terribly alone.

2. A 29 year old single male sought treatment because he was afraid his heavy smoking and drinking were going to kill him at an early age. He lived alone and made occasional Sunday visits to his family for dinner but never really felt welcome; it was as if he was an intruder. His father didn't like him he felt, and there was nothing he could do to please him. In high school his father had pushed him to achieve but somehow he always failed those courses in which his father had most invested. His mother was seen as quiet and passive and he wasn't really sure where he stood with her either, although his major concern was with the overt rejection which he felt from his father. He had gone steady with a girl for a few months but she became pregnant, had an abortion without consulting him and then broke off the relationship. At the time he sought therapy she had become engaged to another man. The patient reported that he felt angry all the time and that the smoking and drinking kept him sedated and under control. Although he was afraid he was killing himself (and had sought several medical consultations complaining that he feared he had throat cancer) he believed that he couldn't afford to stop these practices without running the risk of hurting others because of his violent temper. Specifically, his chronic sore throat kept him from screaming and served as a curb on his losing control when he was with others.

3. A 45 year old married woman was admitted to a psychiatric ward following an overdose of tranquilizers and alcohol. This was her third recorded OD, the two previous ones having occurred approximately 15 years earlier. Her chief complaints were that she was lonely and uncared for, had recurrent episodes of depression and anxiety and had been drinking heavily for the past 2 years. In the 6 months prior to admission her drinking had gotten "really bad" and she was also taking 6 or 7 amphetamine tablets daily. She and her husband were both alcoholics; each evening they would sit in front of the TV drinking until passing out. Her husband had recently been told that he had cirrhosis of the liver and that he would die in 5 years if he did not stop drinking. The patient had multiple gynecological complaints, was menopausal and was scheduled for a hysterectomy within a month. One and a half years prior to admission she had been diagnosed as having cervical cancer but a

conization operation had been apparently successful. Within the past year both her mother and father had died, and in fact, she could trace her really heavy drinking to the death of her father who just seemed to go downhill when his wife died. She was now faced with the spectre of her husband's death. Patient was the youngest of 3 children but considered herself to have been an only child because her two brothers were so much older than her. She felt that her parents were old enough to be grandparents and were no longer interested or able to raise children when she was born. In addition, they were fanatically religious and made her feel that normal activities such as dancing, going to the movies and wearing makeup were sins. She recalled being beaten after going to a Shirley Temple movie. Consequently she had little contact with other children. Patient was overweight as a child and felt in retrospect that she had gained weight in order to take revenge on her mother but ended up hurting herself. She lost weight in late adolescence and then hated the boys who then became interested in her but had rejected her when she was fat. She married the first man she ever dated but soon regretted this since there seemed to be no love in the relationship. She felt ignored by him as he pursued his business career and took revenge on him by becoming promiscuous partly in order to provoke jealousy. This only led to further withdrawal on his part and she began to feel more and more isolated and neglected.

During the first nine years of her marriage she was pregnant eight times and carried five children to full term. She expressed a need to feel filled up and her drinking history really began after the last child was born, and she had a tubal ligation. The couple finally divorced eight years later after many separations and reconciliations. The previous OD's occurred at this time. Many men were in and out of the house during this period and finally she married again six years later. Whereas the first husband had neglected her this one physically abused her. This relationship lasted only six months when her second husband ran off with another man, a supreme blow to her narcissism. She did not tolerate being alone and felt that she was losing her physical attractiveness and that this was the only reason why anyone wanted her; her seductiveness was compulsive in an attempt to feel accepted. She attracted then dumped the men who became interested in her. Shortly thereafter she remarried her first husband but found that nothing had changed and that she still felt unwanted. Furthermore, her children were having trouble adjusting to the world and her status as a mother was diminished when three of them became divorced, one was sent to prison and another had a baby out of wedlock. Finally, when her parents died she felt completely alone and a failure.

4. Patient was a 30 year old male who was admitted to an open ward for treatment because of depression and severe alcoholism. He was on his second marriage but this was not working out well; a few months earlier his wife had been admitted to the same ward after he had beaten her up. Patient reported

that he typically ran away from his problems by physically leaving, by shutting himself off socially and by bouts of drinking. In the past he had been a heroin addict for nine months and had used cocaine, hallucinogens and marihuana sporadically. He currently smoked about two packs of cigarettes daily and had a ten year history of alcohol abuse. Patient reports being troubled by out of control feelings, particularly violence and depression, which had led to hospitalization in State institutions several times in the past. Patient also had a criminal record because of assault.

The family background was characterized by an abusive father who would come home drunk and beat the patient. Father was generally unemployed and mother supported the family. She was out of the house a lot and was ineffective in protecting the patient from the brutal beatings which he received from his father. Two younger brothers were not beaten but patient reports that one is an alcoholic and the other is heavily into drugs. Father forced patient to go out to work and he had to drop out of high school. He recalls having friends but could never bring them home because of his father's violence. At age 14 after his father broke four of his fingers he decided to leave home. He hit the road and travelled all over the country doing odd jobs. Although this was a marginal existence he was able to take complete care of himself and was obliged to no one. However, the sense of freedom was diminished by his increasing loneliness. He decided to settle down at age 19 when he married but this relationship quickly ended in divorce. His drinking along with episodes of rage and violence against both objects and people (throwing knives into his apartment wall and beating up a man in a jealous rage) intensified and resulted in incarceration and multiple hospitalizations. After living alone and travelling for several years he married again when he was 28. After his first child was born he enlisted in the service and his wife and child moved in with her parents. It was as if he did not tolerate being tied down. His service record was characterized by insubordination and numerous AWOL incidents. Faced with prison or a dishonorable discharge he entered a psychiatric hospital. He was discharged nine months after enlisting at which time he returned to live with his wife at her family's home but found that his in-laws didn't approve of him. After a short while he was restricted from their home. The episode reminded him of the abusive power which his own father had exercised over him. He became violently enraged and took it out on his wife. It was this beating which led to her hospitalization.

Patient believes that drinking is not his real problem. He drinks when he is depressed but then becomes violent, ashamed of himself and then totally irresponsible. He trusts no one and finds it hard to confide in a therapist. He is currently unable to take responsibility for his behavior, blaming it on his deprived background, but realizes that he is doomed to a life of loneliness and possibly incarceration unless he changes.

These case studies have illustrated the central features of the addictive personality: the past history of neglect or abuse perceived by the person leading to uncontrollable unpleasant affect (such as rage or depression), an impulsive, defiant defensive structure, and an underlying image of oneself as unattractive and unworthy of being cared for in the present and future. With little to look forward to there is no balance against the need to provide one's own gratification via substances even if they are perceived as self-destructive. Underlying passive longings are frustrated in a self-fulfilling way by the counter dependent and emotionally detached life style which these individuals typically adopt to avoid being trapped and at the mercy of others. Others are unconsciously picked to share their lives who are likely to either repeat the parental patterns or be rejected in turn as unsuitable.

The inner sense of emptiness is exemplified in the various reports and drug abuse is increased following loss. In both sexes pregnancy is regarded as supremely important whereas the raising of children is handled poorly as if the process of separation is too much to bear. In this sense turning to substances to fill oneself (e.g., "feel warm inside") takes on added meaning or represents more than a wish to escape.

Spontaneous Withdrawal and Relapse

Spontaneous remission of addictive symptoms is most likely to occur when a medical danger signal is appreciated. A person who has been drinking regularly for years will stop abruptly when a diagnosis of liver cirrhosis is made. Similarly, the detection of emphysema or lung cancer will halt heavy cigarette smoking. In many cases, regeneration of tissue occurs after prolonged abstinence so that the former smoker or drinker gets a second chance. In other cases the damage has been done. Up till that point medical warnings are denied or are not internalized by an individual who is gaining pleasure from his addiction without much other gratification in his life. Denial that one can be hurt by drug abuse is the rule and even continues after damage is detected. Although government agencies and foundations try to alert the public to the dangers of drug abuse, they are not reaching the addicted population who react to this information as impersonal and as mentioned before, enjoy risks and excitement. Unfortunately, people who respond on a rational basis and take their long term welfare into account are most often not the ones who abuse drugs in the first place.

Although such laws as the Harrison Narcotics Act of 1914 and the Volstead Act of 1919 may have prevented many people from starting to experiment with such drugs or alcohol they have little impact on those who feel they have nothing to lose, who gain pleasure in defying authority or who relish thrills and excitement. Legal, moral or ethical reasons alone are too remote, rational and abstract to affect people for whom drug abuse is highly personal. An actual health scare (fear of being crippled or dying) is effective because it is a threat to a person's body and if physical symptoms are apparent is less easily denied.

It is ironic that a clean bill of health is often taken to mean that one is immune to the dangers with which excessive use of a drug is associated. Such individuals also rationalize that everyone dies sometime so one might as well enjoy life to its fullest. Often fear of the bodily sensations associated with withdrawal is more motivating than the more remote dread concerned with physical damage. Thus, only when a real and immediate danger is perceived will action be taken.

The combination of personal illness highlighting the immediate and real danger of drug abuse and a positive event in one's life provides the best setting for spontaneous withdrawal from drugs. The decision based on facts should be made on the spot without procrastination since it has been observed that addicts either act impetuously in a self-destructive fashion or else are so indecisive that they typically do nothing. Both the threat to life and a reason to live combine to bolster motivation to protect one's future. Usually the positive events involve experiencing the possibility of real closeness with another person thus raising self-esteem. The feeling that someone cares helps one to care more about himself. However, the more one has experienced consistent disappointments and letdowns in the past from broken promises and unfulfilled relationships, the less this new turn of events is likely to have an impact. For such people a wait-and-see attitude might prevail before the guaranteed pleasure of an oral addiction is given up for an uncertain reliance on another. In this connection, relapse is likely to occur when the hoped-for closeness ends (as in a broken engagement or divorce), when loneliness and boredom become intensified (such as when a travelling job is taken or more hours are spent at work because of increased responsibilities) and when tragedy or illness interfere with existing relationships (as when a wife becomes ill and requires care, or when a previously supportive person begins to make demands on the individual without being in a position to immediately reciprocate).

During withdrawal the former addict feels empty and experiences the loss of something very close to him. He seeks to replace the given-up substance with another which can be taken inside. Former smokers routinely gain 10 to 20 lbs. following withdrawal and ex-alcoholics increase their comsumption of sweets, particularly chocolate. Whether this is a biologic reaction affecting appetite control triggered by the sudden withdrawal of a drug such as nicotine or alcohol, or simply symptom substitution or a combination of the two is unknown.

The addictive person seems to seek the inner warmth and contentment which was denied him while growing up by providing self induced oral gratification. In order to break this pattern contentment must come from a sense of inner strength and/or a feeling of affection and caring from others. As mentioned, relapse occurs when external constraints and supports are removed, even temporarily.

Treatment Programs

Formalized programs to help the abuser of drugs—from cigarettes to heroin—have ranged from individual physicians prescribing alternative medications to large group meetings utilizing persuasion and scare tactics to therapeutic communities. Initially, a model thought to have much promise utilized ex-addicts as leaders to foster empathy and acceptance in a counterculture milieu which provided a sense of mutual caring. Most therapeutic communities have been organized by dynamic, charismatic ex-addicts (8). Strong belief bordering on religious fanaticism in its therapeutic potential coupled with the sense of sharing serve to help the addict, but problems arise when attempts are made to return him to an independent existence in the community. One attempt to deal with this re-entry problem is to establish a sub-culture where the former drug abuser can reside indefinitely. Similarly, staying on as a leader in such an organization promotes heightened self-esteem and a sense of purpose which replaces the former feelings of worthlessness, failure and pessimism that one has nothing to lose. Loss of this status associated with termination leaves one only with memories of success. Without others to bolster one's resolve and confidence, relapse is the rule.

Alcoholics Anonymous was founded in 1934 on the premise that people help themselves by helping others. This organization recognizes the need for commitment on the part of the alcoholic and acknowledgement that he needs help, prohibits substitute medication, advocates abstinence, provides a sponsor to welcome the newcomer into the group and to be a personal help when needed day or night, and suggests a step-by-step approach to recovery (a day at a time). Again, the most successful abstainers are the ones who gain status by helping others within the program and make it an important part of their lives.

These examples highlight the delicate balance which must be obtained if successful withdrawal is to become permanent abstinence. The sense of closeness and involvement which the addict fears but desires must be established along with a sense of mastery and self-determination or else chronic dependence on the program is required. A therapeutic community or program of the type described often becomes the reason for a person's life and without it he is literally back out on the street alone. His feelings of success and accomplishment become linked with the community and its members and he becomes an unrecognized prophet in his home town when he leaves. There is no one around afterwards to acknowledge his suffering and success nor to provide external constraints. This may unfortunately be true even if he has available (and this is often unlikely) a warm, caring group of family or friends who are willing and able to support his abstinence and recognize his accomplishments. Such people are likely to become tired of reinforcing his achievements and/or become the objects of his frustrations. This problem is mitigated to some extent by transfer to a half-way house. However, in the long run, unless his self-image is changed (i.e., he feels in control and attractive) the former addict will relapse.

Establishment of a concept of self-determination, at its extreme, implies that a person learns to count on himself instead of being dependent on drugs or even other people. As a first step to interdependence with others a person must first feel that he can take care of himself in a responsibile fashion. A sense of mastery and self-control must be established which replaces both the inner sense of incompetence and the facade of hyper-independence, one aspect of which was the need to self-medicate to ward off unpleasant affects. Once a person learns that he can count on himself he is ready to learn to develop closeness. Dependence on others without a sense of real self-regard is frightening and humiliating. (Parenthetically, people keep their distance from others in order to avoid being "found out" to be a phony. Individuals who present a facade of exaggerated self-reliance but who feel incompetent and out of control inside have a secret which will be betrayed by involvement.)

A first step in changing the ex-addict's self-concept is to help him to appreciate his success in a therapeutic group setting. He is entitled to feel good about himself because he is learning to deal with his own feelings and problems without resorting to drugs. In the process of breaking the habit he faces a challenge which many have failed and gains the satisfaction that he is a success and free of a destructive crutch. Many ex-addicts speak of an exhilarating feeling of liberation, being out from under their former habits, and confess that they felt weak and helpless when relying on drugs. This must be followed with a generalized feeling that he can handle himself without warding off, damping down, or running away. With the confidence that success in treatment brings he must begin to face outside pressures, utilizing the feelings that he is in control and coping satisfactorily and that he has the concerned support of the group.

Understanding the dynamics of the addicted person is helpful in planning an action-oriented group; i.e., one which involves both sharing and self-control. Changes in behavior (stopping the symptom) are focused on first; incorporation of the changes in the self-concept, second; and development of closeness, third. Many long-term therapists have found that symptoms persist while the patient is learning to understand himself and modify his reactive repertoire. For some patients time is an important element, for if they continue abusing drugs they might not be alive to reap the gains of insight. Accordingly, a combined behavioral and dynamic approach is advocated which incorporates action along with understanding of the meaning of addictive behavior and its importance to the person's life style. Furthermore, we have found that the defensive structure of the addict can be used in a constructive way rather than reacted to as an obstacle which must be overcome.

For this reason, certain types of behavioral modification have not proved any more effective than any other treatment. First and foremost of the problems is the investiture of control outside the individual, putting power in the hands of the therapist. People who distrust and defy authority are likely to have difficulty with this approach. Secondly, often the treatment situation is removed from the patient's ordinary life so that conditioning occurs within the confines of the "laboratory" but cannot be accommodated in his real world. Use of aversive techniques, such as blowing hot air in a person's face or shocking him when he smokes, which are not replicable outside the treatment setting, have little carry-over once the therapy ends. This is the same difficulty which the therapeutic communities have discovered; establishment of an idealistic milieu which cannot be found outside leads to patients doing well as long as they remain within the community. But essentially, many become "lifers" in order to continue to benefit indefinitely.

Thus, it is advocated that for long-term success a personally meaningful approach be employed, based on the concept of developing a real and effective sense of mastery which is likely to have congruence with the patient's ordinary life. Since the individual leaves on his own when the program ends treatment must begin to positively alter his self-concept. He must feel that he is the one responsible for his success and that he is in control of himself. He must feel pride in having broken a long-term habit which was self-destructive and extend this to other aspects of his life. The drawbacks are the same here as with any other program; outside life experiences may be unrewarding, temptation and the availability of drugs in the community abound, and a feeling of emptiness may prevail if one feels lonely and unappreciated. Accordingly, the program can give the patient confidence and courage but he must develop on his own a sense of competence which is sustaining.

Summary

This paper has described a dynamic theory of addictive behavior. Essentially, the addicted person is thought of as struggling with impulse control and affective lability problems coupled with a fear of closeness. Inner feelings of emptiness are decreased by "filling up" with substances which are self-provided and thus gratification is under one's own control. Turning to others is difficult because of past experiences within the family constellation which have led the person to expect abandonment, abuse or entrapment rather than affection and support. Placing oneself at the mercy of others is avoided because of these experiences and the need increases to be in complete command. The irony is that the addiction is another sign that he is really out of control and in need of a "crutch" (which is furthermore, self-destructive).

A treatment program which utilizes knowledge of this personality structure would be action oriented, limit dependence on authority by providing group treatment and emphasize development of self-esteem through self-control (i.e., focus immediately on withdrawal and abstinence). It was suggested that people with this personality structure benefit most when given an opportunity at the onset to truly feel competent. Resistance typically takes the form of "I don't need anybody" as long as the person feels compelled to hide feelings of weakness and helplessness behind a facade of hyperindependence. Unless the person feels himself to be an equal, dependence on others is reacted to as humiliating, or becomes a long-term treatment issue with relapse likely after termination.

References

1. Jacobs, M.A., Knapp, P.H., Anderson, L.S., et al: Relationship of oral frustration factors with heavy cigarette smoking in males. *J. Nerv. Ment. Dis.*, 141: 161–171, 1965.
2. Jacobs, M.A., Anderson, L.S., Champagne, E., et al: Orality, impulsivity and cigarette smoking in men: further findings in support of a theory. *J. Nerv. Ment. Dis.*, 143: 207–219, 1966.
3. Jacobs, M.A. and Spilken, A.Z.: Personality patterns associated with heavy cigarette smoking in male college students. *J. Consult. Clin. Psychol.*, 37: 428–432, 1971.
4. Jacobs, M.A., Knapp, P.H., Rosenthal, S., et al: Psychological aspects of cigarette smoking in men: a clinical evaluation. *Psychosom. Med.*, 32: 469–485, 1970.
5. Jacobs, M.A., Spilken, A.Z., Norman, M.M., et al: Interaction of personality and treatment conditions associated with success in a smoking control program. *Psychosom. Med.*, 33: 545–556, 1971.
6. Jacobs, M.A.: The addictive personality: prediction of success in a smoking withdrawal program. *Psychosom. Med.*, 34: 30–38, 1972.
7. Leary, T.: *Interpersonal Diagnosis of Personality*. New York: Ronald Press, 1957.
8. Ramsay, A.: Therapeutic community rap. in *Drug Abuse Prevention Report*. Rockville, Md.: National Clearinghouse for Drug Abuse Information, 1: No. 3, 1973.
9. Schutz, W.C.: *The Interpersonal Underworld*. Palo Alto, Calif: Science and Behavior Books, 1966.

Chapter 5

UNDERSTANDING THE NEUROSIS IN ALCOHOLISM
A Study in Office Treatment

Milton S. Gurvitz, Ph.D.

Milton S. Gurvitz Ph. D.

Dr. Gurvitz is Clinical Professor of Psychology in the Postdoctoral Program, Institute of Advanced Psychological Studies at Adelphi University. He is Director of the Great Neck Consultation Center, a Senior Member of the National Psychological Association for Psychoanalysis and is in private practice of psychotherapy and psychoanalysis.

The selection of patients for office treatment of alcoholics must be based on careful criteria. It is vital to eliminate the essential alcoholic as defined by Knight. Of the remainder, those with a very high W% on the Rorschach attending to the whole card and expressing what is seen in an unintegrated fashion, indicate an extreme variance between their idealized self image and reality, and so a poorer prognosis. The essential alcoholic can be treated but needs Alcoholics Anonymous, drying out and or supportive therapy.

Reactive and neurotic alcoholics also need to "hit bottom"; but more in a psychological sense than the complete social collapse of the essential alcoholic. When this descent does occur, it is a hopeful sign of progress in therapy. This is the alcoholic's way of making his alcoholism ego alien, seeing it clearly as a product of neurotic motivation.

Alcohol is a compensation in various ways for social and psychological defects. It enables the individual to detach himself from an unhappy reality and superego sources of criticism as his self esteem is devalued. This pattern can be observed on a large sociological basis as well as by the effect of culture shock on societal groups such as the American Indian, or on any deprived economic group with limited opportunities, particularly in our Western culture.

In 1937, Knight differentiated the essential alcoholic from the reactive and neurotic alcoholic.

The essential alcoholic begins drinking in early life after a chaotic and unsuccessful adolescence or young manhood and is never able to resolve the identity crisis. Alcohol is a way to blurr his awareness of life by drinking into oblivion. The object here is to secure the nirvana of stupor. Their ultimate objective is to hit bottom and stay there as a defense against the realization of their unacceptable loss of self esteem. The regression to the blissful sleep of the infant is oral; hence the rhythm of alcohol intake, satiation and sleep.

Reactive alcoholics lead reasonably successful lives until they experience a crisis that triggers an emotional conflict that leads to regressive solutions including the use of alcohol. When the individual is relatively healthy, the episode can itself be a form of a self healing release, especially where the social group is tolerant of such behavior. When the crisis is seemingly prompted by an external situation, the loss of self esteem may be replaced by drinking. When the crisis is internal, the drinking problem is often made the cause rather than the effect, i.e., when a job becomes too difficult the ego is bolstered by drinking. When the support becomes insufficient and alcoholism results, the poor job performance is blamed on the drinking rather than vice versa.

Neurotic alcoholics, on the other hand, deal with neurotic symptoms and behavior by drinking until the inevitable down hill cycle takes its toll. Another hazard is presented by the person who is not psychologically disabled by his drinking but develops physical problems such as cirrohosis which makes drinking life threatening and suicidal. Typical conflicts, symptoms or behavior that is replaced or resolved by drinking includes homosexuality, inadequacy, hostility, withdrawal, inadequate sexuality and an inability to be assertive.

The reactive alcoholic needs special handling with emphasis on brevity. Once the acute phase is over, and the reality problem dealt with, self esteem is usually easily restored but the problem of separation becomes crucial. Otherwise, dependency is simply shifted from the parental figure to the therapist. If dependency is not dealt with, prolongation of therapy leads to further alcoholic episodes as an unconscious protest against the oral dependency. If separation can be achieved without great difficulty even social drinking can be retained though it is not desirable.

The neurotic alcoholic needs long term therapy because alcohol is a symptomatic response to the anxiety engendered by the neurotic conflict. Until the underlying neurosis is dealt with there is no real help for the alcoholism. Alcoholism with underlying psychosis represents a much poorer prognosis. Simple aversion therapy in these cases is very dangerous. The stress that is set up may lead in neurotics to overwhelming somatic symptoms such as bleeding ulcers, asthma or mucous colitis. Borderline patients tend in this situation to develop frank psychotic symptoms as regression is forced, reality testing lowered and schizophrenic and depressive restitutional symptoms emerge.

The treatment noted in this paper was analytic psychotherapy combined with abstinence. More support than usual at the beginning is needed to maintain initial abstinence. Patients with character disorders achieve abstinence more easily but need longer therapy because the character probelms need time for the behavior to become ego alien.

This therapist's experience with alcoholics began as consultant to the Connecticut Commission on Alcoholism he tested and evaluated some 300 cases from 1948 to 1953. The treatment cases from 1950 to 1964 totaled 8 reactive and 13 neurotic. On personal follow up, 6 of the 8 reactive cases are recovered to this date although 2 needed further brief therapy. One relapsed after another business failure and has recurrent drinking bouts and the last was killed in an automobile accident while driving when intoxicated. Of the 13 neurotic alcoholics 9 are symptom free of alcoholism and neurosis and have had no therapy for a minimum of 6 years. One recently returned for help with neurotic problems but has been non-alcoholic for 8 years. Three broke off treatment before completion; two are drinking heavily but are in Alcoholics Anonymous. The last is not drinking but is severely disabled psychologically, cannot work, abandoned his family and is living off the financial settlement with his former wealthy wife.

Two cases will be presented to illustrate a typical reactive and neurotic alcoholic case.

Case A—Reactive Alcoholic

Mr. A. was referred because he had struck a child with his car when he was drunk. Court was ready to impose a severe sentence.

Patient was examined because he reported that he did not remember the incident and claimed he had not drunk since. A, a man in his 50's, was a self employed delivery salesman who had a perfect driving record and no history of drinking prior to the death of his only older sister three months before the accident. He and his sister were both childless and the two married couples were very close. Six months before the accident the two couples had been away on a cruise and it was during this time that the sister discovered the condition which led to her quick demise.

He was very different from his sister, she was college educated and a business executive. He was bright, a high school drop out but a good business man, and a bluff, hearty blunt man not interested in intellectual matters. He relates his educational difference to his family suddenly moving away to benefit the sister leaving him adrift in a new school and friendless in the neighborhood. He quit school and slowly worked his way up in the business world "the hard way."

On his sister's death, A felt very depressed based on the emergence and rerepression of hostile feelings toward his sister, guilt over having for once done better than his sister in surviving and again resentment at being saddled with his depressed and alcoholic brother-in-law. He described his brother-in-law as weak and couldn't allow himself the weakness of depression. He began to drink suddenly to relieve the depression, guilt, and hostility and the tragedy followed. Actually A needs treatment for his depression at this point since "hitting bottom" with the accident made further drinking unlikely. Although he was clinically very depressed and at times on the verge of tears he had to maintain a "front" that masked his true adjustment and was ready to go to jail rather than admit his weakness as he saw it. Interpretation of A to the probation officer and the court lead to treatment rather than punishment. Had the psychologist not intervened A would have neurotically punished himself by serving a jail sentence that would have disrupted his life. He would have continued his neurotic repetition compulsion that life was unfair to him.

Case B—Neurotic Alcoholic

B was a physician who came to see me originally because of his problem children. Although he was skilled and respected he never did well economically because of the drain of his divorced wife and his insistance on giving his four boys a private school education and psychotherapy.

He started life as a farm boy on a subsistance farm in Western New York and pulled himself up by his bootstraps and the G.I. Bill through Medical

School after World War I. He was determined to give his children a better life but crippled this by his driving them to social standards befitting his aristocratic, wealthy mistress. These were in hopeless contrast to the working class mores of his schizophrenic ex wife with whom they lived. As he became aware of the degrading relationship to his lover he began to drink more and more and his practice suffered.

Treatment was refused until his mistress was forced to hospitalize him and his colleague had the good sense *not* to use a political diagnosis but called it acute alcoholism.

Since "hitting bottom" with the help of psychotherapy B has not had a drink since. He has not always managed his life well and in one of his resistances to psychotherapy entered another disastrous marriage, soon ending in divorce. He has been able to continue his profession and to lead a life of recognized public service. He struggles with his new daughter who is doing well and he has seen his most disturbed son make an outstanding adjustment and success in life. He is attractive to women but cannot make a permanent adjustment. He still finds it difficult to accept himself and struggles for the outward trappings of self esteem that always just barely elude him. In this he unconsciously still follows his unsuccessful father.

There is a certain equilibrium. He does not drink and he doesn't fail. Therapy has not been successful in truly liberating him so he can fulfill his potential. He is limited by his inability to break from the seductive mother and he is too close to his internal father to resolve his unconscious wish to destroy him by being successful. His ego could only bear the pain of partial truth and the working alliance could not sustain the burden of analyzing the resistance. Unfortunately, lack of money and time made more intensive analysis, at least in B's judgement, impossible.

B's case does illustrate the therapist's necessity to settle for limited objectives without loss of his own self esteem.

Alcohol is the only drug known which is absorbed in significant amounts through the stomach lining; reaching measurable blood levels in 15 to 20 minutes. The general effect on the brain is as a depressant diminishing the psychomotor activity level and therefore anxiety or tension. This in turn gives relief from those conflicts which generate anxiety. There is, however, a secondary or delayed effect of increased activity level. The effect of every sedative drug is followed by increased agitation. There is, then, a tendency to drink more alcohol to suppress the long term agitation with short term relief of anxiety leading to increased drinking. Finally the short term effect even though repeated can no longer relieve the long term agitation resulting in chronic pain, popularly known as hangover.

One of the reasons that essential alcoholics need to be treated differently is that they may very well have a physiological component of anxiety on which the alcohol has an immediate but temporary tranquilizing effect. A typical essential alcoholic who began at 18 said: "I finally found out what it was to feel normal." "I felt abnormal all my life but after the first drink I felt like everybody else."

Unfortunately, to take a new dose of alcohol to control the agitation of yesterday's intake results in an individual close to sleep or extremely uncomfortable and at best functioning minimally. The alcoholic is constantly drinking more than yesterday's plateau, losing functional capacity in the process.

The alcoholic is truly the oral personality, looking for love, comfort and security and yet always losing it because he diminishes rather than develops his capacity for giving to others. He can maintain relationships only in terms of a passivity which he resents. While he is prone to melancholia, the choice of symptom is not depression because the superego is not as punishing, allowing the use of alcohol to control symptoms such as anxiety and depression. The depressive is more directly self punishing on a moralistic; introversive level.

If we think of the superego as a threatening parent, the depressive stops trying to satisfy the parent and turns his anger inward. The alcoholic tries to placate the parent with passivity and compliance and uses the alcohol to deal with the anxiety and tension allowing wish fulfillment and rationalization to temporarily reinforce self esteem.

Bibliography

1. Callner, D.A. 1975. Behavioral treatment approaches to drug abuse: A critical review of the research. Psychol. Bull. 82:143–64.
2. Chafetz, M.E. Alcholoism in the United States. Interam. J. Psychol., 6: 137, 1972.
3. Davies, D.L. Normal drinking in recovered alcohol addicts. Q. J. Stud. Alcohol, 23:94, 1962. Responses: Q. J. Stud. Alcohol 24:109, 321, 1963.
4. Gerard, D.L. and Saenger, G. Out-Patient Treatment of Alcoholism. University of Toronto Press, Toronto, 1966.
5. Gurvitz, M.S., W% As a Measure of Orality, Eastern Psychological Association, April, 1953, Boston.
6. Gurvitz, M.S. and Thomas Kavazanjian, W% as a Measure of Orality, Journal of the Hillside Hospital, 1953, II, pp. 213–218.
7. Gurvitz, Milton S. "Socially Rewarded Pathology" in the Neurosis of Our Time: Acting Out. George D. Goldman and Donald S. Milman ed. Springfield: cc Thomas 1973.
8. Gurvitz, Milton S., "Psychoanalytic Psychotherapy, an Historical Perspective" in Psychoanalytic Psychotherapy. George D. Goldman and Donald S. Milman ed. Reading: Addison Wesley, 1978.
9. Gurvitz, Milton S. "Psychopathy: Suicide and Homicide as Unconscious Expressions of Aggression" in Psychoanalytic Perspectives on Aggression. George D. Goldman and Donald S. Milman ed. Dubuque: Kendall/Hunt, 1978.

10. Jellinek, E.M. The Disease Concept of Alcoholism. Hillhouse Press, New Haven, 1960.
11. Knight, R.P. Psychodynamics of chronic alcoholism. J. Nerv. Ment. Dis., 86: 538, 1937.
12. McClelland, D.C., Davis, W.N., Kalin, R., and Wanner, E. The Drinking Man. Alcohol and Human Motivation. Free Press, New York, 1972.
13. National Council on Alcoholism. Criteria for the diagnosis of alcoholism. Am. J. Psychiatry, 129:127, 1972.
14. Sobell, M.B., Sobell, L.C. 1976. Second year treatment outcome of alcoholics treated by individualized behavior therapy: Results. Behav. Res. Ther. 14:195–215.
15. Wolff, P.H. Ethnic differences in alcohol sensitivity. Science. 175:449, 1972.

Chapter 6

THE EXTENSION OF EARLY DEPENDENCY PROBLEMS IN THE DEVELOPMENT OF DRUG ADDICTION

Richard L. Vickers, Ph.D. and Dolores Etrog, C.S.W.

Richard L. Vickers, Ph.D.

Dr. Vickers was trained at the University of Minnesota. He is a candidate in the Postdoctoral Program in Psychotherapy at Adelphi University; is affiliated with the Community Hospital at Glen Cove and is in private practice.

Dolores Etrog, C.S.W.

Dr. Etrog has been employed at Mt. Sinai Hospital as well as in Social Services at Elmhurst General Hospital and the Glen Cove Community Hospital Drug Program and she is presently at Long Island Jewish-Hillside Medical Center. She is a field instructor for Adelphi University Graduate School of Social Work. She received a BA degree at Hofstra University and a MSW degree at Wurzweiler School of Social Work at Yeshiva University.

Introduction

As children, most of us listened with rapt attention to stories about our parents' childhood, and their parents' childhood in turn. This was our first contact with history. Eventually our frame of reference expanded and crossed family boundaries: we became aware of the larger scope of history in the world. At the same time we began to lose track of our own beginnings, our childhood experience. Our mature relationship with history is two-sided, encompassing our intellectual orientation to the outside world and our personal orientation to our individual past, including our family history. Understanding the impact of early experience increases our capacity for freedom of choice.

During the last two years, we have explored the use of early recollections (ER's) with individuals and families who do not appear interested in the past nor its effects upon them. These are adolescent drug abusers and their families who come for treatment at our clinic.* This paper discusses our experience with ER's obtained from drug users and their families and explores the use of ER's as a diagnostic tool and facilitative technique.

Our clinic treats adult addicts and high risk adolescents, age thirteen to sixteen. Characteristics of these two groups are similar: they are white, suburban, polydrug users with histories of behavior disorder and school failure. Their families have histories of disruption and discord. They are exposed to drug and alcohol abuse early in life, and many of their families contain multigenerational alcoholism. We view their drug abuse as symptomatic, but also specifically learned in the family and from peers. This behavior grows progressively compulsive during adolescence, becoming physically reinforced with addiction. Many of our adult patients have progressed stepwise, through experimental, habitual, and finally addictive drug abuse. Much of our work is directed toward the goal of abstinence, especially with the adult addict. Youngsters in our adolescent programs are less enmeshed in a drug-oriented life style and more connected with their nuclear families. We work with them and their families in attempting to understand their struggle with adolescent separation.

Drug abusers hold inaccurate representations of others, leading to their characteristic mistrust, evasiveness, fear, and manipulation. Their wariness and use of nonverbal defenses makes them poor candidates for intensive therapy, both as adolescents and adults.

In 1972, Reuben Fine (14) reported only one case of successfully treated addiction in the psychoanalytic literature. Gottesfeld et al. (17) also noted that there is little clinical writing about the preaddictive client, in contrast with extensive literature on narcotic addiction. His observation applies to the family therapy literature as well.

*Community House, Drug Abuse Treatment and Prevention Program, at The Community Hospital at Glen Cove, Long Island, New York.

One goal of treatment with drug involved adolescents is to help them remember, rather than act out feelings and needs; and synthesize the past, present, and anticipated future. We began using ER's in the first interview as a simple technique which might contribute to diagnosis and would introduce the concept of historical exploration. We also began collecting ER's from each family member in the first family interview.

Early Recollections as a Diagnostic and Facilitative Technique

First memories can be obtained easily, and are considered clues in understanding personality. Most of the literature in this area has focused on ER's given by patients in individual treatment. Early memories appear as a matter of course in psychoanalytic treatment and can lead to an accurate reconstruction of childhood experience. The path backwards is indirect, and memory fragments which filter through childhood amnesia are falsified and reworked. Psychoanalytic theory conceptualizes ER's as screen memories which cover more emotionally laden material. Memories repress, rather than express conflict laden experience, and ER's change in the course of treatment as repressive defenses are lifted. In this view the manifest content of these memories, like the manifest content of dreams, are less significant than the repressive mechanisms which disguise latent meaning.

The second major approach to ER's stems from Gestalt psychology and Adler's use of ER's as a specific diagnostic technique. Adler considered ER's "one of the most trustworthy approaches to the exploration of personality."(3) He believed certain memories were selected because of their consistency with the individual's life style. *Life style* is a complex notion encompassing the unity of a person's expectations, and major guiding assumptions about life. In this view the manifest content of such memories is interesting in its own right. Both the analytic and Adlerian approaches consider ER's to be symbolic condensations in which personal meaning is more important than historical accuracy; and indeed ER's often have a vivid, eidetic quality similar to dreams.

Clinical interpretation of ER's involves the structure of the memory and form of presentation, regardless of theoretical approach. The form of presentation sets the level at which the interpretation is made. Is the patient cooperative or guarded, exhibitionistic or withholding, hesitant or decisive in his approach? The structure of the memory includes the individual and his environment as presented in the ER. Diagnostic focus is in three areas.(31)

1. How does the individual see himself? Is he healthy or sick, realistic or grandiose, ineffective or powerful?

2. How does he deal with the environment? Is he conforming or deviant, passive or assertive, clear or baffled?

3. How does the environment treat him? Is it supportive or hostile, accepting or intolerant, understandable or confusing?

Early Recollections Given by Drug Abusers

ER's are advantageous with drug users because they appear nonthreatening and are obtained more easily than other symbolic productions such as dreams. (Most of our adolescents report that they do not dream.) Memories given by our patients are similar to memories reported by other patients with character disturbance.(21, 23) They reveal depreciation of others, and sensitivity to harm. Memories obtained from drug abusers share common features. Many traumatic scenes are recalled. Adults are remembered clearly; for example; names of grade school teachers are frequently mentioned. Adults are seen either as angry and rejecting, or supportive and protecting. This division is sharp and exaggerated. Ordinary and pleasant experiences are reported infrequently. Tragic stories may be disarmingly blunt. One patient said simply, "When I was five, my brother died in a fire, Christmas eve or Christmas morning." Traumatic incidents are often reported in a flat, journalistic narrative, as in this example:

> My mother locked me out of the house once when I used too much bubble bath. I was locked out of the house without any clothes on. A neighbor found me on the back porch, semiconscious, at eight PM. My mother refused to take me in and my neighbor called the police. They took me to Meadowbrook Hospital, then to the Children's Shelter.

Both of these examples reflect detached compliance and isolated affect. Many of our patients show this kind of emotional withdrawal. Occasionally, ER's given by drug abusers are poignant and revealing in contrast with other clinical material. Consider the example of a nineteen year old chronic abuser who comes to the clinic following an arrest for burglary. He says he wants help, but seems unconvincing. He smiles throughout the first interview, and he antagonizes staff and other patients with his mocking laughter. Personality tests indicate primitive development with hebephrenic affect. The patients frightening imagery is demonstrated in the first dream he reports:

> It was a funeral. The woman in the casket wasn't dead and had to be killed. She had a tomato head, and all the people around her had tomato heads. I had to kill her. I had to throw a tomato at her head in order to kill her. I did that, and she still wasn't dead, but she only had half a head, all squished.

There is a cartoon-like quality to this dream along with primitive expression of aggression. In contrast, the same patient reports this vivid ER:

> I was in kindergarten and the teacher asked us to draw self-portraits. When she picked up mine, she said, "Look at what this fool thinks of himself," and everyone started laughing. I started crying, all day and the next day. The sun was burning in my eyes. The next day I pushed one of the kids off a swing. I hardly ever returned to school.

The patient's pain and vulnerability appear only in this memory, making him more available to us. The structure of this ER can be described as follows. The patient sees himself as victim; he is upset and angry. He conforms with the environment by drawing his portrait, fights back ineffectively after he is injured, and finally withdraws by staying home from school. The environment contains a powerful female figure who demands that he cooperate with the class project and ridicules his performance. The environment then isolates and burns him. The harm escalates: first only the teacher is involved, then the entire class, and finally the power of the sun burning in his eyes.

These examples demonstrate the preponderance of powerful, hostile, rejecting adults in the ER's of drug abusers. Protective, supportive adults are described with similar hyperbole. Such discrepancy is explained partly by the drug abuser's rationalization of behavior, but also attests to the archaic defensive organization described in these patients; that is, their inability to tolerate ambivalence, and their split object representations.

ER's obtained from younger patients in family interviews have a different quality. This may be the result of different personality configurations in preaddictive drug abusers, or more likely, the interview situation which creates a different set. In the following section we will describe the technique of family recollections, and present two examples.

Family Recollections

We introduce family recollections (FR's) by stating, "We often get a better understanding of a family by asking each person to recall their earliest memory." We usually begin with a sibling of the identified patient. Brief questions elicit details and ease the transition to the next family member. Inquiries should avoid interrupting the developing projective theme. The purpose of controlling the family this way is to encourage open-ended responses while limiting family interaction. Families cooperate well with this exercise, although individual members sometimes block or object. The technique is helpful in redirecting a session which has become fixated on problem description, transfer of blame, or scapegoating. The procedure calls for individual responses by asking each person for his own memory, and is consistent with the treatment goal of differentiation of family members.

FR's can also be interpreted by examining the structure of memories and form of presentation. As with individual ER's, three questions can be considered: (1) How do individuals see themselves? (2) How do they deal with the family? (3) How does the family treat them? Extended families become involved because the FR typically describes three families: the nuclear family, present in the interview, and the families of origin of both parents. ER's given by family members structure the roles of significant figures in the family in different ways. The form of presentation of the FR is affected by other family members, as well as the therapist. Members are cued by proceeding responses. They listen carefully, react nonverbally, and sometimes interrupt one another. For example, parents may challenge a memory which places them in an unfavorable light and adolescents involved with power struggles often become anxious when listening to reports of their parents' helplessness in childhood.

Assessment of family interaction is a complex enterprise, and needs to take into account transpersonal defenses. Among these defensive operations are family myths, defined as "the pattern of mutually agreed, but distorted roles which family members adopt as a defensive posture and which are not challenged from within the family."(13) Recollections of individual family members may support or expose the family myth, as in the following example.

The patient in *Family 1* is an awkward, blond haired fifteen year old boy. He was referred to our program when suspended from school for behavior problems and drug abuse. He ran away twice in recent months to stay with relatives but was returned by the police. The patient says he is "hassled" by his father, and wants to get away from home. The FR was reported as follows:

Family 1

Brother (age 17): We were visiting a relative's house, my uncle's. I was riding a red tricycle. I remember the big black tire on the front.

Stepmother (age 36): I grew up in Holland. I don't know if this is a memory or my father told it to me. I was about two, and I fell into a canal. My father pulled me out. The water was green, and I liked it. I wasn't afraid of it. Everybody was all upset but me. Mainly I remember liking the green in the water.

Father (age 44): In Lapland, I was a little boy and I was sledding the whole day by myself. I came home, in the front door, and my parents were mad at me. They didn't know where I was. The snow was on my pants up to my knees.

Patient (age 15): I came home from kindergarten. I had this drawing I wanted to show my father. He was in the driveway fixing the car, and he didn't notice me.

Brother (age 8): I shut the door in the bathroom and the mirror broke. They were all mad at me and I was afraid.

The stepmother is surprised by her own lack of concern about her falling in the water, compared with the reactions of those around her. The father's memory also describes parents who express concern when he does not. The patient's brothers, likewise, report themes of self-sufficient enjoyment and parental overreaction. Only the patient reports that he wanted something from someone else, and he didn't get it. The myth in this family is self-sufficiency, which the patient shares overtly but challenges in his ER. The specific parent-child interactions in this family were organized around premature separation. Stierlin (36) describes such families as "expelling." Unsurprisingly, the parents would not agree to family treatment and their son ran away from the program after several months. He returned and ran away a second time, after which the stepmother told us "Either he goes or I do!" This was a case in which we were unable to engage the family in treatment. Mosak (27) has found ER's predictive of the therapeutic relationship in individual treatment. FR may sometimes be used in the same manner.

The patient in *Family 2* is a lanky, fifteen year old boy who failed ninth grade twice and drank and smoked marijuana excessively. He appears more isolated and paranoid than most youngsters in our program who are more sociopathic in character. He talks little when seen individually or in group, but conspires secretly with other patients in some frightening plans. One plan was to derail a commuter train with explosives; another was to booby-trap his room at home with razor blades in case of intruders. The patient doesn't act on these fantasies, which are reported to us by others. He soon became ostracized by other patients who taunted him. The mother carries much of the family responsibility and the father appears more in the background. She is a chronically depressed woman; the father is more of an adolescent type whom the children call "the instigator." The FR is as follows:

Family 2

Daughter (age 16): I remember roller skating. I used to chase the bigger kids and try to catch up with them. I never could.

Mother (age 39): I was a little girl in Argentina. I was with my sister and we were picking flowers. A bee came up and stung me in the leg. It swelled all up. It almost had to be amputated. It was awful. *(Appears upset and tearful at this point.)*

Father (age 36): I remember when I grew up in town here. I must have been three or four. I used to repair the erosion in the street after the oil trucks went by. I would make little dams to stop the oil from running in the sewer.

Brother (age 12): I fell on the sidewalk at home. There was a piece of slate stuck in my knee. That grey stuff from the sidewalk.

Brother (age 10): A swing hit me on the head. *(Becomes giddy.)* I wasn't looking. I had to go to the hospital to get stitches. *(Cries, is comforted by father.)*

Patient (age 15): I don't remember anything. I used to ride my bicycle last year.

The patient's ER does not appear to be a memory at all, but a scornful avoidance of the task. The emotional tone in the family was tense by the time the patient had his turn to speak. His ten year old brother had just become very upset, first laughing about the memory of the swing striking his head, then suddenly crying. The context of this ER in the FR may explain such a reaction. The first family member to become upset is the mother, while reporting her memory of being stung by a bee. The theme of her ER concerns vulnerability, and sudden injury. This theme recurs in two other memories: the fall on the sidewalk, and sudden strike on the head while not looking. The affective tone of the mother's memory appears to have a strong influence on the subsequent responses. An emotional contagion of this sort appear as a consensual sensitivity among certain family members, particularly in families described as enmeshed (26), intersubjectively fused (5) and undifferentiated.(8) The influence of the mother's distress emerged in treatment. Her fear that some catastrophe would befall the family had been acted upon for many years by fears of burglars. Often the mother would stay up all night to make sure the house was safe without being able to explain her concern. The background of her multiple fears appeared related to traumatic childhood experiences in prewar Germany, before her Jewish family moved to South America. The ER of being stung by a bee is very likely a screen memory representing more disturbing childhood experiences. The mother's depression and survivor guilt are transmitted to the patient, who becomes preoccupied with fantasies of vengeance. This family is emotionally undifferentiated, and trapped by contagious fear. Stierlin (36) describes such families as "binding." Members cannot emotionally separate without destroying the family equilibrium.

In summary, the technique of FR's demonstrated in these two cases may serve as an adjunct to family diagnosis, and serve to introduce the family to the concept of historical exploration. Themes present in the ER's of family members may show discrepancy with expressed beliefs about family life. Similarities in ER's may reveal alliances in the family; the interplay of themes may reveal domains of mutual validation or disagreement, and sometimes of undifferentiated family belief systems. The technique is limited in that information obtained in the FR is sometimes impossible to interpret meaningfully without much additional information.

Memory and the Goals of Treatment with Drug Abusers

We believe that both early genetic and current family dynamics contribute to adolescent drug abuse and determine its outcome. For many patients experimental and preaddictive drug abuse follow an extended course in early and middle adolescence. Preaddictive drug abuse is symptomatic of the failure to accomplish phase-specific tasks of adolescence. Traditional psychoanalytic approaches (6, 7, 19) to adolescence focus on the resurgence and recathexis of libidinal and aggressive energy, leading to a "drastic overhauling of the entire psychic organization."(19) Ego structure established during early development sets limits on adolescent adjustment. Addictive pathology results from very early deprivation, leading in many cases to life-long dependency problems. Tasks of adolescence involve current family life as well as intrapsychic structure, with separation-individuation as the dominant theme. Parents are involved in this process, and in Jacobson's words, "Whenever parents refuse to accept the impending final separation from their children in adolescence, chronic pathology is bound to develop."(19) The struggle to separate determines the final form of adjustment, and this may mean the difference between extended dependency problems and addicition for some adolescents. Successful separation involves truly individualized understanding of experience, rather than imbeddedness in the family's definition of reality. Family myth and ideology are defensive functions which inhibit separation and contribute to regressive adjustment. They are formed by the impact of historical experience on the family, and need to be understood in historical perspective by the adolescent. "There is a time in the life of every boy when he for the first time takes the backward view of life," says Sherwood Anderson in his novel, *Winesburg, Ohio.*(1) "Perhaps that is the moment he crosses the line into manhood." Most of the adolescents we treat avoid this backwards view because their lives contain pain and neglect. They avoid remembering the past, which is painful, and they seek excessive gratification in the present. Some pursue this goal through use of drugs offering arousal and pleasure; others deny their needs with drugs which dampen and depress. Like all adolescents, they strive for self-sufficiency and independence; but they do so in a self-defeating way. Their behavior is self-deceptive because it is not connected with an awareness of their individual and family history. Early recollections are useful in facilitating a more accurate awareness of the present through an understanding and acceptance of the past.

References

1. Anderson, S.: *Winesburg, Ohio,* New York, Viking, 1919.
2. Ansbacher, H.L.: Adler's interpretation of early recollections: Historical account. *J Ind Psychol,* 29: 135, 1973.

3. Ansbacher, H.L., and Ansbacher, R.R. (eds.): *The Individual Psychology of Alfred Adler*. New York, Basic Books, 1956.
4. Barnett, J.: Dependency conflicts in the young adult. *Psychoan Rev, 59:* 111.
5. Boszormenyi-Nagy, I.: A theory of relationships: experience and transaction. In Boszormenyi-Nagy, I., and Framo, J.L. (eds.): *Intensive Family Therapy*. New York, Harper & Row, 1965.
6. Blos, P.: *On Adolescence*. New York, The Free Press, 1962.
7. Blos, P.: The second individuation process of adolescence. *Psychoan Stud Child, 22:* 162, 1967.
8. Bowen, M.: The family as a unit of study and treatment. 1. Family psychotherapy. *Amer J Orthopsychiat*, 31: 40, 1961.
9. Byng-Hall, J.: Family myths used as defense in conjoint family therapy. *Br J Med Psychol, 46:* 239, 1973.
10. Ehrenwald, J.: Family diagnosis and mechanisms of psychosocial defense. *Fam Proc*, Vol. 2 (#1) 128, 1963.
11. Eisenstein, V.W., and Ryerson, R.: Psychodynamic significance of the first conscious memory. *Bull Menninger Clin 15:* 213, 1951.
12. Ferreira, A.J.: Family myth and family life style. *J Ind Psychol, 23:* 225, 1967.
13. Ferreira, A.: Family myth and homeostasis. *Archiv Gen Psychiat, 9:* 457, 1963.
14. Fine, R.: The psychoanalysis of a drug addict. *Psychoan Rev, 59:* 585, 1972.
15. Freud, S.: Repression In *Collected Papers*, Vol. 4. London, Hogarth, 1925.
16. Freud, S.: Screen memories, In *Collected Papers*, Vol. 5. London, Hogarth, 1950.
17. Gottesfeld, M.L., Caroff, P., and Lieberman, F.: Treatment of adolescent drug abusers. *Psychoan Rev, 59:* 527, 1956.
18. Hedvig, E.G.: Children's early recollections as a basis for diagnosis. *J Ind Psychol, 21:* 187, 1965.
19. Jacobson, E.: *The Self and the Object World*. New York, International Universities Press, 1964.
20. Kaldeag, A.: Interaction testing: an engaged couple of addicts tested separately and together. *J Proj Tech Pers Assess, 30:* 77, 1966.
21. Langs, R.J.: Earliest memories and personality. *Arch Gen Psychiat, 12:* 379, 1965.
22. Loveland, N.T., Wynne, L.C., and Singer, M.T.: The Family Rorschach: A new method for studying family interaction. *Fam Proc, 2:* 187, 1963.
23. Manaster, G.J., and King, M.: Early recollections of male homosexuals. *J Ind Psychol, 29:* 26, 1973.
24. Mason, P.: The mother of the addict. *Psychiat Quart Supp*, 32: 189, 1958.
25. Meissner, W.W., Thinking about the family-psychiatric aspects. *Fam Proc, 3:* 1, 1964.
26. Minuchin, S.: Structural family therapy. In Arieti, S., and Brody, E.B. (eds.): *American Handbook of Psychiatry. Vol. III.* New York, Basic Books, 1974.
27. Mosak, H.H.: Early recollections: Evaluation of some recent research. *J Ind Psychol, 25:* 56, 1969.
28. Mosak, H.: Early recollections as a projective technique. *J Proj Tech, 22:* 302, 1958.
29. Mosak, H.H.: Predicting the relationship to the psychotherapist from early recollections. *J Ind Psychol, 21:* 77, 1965.
30. Rapaport, D.: *Emotions and Memory*. Baltimore, Williams and Wilkins, 1942.
31. Renshaw, D.C., First memories as a diagnostic aid, *Dis Nerv Sys, 30:* 267, 1969.
32. Salman, R., and Salmon, S., The Causes of Heroin Addiction—a Review of the Literatures. International Journal of the Addictions 12(7) 1977.

33. Saul, L., Snyder, T. Jr., and Sheppard, E.: On earliest memory. *Psychoan Quart,* 25: 228, 1956.
34. Serrano, A.C., McDonald, E.C., Goolishan, H.A., MacGregor, R., and Ritchie, A.M.: Adolescent maladjustment and family dynamisms. *Am J Psychiat, 118:* 897, 1962.
35. Stierlin, H.: Group fantasies and family myths: some theoretical and practical aspects. *Fam Proc, 12:* 111, 1973.
36. Stierlin, H., *Separating Parents and Adolescents.* New York, Quadrangle, 1974.
37. Wells, C.F., and Rabner, E.L.: The Conjoint Family Diagnostic Interview and The Family Index of Tension. *Fam Proc, 12:* 127, 1973.
38. Wynne, L.C.: Consensus Rorschach and related procedures for studying interpersonal patterns. In Farberow, N. (Chmn): Synposium, consensus Rorschach and the study of problem behavior. *J Proj Tech Pers Assess, 32:* 338, 1968.

Part II

Manifestations of the Addictive Personality

It is conflict and the need for resolution that provokes an individual to turn to some external substance for temporary gratification as an artificial means to satisfy this need. In part then, as the real need is not relieved, an addictive pattern develops. This way of coping influences new behavior and changes within the personality structure of the individual. The different behaviors resulting from the integration of particular addictive patterns are examined in the chapters of this section.

Dr. Lawrence Hatterer distinguishes between obsession, compulsion, habituation and addiction as he defines the "addictive process." He formalizes the process as he describes the responses that motivate a shaping of the structure that perpetuates the addiction. Such responses are initiated by "triggering mechanisms," the external cues that stimulate the addict's drive for his substance. Such cues are operative constantly, though the addict remains unaware that his addictive behavior is reactive to external pressures. This is a process of conditioning, whereby the addiction becomes as unconscious and permanent as a reflex. An addict usually finds an "addictive complement," that is, a person who serves as a complement to the addict's problems, reinforcing his addiction. This person may be another addict, or a hypercritical person whom the addict incorporates against whom to rebel. As the addict's relationships are narrowed within a circle of fellow addicts, he becomes more and more isolated from warm, close contact with others. The further he establishes his addictive structure the more frustrated he becomes. The problems which at the outset to relieve magnify tremendously, and as the addict continues to suppress his awareness, he becomes conscious only of his addiction as his identity.

The image the addict projects is one he tried to introject, to supersede the awareness of his actual conflict. The following chapters describe different behavioral stances, which are addictions, through exploring the nature of the identity the addict means to impress on the outside world as his own.

Dr. Jay Livingston analyzes the compulsive gambler "type," and the societal influences that affect him. In this "type," these influences are easily recognized, as his compulsion focuses upon the phenomenol acquisition of money, which is his means of accommodating to his perception of the meaning of success in Western society. Addictive behavior is not as unusual an activity as conventional stereotypes seem to imply; frequently it can be viewed as an adoption of prevailing social values. The environmental and internal factors leading to the development of the compulsive gambler are considered in this chapter.

In *Don Juanism,* Dr. Irving Solomon employs the story of James Bond to depict the character he examines. The Don Juan personality chooses women to use in an exploitative fashion, manipulating them as this manner of interaction was demonstrated to him by an inattentive mother. He maintains a demeanor of narcissistic tranquility, emanating from a sense of a grandiose self, distancing himself emotionally from women though engaging in numerous affairs with them. He is unable to fulfill himself in love. This article traces the feelings that were activated by the early rejection of his mother and then reexperienced through his addictive behavior.

Dr. Ted Saretsky discusses the central importance of the early mother-child interaction to the later development of masochistic tendencies to mediate between the fear engendered by the latent threat of separation in the former experience and the need for the closeness of love. In *The Comfort of Loneliness, Depression and Self-Destructiveness and Its Relation to Ego-Autonomy,* self-inflicted pain is analyzed as a self-preserving mechanism, as for one who feels such paralysis in the search for an identity, pain becomes a sure guide to feeling of self. Cases are illustrated as insight to the personality that is typified by his behavior.

Social, Behavioral and Adjustment Factors in Obesity, is a report by Dr. David L. Snow's findings, in his in-depth study of the problem of obesity, encompassing the possibilities of both physical and psychological origins. He finds that obese individuals are less attuned to their own internal cues than to external stimuli, and hints that obesity has a psychosomatic base. However, he does assert that compulsive eating may be responsive to certain triggering mechanisms, and reactive to feelings such as anxiety, frustration and depression.

Dr. Martin N. Fisher's article, *Addiction as an Avoidance of Depression,* concludes this section. The traumatic separation from mother at birth is understood to cause fear and to motivate a depression that is recurrent throughout the life cycle. Addictive behavior is seen to be one defense against such depression that is regenerated by conflict. This coincides with the beginning chapter by Dr. Lawrence Hatterer, in which he outlines the addictive process as one that is demonstrated in so many of our so called normal activities.

Chapter 7

THE METAMORPHOSIS OF ADDICTION

Lawrence Hatterer, M.D.

Lawrence Hatterer, M.D.

Dr. Hatterer is Associate Clinical Professor of
Psychiatry, on the Alcohol and Drug Abuse
Service Cornell University Medical College;
Associate Attending Psychiatrist, Payne Whit-
ney Psychiatric Clinic and is a Fellow of Acad-
emy of Psychoanalysis.

This chapter is an analysis of the nature of the *addictive process* that has become integral in every aspect of American life today. Each of us feels the impact of addiction in some form, whether through family, friends, lovers or passing encounters with strangers. No day goes by without one's being bombarded by every media to engage in some excess or to curb some excess, whether it is food, alcohol, drugs, sex, smoking, gambling, acquiring or simply work itself. America has a billion dollar diet business and a billion dollar business advertising the joys of eating.

This article does not describe the addictive personality per se, because there is no such single type of addictive person, but rather people who have varying degrees of addictiveness because of their vulnerabilities to the varieties of addiction. These facts are self evident in the histories and crises of the individuals I treated who manifested the addictive process.

This process can be defined, diagnosed, and has common etiologies and psychodynamics. It has early, middle and end stages. What follows is based on thirty years of diagnostic evaluation and naturalistic observation of addictive patients seen while Admitting Psychiatrist at the Payne Whitney Out Patient Clinic (1953–1961) on the Alcohol and Drug Abuse Service and in private practice.

They were also culled from fifteen years of individual psychoanalytic psychotherapeutic investigation and therapeutic experimentation with one hundred and thirty three patients addicted to drugs (alcohol, nicotine, caffeine, heroin, demerol, amphetamine, cocaine, barbituate, polydrug), food (obese, anorexia nervosa, compulsive vomiting), sex (hetero/homosexual, satyriasis and nymphomania), gambling, and work, and on one year's group therapy (audiotaped) of two gambling, one gambling/food, two food (obese and compulsive vomiting), one alcohol/smoking, one sex/amphetamine, and one work/sex addict. Each addicted individual has his or her own unique history with its ebb and flow, its remissions and its relapses which are dependent on the stress of life crises, pressures, and what I believe to be an almost cyclical nature of any addictive syndrome.

The germination for conceptualizing addictions as a process with common denominators began for me one day when a young bisexual man came for treatment. He had fallen in love with and was having an affair with a very beautiful, but troubled, young girl; and had come to the clinic for help in ridding himself of obsessive homosexual fantasies and an insatiable need to seek homosexual release in subway urinals. His life situation and his aggressive motivation convinced me that he desperately wanted to be rid of his compulsive homosexual practices. I decided that the only truly effective way to learn about what could be done to document the therapy would be to tape-record and study each session which we had together. In addition, I asked this patient to sit in a room alone before each session began and record his free associations about his reactions to the impact of the therapy—what he thought was helping him, and what, if any, change was taking place. Because of his involvement with the girl I felt he had an excellent prognosis despite an extensive homosexual history, starting at the age of six when he had begun homosexual fantasizing. Soon after that age he had begun behaving homosexually, and by the age of twelve, he began to visit subway urinals in order to consummate depersonalized homosexual contacts. During the entire therapy he defended the rights of others to engage in all forms of more humanized homosexual activities and life styles, feeling that they were perfectly normal, but unfortunately not attractive to him as a permanent way of life.

This patient realized that his own activities were in part pleasurable, but he also realized that they eventually made him anxious and depressed, and were totally destroying his love relationship with his girlfriend, as well as blocking his ability to create.

Two-and-a-half years, and hundreds of hours, later, his analysis terminated in a stalemate. He told me he felt he might still rid himself of his compulsive unintegratable practices. He ran away with a married woman whom he subsequently married and with whom he had a child. I filed away 600 pages of a taped transcript which became a manuscript that for reasons of professional confidentiality was never published.

However, the particular project stimulated my imagination enough to the extent that I spent the next ten years discovering why I had failed to help him, and learning to help other bisexual and uncommitted homosexual men who were highly motivated to rid themselves of their homosexuality because they could not adapt as homosexuals in our society. I began to realize that there are almost as infinite a number of gradations of homosexuality, as there are of heterosexuality. I also learned that both heterosexuals as well as homosexuals can become *sexually addicted*. More recently I learned that even within the enlightened homosexual community, a need is seen to separate adaptive from maladaptive forms of homosexuality which are viewed as addictive.

"AA" for Tearoom Addicts

"Sex can be suicidal. At least some sex is," say the members of a self-help group newly formed in Los Angeles under the wing of Metropolitan Community Church. The group calls itself Sexual Compulsives Anonymous. Its program is directed particularly toward those addicted to seeking sex in public restrooms in spite of the threat of arrest. In a press release, SCA said its program is "structured to provide a step-by-step program of behavior modification for this and other sexual compulsions. It is constructed to re-gear sex drives into healthier ways that will place emphasis on long-term relationships, utilizing the basic tenets of Alcoholics Anonymous-type groups. The goal is to modify sexual behavior to a socially acceptable point." *The Advocate 1973*

I soon realized that my first taped analysis was not of a failed heterosexual adaptation, but of an unrecognized sexually addicted person. I understood the importance of the steady positive reinforcement my patient received almost daily from fellow addicts in subway urinals. In retrospect I came to understand that these contacts, his father's obesity, his mother's heterosexual hypersexuality, his girlfriend's acute and chronic addiction to alcohol and other drugs, all contributed to his becoming and sustaining his addiction and explained his profound resistances to the therapy which was destined to fail.

During the following years I have treated heterosexual and homosexual sexual addicts and also turned my efforts to the study of other addicts, those who eat, drink, smoke, take other drugs, gamble, work, spend, and were acquisitive in ways that relieved their pain by bringing them pleasure which could only temporarily ease and mask their symptoms. What I learned from my work with these individuals is the substance of this chapter. It is vital to understanding the contents of this book and the nature of my hypotheses to define what I mean by the *ADDICTIVE PROCESS* and to distinguish its characteristics from those of a habit, a drug addiction or habituation and neurotic obsession or compulsion.

A Habit

A habit is something we do almost every day, the same way we did it the day, week, month or year before. It can be something we've been doing since birth. Whether or not we like it or dislike it, feel it is good or bad for us, do it voluntarily or involuntarily, or even acknowledge it, it does exist. And it does hang on. In essence, our habits are the *repeated, predictable forms of behavior* we exhibit in our living. They can emerge at almost any time in our lives, they can be constant, or they can come and go. Our awareness of them can range from complete consciousness to absolute denial. They can emerge from our constitutional makeup, or be developed in imitation of our identification with our families, friends, teachers, strangers, and environment—from anyone we are close to or anything that influences our lives.

We are not aware of developing our earliest habits, they just seem to come naturally, or they get handed to us without our having much choice. Whether they are determined by nature or nurture, they are all set into motion by our chemistry, conditioning, conviction, motivation, feeling, fantasy, thought, and impulse. We take most of them for granted, unless they result in some form of physical or psychological failure, get in our way, or cause someone else to announce they can't stand them. They are the foundation of our lives and the core of our physical survival, our work, our play, and our human relationships.

They build or destroy our lives, according to the way we use or abuse them. The best of our habits represent the rhythm that enables us to lead ordered, predictable, socialized, hygienic and anxiety-free lives; in short, the base of discipline from which we reach to our highest achievements. The worst of them can do anything from mildly interfering with our successes to completely destroying our psyches and somas.

We are in danger when one of our habits hold the potential to develop into an addiction, habituation, or into the Addictive Process. Let me distinguish these from a neurotic obsession or compulsion.

Addiction (Drug)
(Behavior)

A state of periodic or chronic intoxication produced by repeated consumption of a drug (natural or synthetic).

Characteristics:

An overpowering desire or need (compulsion to continue taking a drug and to obtain it by any means).

A tendency to increase the dose; (tolerance and abstinence) (withdrawal symptoms) phenomena occur.

A *psychic* (psychological) and generally *physical* dependence on the effects of the drug.

A psycho-physiologic high *tolerance, abstinence, withdrawal*

Invariably a detrimental effect on the individual and on society.

Criminal (hard core) more frequent in occurrence.

Habituation (Drug)
(Behavior)

Is a condition resulting from the repeated consumption of a drug.

Characteristics:

A desire, reflexive, activity to continue taking the drug for sense of improved-well-being which it engenders.

Little or no tendency to increase the dose.

Some degree of psychic dependence on the effect of the drug, but with the absence of physical dependence and hence on an abstinence syndrome

Detrimental effects if any, primarily on the individual.

Official definition of World Health Organization

Obsession
(Thought)

A condition of repetitive
unwelcomed thoughts.

Characteristics:

The individual feels impelled to
perform actions which not only
afford *no pleasure* but from
which he is powerless to desist.

He experiences loss of energy and
curtailment of freedom.

Opposite values and ambivalences
prevade.

It produces a doubt in his
intellect which spreads to other
areas of functioning.

Detrimental effects on the
individual and may or may not
be destructive to those in his
environment.

Compulsion
(Behavior)

A condition of repetitive
unwelcomed behavior that does
not interest the individual and
which are alien to him.

Characteristics:

The thoughts are meaningless
and the strain of concentration
exhausts the individual.

The behavior is against his will.

The behavior can be silly or
terrifying and from which he can
flee or from which the individual
guards himself by prohibitions,
precautions and restrictions
against carrying them out.

They are trivial acts, ritualistic in
nature.

They give *no pleasure.*

Initially they may not have
detrimental effects on the
individual and his intimates, but
ultimately are destructive to
both.

The Addictive Process (Thoughts—Behavior—Interactions): Can involve
Food, (Obesity, Overweight, Anorexia) Drugs, Sex, Work, Smoking, Gambling, Collecting, Spending.

The process has a life history that is related to constitutional, ethnic,
familial, peer and environmental factors. The nature of the particular addiction within the Addictive Process is related to the above factors and is always
based on the particular function* it serves. Certain addictions can serve more
specific functions than others, but invariably serve many functions which

---

*Some Functions Addictions within the Addictive Process can serve)
1. *Alcohol—Barbituates—Minor Tranquilizers:* to reduce anxiety, to relieve depression, to release inhibitions, repressed emotions (i.e. anger, hostility).
2. *Narcotics:* to reduce aggression, rage, relieve psychic and physical pain, deny isolation, achieve
an identity.

overlap from one addiction to another. This depends on the specific psycho-physiologic needs of the individual. The process is initially a coping mechanism which enables the person to adapt, but ultimately proves to be obsessive and compulsive in nature and practiced to such an excessive degree that it becomes maladaptive and symptom producing. Evidences of *tolerance* and *abstinence* (withdrawal) occur in the earliest stages of the process which can plateau or be consciously or unconsciously extinguished at the end stages of the process. This depends upon the specific addictive agent and the vicissitudes of the person's psychic and physical life history.

Characteristics

An overpowering desire or need for a substance, or to experience a fantasy, impulse, and/or act, psycho-physiological reaction or interpersonal interaction and milieu, by any means whatsoever.

A psychic (psychological) and/or generally physical dependence upon the substance and/or fantasy, act, milieu and/or interpersonal interaction.

It always relates to the *pleasure* versus *pain* and *work* versus *play* (sensuality) axis of the person's life.

There are varying degrees of disturbed and impaired ego and superego functioning in the individual's early life history.

Within the process there can be a shift from one addiction to another, which is determined by that person's history, addictive contacts, the individual life circumstances and the availability of addictive agents.

Initially there is *total* or *partial coping* with and/or resolution of needs, conflicts, and pain which is *masked by pleasure* (psychic and/or physical).

This pleasure ultimately diminishes over the life history of the process until there is neither coping, masking, resolution, relief or the ability to consciously deny the pain (i.e. symptom formation).

The process can be continuously cyclic, predictably sporadic, periodic or become a *life style*.

There usually exists an *addictive model, compliment, collusion, interlocking person.*

---

3. *Amphetamines:* to remove fatigue, to increase energy level, to enhance action, increase speed and ability to perform and to extend time span.
4. *Hallucinogens:* for escape, phantasy, to resolve identity and body image disturbances, inability to experience emotion, and to permit oceanic feelings.
5. *Food:* to reduce tension, relieve depression, anxiety, to resolve inaction.
6. *Work:* to increase self esteem, to deny isolation, to avoid intimacy, gain acceptance.
7. *Sex:* to remove isolation, to reduce tension, to resolve conflict.
8. *Smoke:* to reduce tension, to take or replace needed action, and control, replace or express emotions indirectly.

Characterologic defects can contribute to or be provoked by the process. Sociopathic behavior and less frequently overt soft and hard-core criminal behavior, can occur depending on the specific addiction.

Summary: Definition

Any repetitive, obsessive fantasy and/or feeling which leads to *impulsive, compulsive* and *excessive* behavior (i.e., acts, interactions, substances) practiced at varying levels of consciousness (conscious—preconscious—out of consciousness) for *multimotivational reasons* which become psychologically and biologically maladaptive.

Initially this behavior is always experienced as a *pleasurable* and a coping mechanism that temporarily serves many psychic and somatic functions. Ultimately this behavior *always* becomes destructive and/or painful (i.e., consciously or unconsciously symptomatic) and does not resolve, reward or afford sustained gratification.

Escalation (tolerance) and *withdrawal* (abstinence) phenomena can occur due to an absence of continuous pleasure and/or any conscious-unconscious psychological resolution (i.e., relief) or painful psychic and somatic conflict, pressure and/or stress.

It is these last ten factors in the addictive process which distinguishes it from a neurotic obsession and a compulsion. The element of *pleasure* in particular invariably makes it almost impossible for someone who is becoming addictive to recognize his specific addiction in the earliest phases of their addictive process.

In our society we are all faced with high potentials and vulnerabilities to becoming involved in the polarized excesses of such pleasurable activities as eating, drinking, taking drugs, sex, making and spending money, smoking collecting, and gambling. Unfortunately most of these activities also provide us with the things which make life worth living; they are our pleasures. They also do relate to our natural appetites, and have to do with our everyday survival. They relax us, remove our cares and tensions, revitalize us and help us to deal with and enjoy people.

They keep us alive, in love, and propagating our race. This is what makes dealing with them so difficult when one becomes addictive. When one uses one or several addictive forms of behavior over a lifetime to cope with isolation when everything and everyone around him become too ugly to bear, or in order to get back to and in touch with people or to feel, or to experience feelings we never had before, it can appear to be the only kind of pleasure possible, when all other pleasures and people have failed them. The addiction becomes the only reward to relieve that person of the pain of failure or rejection.

When this urgency to eat food, take a drug, have sex, or escape into work has become so encompassing that it replaced everything else in someone's life, then it has become not only his body's deepest physical craving, but also his emotional life's blood. That is when someone has reached the stage in his addictive life where nothing is ever quite enough and he keeps needing more and more to get satisfaction, or no satisfaction or sometimes only to feel the pressure of having to look for that elusive better feeling. That is when someone is looking for a pleasure to soothe a pain he may not even be aware is bothering him. He then eventually reaches that point when his mind and body are no longer experiencing the pleasures of addictive behavior. The addictive process has taken charge and interferes with survival, brings no relief, resolution or reward. The process is dysfunctional and only motivated by success, failure, status, power, money, social mobility, controlling and being controlled, authority, problems with one's family and people, not being able to feel or think and sometimes not even having values or a life style, or worst of all, an identity.

In some cases one's addiction eventually becomes one's identity. A person's known as "fatty," "a head," a "lush," "trick," or "work freak." What started out as a way to cope or just a good, bad or indifferent habit has gone wild. The behavior is not pleasurable but consciously or unconsciously painful," a pain that is often contagious causing suffering for those close to the addictive person.

Inside the Addictive Process

It is almost impossible to explain exactly how, when or why someone becomes involved in the addictive process. The shifting combinations of influences which breed addictiveness become even more complex and elusive once vulnerability evolves into a recognizable full fledged addiction. And so we find ourselves faced with a problem both painfully unique and frighteningly autonomous. To explore it in a way which will be comprehensible and helpful for all of us, we must begin with *vulnerability*. It is a problem we all share, we are all more or less vulnerable to addiction in our society. We live so surrounded by excess and contradiction that vulnerabilities which might lie dormant in a less stressful environment are daily being forced into malignant bloom. Hence it is vital to recognize what factors make a person vulnerable to the addictive process.

Being Born with Too Much or Too Little

What someone is born with and how people react to it can be a powerful determining factor in his addiction proness. Sadly, it is also the single factor over which he has the least control, and is often the last to be recognized as the precipitating factor for his addiction.

We do not know how much genetic or constitutional makeup contributes to addiction proneness. We have no way of testing for such vulnerabilities at birth. It is difficult to detect emerging genetic or constitutional addictive signs in an infant who has not yet developed a conscious ability to control her impulses or behavior.

We must rely on hindsight, or on the reports of family members who have observed or responded to those physical or emotional endowments which may have contributed to an addiction.

The interactions become further complicated when the responses are evoked from an addiction-prone or addictive person. We have not been able to separate nature from nurture, as each must play upon the other; but we do know that vulnerabilities to addiction seem to run in families.

Being Given Too Much or Too Little

Every addictive adult I have treated has given me some history either of excess or of inconsistent deprivation and overindulgence in her early history. Every addict's childhood is marked by shifts from too much or too little love, protection, or discipline.

Seeing Someone Else Do It

The addictions which become firmly fixed, longest-lasting, and most malignant are often formed through identification with or reaction against someone who has had a strong and early influence in a child's life.

The sights, sounds, smells and movements of excess or addiction can be sensed by a child during his first days of life when he is cared for by an over-smoking—drinking—eating—working—drugged, or—eroticized parent. Addictive messages can be experienced subtly—the constant smell of tobacco, a tense, over-worked body—or over-whelmingly-being left hungry and neglected by an alcohol—or drug-intoxicated parent. How ever it is first experienced, this kind of early exposure leaves a deep mark that is passed along in various modes of identification and reaction, usually from generation to generation.

When an addiction prone child is unable to practice the addiction to which he is exposed—gambling, alcohol and drugs, smoking or sex—he may approximate it by turning to something that is available—eating—or he may turn to excessive and compulsive work at school or at home in order to get praise from the addictive adult and the other people around him.

Not Getting Along with Anybody

Very early in life, preaddictive people start having difficulty adapting to problems within their families and outside their homes. They are unable to deal with most forms of authority—parental, peer, social, and often legal—which can result in inappropriate aggressivity or passivity, hostility, lying and withdrawal. The most common reaction, however, is a sense of isolation and of not belonging to their family and peer groups for any number of reasons. This isolation, whether externally—or self-imposed, produces a feeling of being different and a subsequent increase in tension.

As soon as a preaddictive person finds a practice which pleasurably relieves his tension, he can assume his isolation has ceased to exist, or can find an illusion of contact through group addictive activity.

Loving or Hating One's Self Too Much

If problems with self-esteem do not appear early in a preaddictive person's life, they are certain to emerge once his addictive pattern has been set into motion. All too often, an addictive practice seems like a good way of dealing with feelings of physical, social, emotional or interpersonal inadequacies, because it can anaesthetize all the tensions involved. However, it soon proves to be maladaptive as it begins to compound one's problems, and eventually only adds to developing a distorted self-esteem system. When one resorts to addictive practices instead of trying to get along with people, intimate levels of interaction become impossible. People begin to see the addicts as selfish, disinterested and uninvolved, and may become intimidating, hostile and rejecting.

Not Knowing One's Self

Identity problems of one sort or another invariably play a part in starting and perpetuating addictive behavior. Gender and erotic problems usually appear first, followed in due time by difficulties in establishing social, interpersonal, status, intellectual and career identities.

Finding a Way to Feel Better

Addictive patterns first begin to emerge when someone feels he has no other options available for the release of tensions. He can feel this way because he has been overdisciplined and genuinely has no options; or because he has been overindulged with an *excess* of options. Either way, he has not learned to make conscious constructive choices, and when he is tense, only an addictive avenue of relief seems open to him.

The Addictive Process

When an individual develops an addiction, he develops along with it a set of trigger mechanisms which make the addiction self-perpetuating. A trigger mechanism is any psychological, physical, environmental or interpersonal stimulus, conflict, pressure or crisis which provokes a fantasy, feeling or thought, which in turn leads to an addictive act.

Invariably, the trigger mechanism becomes an intergral part of the addictive process. The sequence becomes circular, each trigger leading to an addictive act, and each addictive act sensitizing the addict more acutely to future triggers. The entire process escalates, not only because of its circular nature, but also because an addictive act produces fleeting physical pleasure or psychological euphoria, without ever resolving the problems which have caused the addiction.

Trigger mechanisms occur in clusters, and vary with each person. Their number and nature may change over an addict's lifetime, but more usually they are repetitive and predictable. They relate to his early family history, and to the circumstances and pressures he has to deal with at the present moment.

Invariably, the addict is completely unaware of the multiplicity of his trigger mechanisms. Even if someone tells him, or more likely, complains to him, about his addiction, or if some situation throws the connection between a particular trigger and his addiction into focus, he will quickly deny or repress this unwanted insight. Under ordinary circumstances, the pleasure of anticipating, carrying out and experiencing the gratification of an addictive act completely wipes out any awareness of what might have triggered it.

The trigger mechanisms we will explore in this section are those I have observed most frequently in my practice. Anyone studying other addicts, particularly in other environments, might find any number of equally important triggers. What I hope to illustrate here is what is most important about trigger mechanisms; to help any addict, it is necessary to help him identify which specific triggers set his addictive practices into motion.

The Fuel Becomes the Fire

Ask any addict why he does what he does. The first and often the only sort of answer he can give is,

"I do it because I like it,"
"It makes me feel better,"
"It makes me feel good,"
"It's my thing."

He reduces the entire process to pleasure. It is this awareness of only the pleasurable aspects of an addiction, coupled with the ability to deny its pain, which makes the pleasure trigger paramount and makes the addiction autonomous.

Every addictive practice initially appears to give an addict more pleasure than pain. Often this pleasure heightens one's senses and does create the illusion that one is freed from pain. It also creates the illusion that by reducing the painful elements in life, one has resolved one's pressures and conflicts.

Pleasurable fantasies can lead to impulses and then to addictive acts without any other trigger mechanisms; yet no other trigger operates without an initial pleasure trigger.

Eventually, fantasies become less and less important, and the act itself becomes more important but less pleasurable. The addict must find ways to deny the pain an addiction is beginning to cause, and to reinforce the illusion that he is experiencing greater highs.

Denying the Addiction

In the beginning, addictions always seem to work. As we have just seen, they are pleasurable, and they seem to reduce anxiety, depression and pressure. Once an addiction begins to interfere with important parts of one's life, however, the addict must find ways to deny the trouble it is causing him. Usually he is helped by the people in his life. If they are fellow addicts, it is as important for them as it is for him to deny the addiction. If they are family members, they may need to deny the guilt, pain and fear his addiction is causing them; or they may have psychological needs of their own which are best satisfied by allowing him to remain addicted.

At first, an addict is able to deny his addiction by shifting to another activity immediately after any addictive act. He often completely forgets, blocks or represses any memories of his addictive fantasies or acts.

His denial is always accompanied by rationalization. If someone tries to make an addict face the degree of his addiction, he will be able to produce a host of explanations for his actions. He may deny that the practice is addictive, and say he only did what he did because someone upset him. Or he may say that he is only doing what everyone else is doing. Or he may go so far as to admit that the other people he knows may be addicts, but that he can always stop.

When his addiction has really begun to remove him from his usual work and social life, his ability to deny removes him from any realization of what has happened.

If he is asked to describe how he has spent his day, he will not be able to account for much of his time, and will not be aware that it was spent in addictive reveries and activities.

In the final stages, he is unable to make the connection between a life that has reached the point of paralysis and the addiction which has brought it to a halt.

The Environment

By the time he becomes addicted, an addict has built up an environment of personal stimuli—other people, his own fantasies, the paraphernalia he uses in his addiction—and must also live in an extended world of stimuli—

ads, movies, reading matter, bars and other social settings—all of which are powerful environmental triggers.

Trying to Cope

All of us have to deal with ordinary and extraordinary pressures in our lives. If our egos—our sense of self—and our superegos—our consciences— are in good balance, it makes it easier to cope.

An addict's ego can be too weak, so that he thinks too little of himself, or too strong, so that he has an unrealistically high opinion of himself. His superego can be too weak, so that he is not able to control or discipline himself very well, or too strong, so that he controls himself too rigidly.

Any combination of these sorts of imbalance makes it very difficult for an addict to cope with his problems. Naturally, he is most vulnerable when he is subjected to many kinds of pressure at once, or to an unusually intense pressure. It is then that trying to cope becomes a trigger: if he fails in his efforts to cope, his mounting failure creates greater tension which he finally tries to resolve with addictive behavior. Initially, and in the early life history of the addictive process the addictive behavior appears to serve as an effective and totally pleasureable coping mechanism. That drink, that candy bar, cig- arette, or masturbatory act dissolves the tension, relieves the depression, re- solves the conflict, provides the energy to re-engage oneself in a challenging life situation or merely allows one to take the action that was impossible to initiate. What distinguishes it from the normal use of such everyday coping practices is its *excessiveness* and its *repetitiveness in serving too many func- tions too often, instead of directly dealing with life.* In the advanced and end stages of the process the addictive practice becomes the sole coping mechanism and precludes all other forms of pleasure in that person's existence. It then serves no function as a way to cope but has begun to produce symptoms which multiply the problems with which the individual must now cope. The cycle becomes vicious. The cure becomes the disease.

Addictive Complements

An addict is always an excessively dependent person whether this is overtly or covertly apparent. The emotional excesses, deprivations and swings to which he was subjected as a child, his imbalanced ego and superego, and a variety of resulting problems, always leave him with dependency problems of varying degrees which others cannot accept or tolerate. He usually is unaware of how dependent he is in the many areas of his life, how paralyzing his dependency is and how insatiable his needs appear to people. All he feels is a series of painful rejections and failures when these dependency needs are not met by the society and those close to him.

As we have seen, an addict is someone who has become not only dependent upon various substances and practices to try and replace some of his needs, but dependent upon people. There is another, older meaning for the word "addict," one which I feel is as valid today as it was thousands of years ago. It comes from the Latin word addicere, which means to assign or surrender. An addict, or addictur, was someone who was bound over to another person, as a captured enemy, slave or serf.

An addict looks for a person as well as a substance or practice to help him satisfy his dependency needs. He needs someone who will be able to provide something he feels is lacking in himself; or with whom he can make an exchange of what each is lacking. Thus, he becomes bound to other people, with his chosen addictive substance or practice serving as the catalyst.

Addictive complements are among the many ways in which other people contribute to one's addiction; the addict, in turn, has many ways of getting others to help perpetuate his addiction. The *addictive complement* is a person, group, or sometimes an environment which keeps the addictive process alive in the addict and insures the propogation of the addiction. For example, the work addicted nagging parent whose excessive super ego becomes the complement to the drug (play) addicted child who consciously ignores and denies that parent's practices and controls or the spending addicted wife who keeps her husband's work addiction alive.

Controls

If someone tries to exert excessive controls on an addict, either overtly or covertly, he will consciously or unconsciously perceive it as unjust, and, in reaction, can be triggered into addictive behavior. They very best example of that is the one way to provoke an addict to become more enmeshed in his addictive process is to either exert over controls or engage in unrealistic excessive denials of the existence of their addictive practices.

Interlocking Addictions

Obviously, if an addict has another addict in his family or exerting a strong influence on his life, the complement relationship can be very powerful and very damaging. Character traits, character reactions and addictive lifestyles can be passed on from generation to generation.

An addict can also find another person who has an addiction which seems to justify the existence of his own.

When someone has lived with an addict, he often searches for another addict, or addictive group to serve as a complement who will resolve his guilts, anxieties, hostilities and vulnerabilities, or balance his excess or lack of ego or superego. The addiction does not have to be the same in nature or degree.

The addict can find a person whose severe superego alone is sufficient to keep his addictive behavior alive. The parent can reverse a child parent role by parentalizing the child into an adult superego so that when that child grows into an adult he will find an addicted adult with whom he can interlock and perpetuate his early life addictive complementary behavior.

Collusions

There are many people in an addict's environment who find him a convenient scapegoat. These persons can be consciously or unconsciously in collusion with the addictive person for a host of their own needs which in turn perpetuate the addictive behavior.

In the earliest phases of the addictive process the first persons who invariably involve one in collusion are addicted parents, peers and others who are in daily close contact who need an *Addictive compliment* or an *Addictur* i.e., someone they can become dependent upon to support or provoke their addiction or in some instances actually engage in the activity as a form of collective reassurance that reduces any guilt, fear or tensions related to their addictive behavior. Later on the addictive person can find other collusions in the form of media, environment, social attitudes and varieties of addictive subcultures to support their addictiveness.

Finding a Subculture

When an addict finds his subculture, he finds not only collusive partners to support his addictive cycle but a host of people who become a steady source of complements. Sometimes the complement is not a group but simply a milieu which supplies what he needs—a bar, a porno shop, an ice cream parlor, a steam bath. Our society considers many of these socially acceptable, since they are also used by nonaddicts, or semiacceptable, since they are places of business. An addict may not realize how persistently he seeks his fellow addicts or addicting environments. He only knows that with them he feels stronger, more adequate, and is relieved of whatever has triggered him to turn to them.

Usually, an addict who is just coming out into his subculture finds his complement in a peer addict who is in a more advanced stage of addiction, or in an older, more experienced addict who will help him establish himself. These seemingly well-functioning addicts provide him with the rationale that his addiction is essential to his emotional survival and serve as "healthy" models.

Once he is fully at home in his subculture, he will spend more and more time with peer addicts, who will trigger increased addictive behavior by making it seem more real and valid. In their company, with their mutual addiction as a catalyst, it seems easy to deal with all sorts of social interactions and tensions. He sees his fellow addicts as adjusted to their problems, and they convince him that he, like them, has found the best way to deal with the injustices and difficulties which seem to beset them all.

Soon the only people the addict feels comfortable with are those to whom they can relate in a state of excess. Moderate people are considered dull, when in fact their real shortcoming is simply that they are incapable of the levels of excess that can turn an addict on.

Eventually, the addict will begin to serve as a complement to other neophyte addicts. He has acquired an addictive identity which he can use to rationalize all his addictive acts. He soon figures in a more advanced stage of the cycle by being able to bring the neophyte addict "out" and feel the justification of his own practices by the enlarging of his circle.

Making One's Own Subculture

Sometimes, an addict does not become absorbed into an addictive subculture, and must find his complement with just one other addict, with whom he forms a closed and symbiotic relationship. Since he is already unable to experience any kind of emotional contact or feelings of aliveness except during addictive acts, he is in great danger when he invests his entire emotional life in only one other addict.

Addictive relationships, no matter how intense they may seem during a high, are by their very nature fleeting and transient. An addict is not really interested in the other person, but only in the pleasure dependency needs the other person can provide.

When two people become locked in an addictive relationship, they become removed from the mainstream of life. Although they may be able to totally justify each other's addictive behavior, they begin to feel suspicious of and removed from the rest of the world.

When an addict becomes too acutely aware of the danger of harsh disapproval, he may withdraw completely from society. Or, when the people around him are unaware of his addiction, their hostile, rejecting, intimidating reactions may seem very guilt producing and unjust to him. This can drive him into an isolation which can only deepen his problems and aggravate his addiction. No longer able to use his sole means of emotional contact, he practices his addiction alone, feeling unreal and detached from other people and the rest of the world.

Manipulating the Environment

Sometimes an addict is able to make the people with whom he has close and interdependent relationships his addictive complements by manipulating them into providing whatever sort of trigger he needs to justify his addictive acts. He may force someone to reduce his self-esteem, make him feel guilty, overprotect him, reject him, or arouse in him any number of other negative reactions.

Then, instead of expressing his anger directly to the person who has aroused it, he feels justified in going out and acting out his addiction. Sometimes, the addict seduces people into exploiting him or abusing him, and then submits to them or encourages further punishment in order to justify his addictive needs.

Needing It Instantly, No Matter What

Sooner or later, an addict becomes someone who must have what he wants when, where and how he wants it. He is unable to delay his gratification, and his need must be met in spite of any unpleasant consequences to himself or anyone around him. He also needs to be instantly and lavishly rewarded for his relatively small emotional exertions towards others, and his own selfishness.

These are examples of narcissistic behavior. We are all narcissistic to some extent, but an addict must develop this trait to the point of character defect in order to provide continuing justification for his addiction. It is unrealistic, inappropriate, detached and selfish behavior, and it arouses hostility, guilt, and the wish to retaliate in the people who must cope with it. Most of them ultimately see that he is insatiable, and refuse to cope with his demands, triggering him into trying still harder to get his instantaneous fix.

His ego and superego become still further damaged, and he has to turn to rages, withdrawals, dishonest manipulations and pathological lies to try and satisfy what has become his truly insatiable need.

Having Problems with Sex

An addict begins to try and solve the problems caused by faulty, impaired or destroyed gender and erotic identity as soon as he begins to suffer from their conflicts. If he is not able to establish a satisfactory gender role, the pain of his sexual problems will continue to be a trigger for addictive practices. The addictive act can become either a form of sublimation or a diversionary activity to avoid sexual participation and confrontations or the ability to establish a satisfactory gender and/or erotic identity.

Failing, Being Rejected, and Being Criticized

The first triggers an addict can learn to identify are failure, rejection and criticism. His impaired ego and superego make it difficult for an addict to deal with any of these, so they become frequent addictive triggers.

He is most vulnerable when his childhood has been marked with periods of unrealistic, excessive praise or criticism from the people he was closest to. He continues to search for the totally accepting relationship he had, or wanted, as a child, and begins to distort the real nature of the rejections he receives. He may not be able to see that people reject his demands because they are excessive, or because he makes them under circumstances which make them difficult to fulfill.

Trying to Feel Real

An addict feels his addiction is well-justified if it increases his pleasant emotions and diminishes his unpleasant ones. Because it seems to work well for him, this method of keeping his emotions at manageable levels becomes a trigger he cannot easily abandon.

An addict who is unable to express or handle tenderness, sensitivity, warmth, or intimacy is easily triggered into using his addiction to dilute his human contacts and keep people at what he feels is a comfortable distance.

An addict is not usually consciously aware of his angry feelings, and replaces them with addictive behavior. Addicts have similar conflicts with their passive and aggressive feelings and with their wishes to be dependent or independent. If he is afraid of asserting himself with someone, an addict can be triggered into an addictive act which becomes his form of assertion or aggression.

Dependency on addictive behavior destroys healthy dependency on people. All of us have to deal with some degree of anxiety and depression. For an addict when the ability to communicate with the people close to him has failed, these emotions can cause almost intolerable pain. Each addict has his own level of tolerance for anxiety and depression, and if he cannot identify it, and deal with these emotions directly, he will be triggered into addictive activities.

Pursuing Pleasure to Avoid Competing

Our highly competitive society urges us all to live up to a variety of ideals, not all of them attainable for all of us. The degree of our competitiveness is heavily layered over with denial. We are supposed to be "nice guys," but we all know "nice guys finish last." These values set in motion an incredible number of competitive and comparative associations for all of us.

An addict may be especially vulnerable to these standards. He may not be aware of the degree to which he is obsessed with the need to compare himself with others, but he is often triggered into addictiveness by the wounds his comparisons deal to his ego.

When an addict is actively devalued and minimized by his family, close peers, and authority the effects are especially destructive and can be the most profound triggers of addictive behavior.

Needing More Money

Money can bring us so many things in our society, comforts, educations, medical care, security—and is equated with so many other things, success, power, control, even sexual prowess—that it is no wonder that it, too, can serve as an addictive trigger when an addict is faced with a conflict or excess in these areas.

Getting Future Shock

None of us can protect our life from the increasingly rapid shifts and changes in environments, attitudes, jobs and interpersonal relationships to which we are all exposed. It produces a strain in all of us, and in those most vulnerable to strain, a need for some kind of anesthesia.

For the addict, this means turning to his addiction. It is this kind of pressure which often triggers the binge addict, and which causes a recurrence of addictiveness in an arrested addict.

On Value Systems

Most of us feel that ours is a democratically-oriented, middle-class society which places a high value on moderate living. Actually, our value systems are often contradictory and hypocritically held, provoking highly polarized behavior and attitudes.

We value highly physical, aggressive, even violent, youth-oriented, power—status—and materialistically-oriented behavior; but we praise the intellectual, peaceful, nonmaterialistic life.

We represent ourselves as a peace-loving nation, but for almost a decade, our children have been able to watch us on television, waging a pointless and dehumanizing war.

We are a perpetually dieting society, perpetually glutting ourselves. We are a smoking society with cancer and heart warnings printed on our seductive tobacco advertisements. We are a drinking society, busily devising soda pop flavored wines that will be palatable to younger and younger adolescents, while we post notices of Alanon meetings on school bulletin boards. We talk about sexual freedom while we support the production of boring, devitalized pornography which arouses only our voyeuristic interests or dehumanized excesses.

Addictive value systems emerge from and reflect these contradictions. When we examine them, we find distortions of the best, but most often the worst, of our social values.

When an addictive person discovers that some of our professed values will not really give him the opportunities they seem to offer, he can distort them still further, valuing his deviance as a form of rebellion, or finding in them a justification for his needs.

We are so excited by and involved with excess that it often blinds us to the beginnings of addiction. We think of addicts in extremes: skid row derelicts as typical alcoholics, ghetto heroin addicts and hallucinating acid trippers as typical drug addicts. We separate them from ourselves by concentrating on their extreme deterioration or the spectacular results of their practices. We isolate them on skid rows and in ghettoes.

It makes it easier for us to ignore the man who can only tolerate the inhuman work demands of his success by heavy social drinking; the woman who anesthetizes herself to the irritations of her life by just the right carefully—worked-out combination of liquor and tranquilizers; the teenager who may take hallucinogenic drugs on special occasions, but usually armors himself against the stresses of school with a sufficiently large, daily supply of marijuana or barbiturates; the other teenager whose parents are relieved to find that she is getting drunk on weekends instead of taking other drugs.

The addict in turn comes to value only those people and things which permit him to live his life in a state of excess. Anyone who is incapable of excess is relegated to the dull and worthless ranks of those who are not a turn-on.

We seem to offer our young people many more options for individuality during their unrealistically prolonged adolescence than are in fact available to them when they enter the adult world. When doing one's own thing collides with keeping up with the Joneses, many young addictive people find the rationale for insisting on continuing to do their own thing. It comes carried to the point of irrational change and deviance, in spite of the Joneses and in spite of themselves.

Individuality becomes quickly distorted into having to have your own thing, no matter what. The addict feels that the rights which seemed to be held out to him—new life styles, sexual freedoms, minority opportunities, meaningful but nonconformist and nonmaterialistic careers—are in fact not easily available. He and his friends may have tried to live in these ways; his parents may have read a lot of magazine articles and seen a lot of television programs on these subjects, but he is faced with a society that is far more rigid and conformist than he thought it would be.

So he finds the rationale for insisting on whatever rights he feels he deserves. He has been led to expect great rewards for little effort, and he continues to insist on greater rewards for still less effort, finding in the end that nothing is ever enough. And if he finds himself in a subculture where hard drugs are the norm, he will find that his addiction is no longer called "having a monkey on your back," with all its exotic and bizarre connotations. It's called "having a Jones."

The speed at which we live can also contribute to our addictiveness. Most of us are incapable of keeping pace with the rapid advances of our technology; and the swift changes we are asked to make in our jobs are more often than not incessant uprootings in the service of a rigid corporate structure.

The faster we move, or are moved, the more vulnerable we are to seeking something which will help create the illusion that we are still on top of things, still managing to beat the clock. As we place more and more value on speed and action, we must devalue the contemplation which might allow us to face our human frailties.

We even extend these attitudes into our opinions on addiction. Addictions which slow people down, such as food, alcohol and opiates, incur far greater disapproval than addictions which speed people up and give the appearance of greater activity, such as work, amphetamines and sex.

Young people become torn between the high value we place on action and excess, and their own reaction against it. They use drugs to slow themselves down or speed themselves up in their attempts to deal with or react against our culture.

Passive and dependent people are most vulnerable to these pressures, as we are most intolerant of these qualities. A passive and dependent person may turn to excessive work, sex or speed-up drugs in an over-reaction to his fears about himself. However, all these addictions have their crash periods, when the addict is overwhelmed by depression, fatigue and sleeplessness. He can then no longer value himself, and is devalued by society, because his addiction has reduced him to the same state of passivity as the addict who has chosen a slow-down addiction.

Each person's addictive pattern has its own unique time sequence, related to her unique needs, circumstances and stresses. While no one pattern occurs in every addictive person, all addictions eventually disrupt the addict's ability to integrate into everyday living.

His addictive patterns lower the addict's level of consciousness and remove him from the mainstream of life. He must spend a lot of time thinking about and practicing his addiction; and at the same time, he must deny it in order to spare himself the pain of recognizing how much of his life it has invaded. He gives this priority over everything else, and his ability to work, be on time, or even spend much time at all with nonaddicts suffers accordingly.

Our time values are reflected in still another way in our addictive patterns. We cast off our traditions whenever they become inconvenient, just as we tear down our buildings when they stand in the way of a new highway, and seg-regate our old people, without honor, from the mainstream of society. We value the fast, the convenient, the here and now.

It is easy to see how the addict finds a rationalization in these attitudes for his own insistence on instant gratification. He forgets his past, with its hours destroyed by his addiction, and values the present and future only for the promise of addictive gratification they may hold.

An addict has usually grown up feeling alienated from his family and peers. If he does try to integrate himself into the social system, he still feels alienated, and will devalue and denigrate it regardless of its real strengths and failures.

More often, since his addiction places him outside the established social structure, he more openly admits the value he places on deviance. He may ally himself with people who are pushing for clearly defined social changes. But the addict's interest is less in genuine, constructive radical changes and advances in human consciousness, and more in the promotion of an anarchistic and excessive life style in which he can pursue his addiction in greater freedom. His aim is the pursuit of his own pleasure, rather than the increased freedom and fulfillment of others.

The addict feels that the counter-culture offers him change for the sake of change, along with a certain amount of protective coloration. He is initially attracted by the promise of a more humanistic tolerance of sex, drugs, play and sensual life, but his real interest is in disintegrative people and activities. Thus, he often denies the real value of counter-cultural groups, and champions the most radical and militant elements, feeling that their excesses justify his own.

Social polarization impairs ego and superego as surely as emotional imbalance. The unnaturally rapid transitions of war; the confusing proliferation of options when highly authoritarian, primitively reactionary forces are engaged in struggle with excessively permissive, unstructured, undisciplined forces, all loosen man's superego and weaken his ego. A society which severly limits human freedoms and censures hedonism may produce strong superegos, but the demands it places on them are too strong, and produces more hidden but equally flourishing forms of addictiveness.

We must stop promoting unreality. When a human being is reported killed in battle, we must know he is a man, and not call him a "troop" or an "enemy dead." We must stop killing people we cannot see because we are flying miles above them in multimillion dollar machines.

We must come to grips with the archaic, unenforced, and currently unrealistic drug and sex laws still on our books. We must seek solutions for our social problems instead of using them to create fear in our population and bludgeons for our politicians. We must seek integrated, constructive, progressive change, rather than abrupt breakdowns of our social institutions.

We must learn to study our strengths and weaknesses, our humaness, and learn how to conduct ourselves as social beings in a humanistic way. Only by admitting to the sources of the pain we cause ourselves and others can we begin to eliminate the plague of addiction along with our other human ills.

An Outline of Current Concepts of the Addictive Process

Before outlining the various factors involved in the Addictive Process, it must be made clear that every factor of this distillate of multidimensional findings presented below *does not hold true for every individual who has become involved in the addictive process.* I have tried to be all-inclusive by presenting the major findings that have been repeatedly reported by the outstanding researchers in the field.

An Outline of the Addictive Process

Definition:

A Process that is:

A dysfunctional, destructive and impulsive coping mechanism practiced obsessively and compulsively to excess.

The process can have stages, degrees, a life history, be cyclic, periodic or plateau.

The existence of excessive degrees of psychic, interpersonal, and/or chemical and physical dependencies.

The *maladaptive* use of *pleasure* to remove psychic pain or conflict and/or physical pain.

The initially pleasurable cure of any disturbed psychic function that becomes a disease; i.e., a pleasurable act which consciously or unconsciously serves functions unrelated to pleasure.

Degrees of tolerance, withdrawal, abstinence and craving phenomena.

Pre and Post *Hangover* phenomena; i.e., prior to, during of after the pleasurable act evidences of depression, anxiety, guilt, fear, panic, withdrawal or any other forms of psychic pain and somatic disturbances.

The process is an involvement in a repetitive, predictable drive for pleasure to serve functions that go beyond pleasure which always are accompanied by some degree of conscious, preconscious or unconscious psychic and/or somatic pain; i.e., symptoms to one's self or to others before, during or after the pleasure.

Diagnoses:

A process that can occur in any psychiatric disorder. An overpowering, repetitive, and excessive need for a substance, fantasy, effect, act, physical experience, milieu or interpersonal interaction.

The attainment of the above at any cost and often with denial of reality, personal, social, economic, or even emotional physical life or death risks.

The repetitive and excessive use of a pleasurable activity when there is a conscious or unconscious inability or block to confront, resolve, be aware of, take action or cope with a pressure, conflict, or psychic pain.

Disturbances in:
    Work versus play (pleasure-pain)
    Self-esteem system functioning
    Dependency-interdependency interaction
    Control-discipline
    Agressivity-passivity
Free associative patterns saturated with excesses of addictive fantasy, impulse and act.
A past and/or present life history of:
    Work maladaptation
    Evident addictive practices of family
    members, peers and milieus.
Quantitive and qualitative interferences by addictive practices into interpersonal, peer, familial, work, economic, social and erotic functioning.

Causes

Constitutional

A real or imagined constitutional factor which causes the person to perceive himself as excessively inferior or superior to his peers or others. Inability to identify himself with family or peers due to a constitutional defect or excessive endowment.

Ethnic—Genetic—Biological

These causes have not been consistently validated, despite considerable research that has pointed to their significance.

Psychogenetic

Disturbances in *orality* during *"oral" period,* and in *narcissistic* phases of psychosexual development.

Parent (or Surrogate) Family—Child Interactions

Significant and continuing inconsistencies in treatment.
Polarized excesses in behavior.
Radical swings from too much discipline and control to too little.
Absence of any discipline—excessive discipline.
Overindulgence.
Double-bind messages, i.e., conflicting messages.
Parental conflict over discipline in which one is excessive and the other is inadequate.

Early and later experiences of a high incidence of provoked, imposed or actual rejections from significant persons (family, peers, authority).

Inability to tolerate intimate or extended social tensions with short or extended periods of withdrawal.

Interpersonal world viewed as dangerous, hostile and isolating.

Overt or covert excessive degrees of dependency or unrealistic interdependence (isolation).

Problems with authority, rebellion, achieving and establishing status, power and self respect within family, with peers and larger social forces, i.e., at school, on the job, with the law and in politics (using the political arena only to act out interpersonal difficulties rather than as a genuine belief in the need for change through political action.

An excessive need to control or to be controlled by others—to be dominated or submit.

Frequent sadi-masochistic interactions based on need to be punished for addictive behavior or to punish others with addictive behavior which has been denied or thwarted.

A high incidence of distrust, fear and guilt interactions.

Immature interactions related to desire to remain, repeat, or gain early interfamilial deprivations or patterns established, i.e., to be the dependent, overindulged child, the omnipotent inappropriate controlling parent, or a reflection of any of the other patterns described in the previous section.

Social disclaimers, hostility to, and/or dissociations from aspects of the establishment that represent discipline, order, the law, and religious and educational institutions that are traditional and conservative.

Faulty development and an inability to achieve due to a high incidence of conflict in these areas: career, social status, and class identity. Being thrust into social and economic environments that were beyond the individual's chronological capacity to deal with provoked serious failure and a loss of self esteem.

Disturbances in Self Esteem
Faulty Ego and Superego Development

All investigators found a high degree of narcissism, i.e., overconcern with the self (egocentricity) and extremes in overevaluation of the self as an elaborate defense mechanism against deep-seated underevaluation of the self.

A gap between expectations of the self and ability or willingness to discipline the self to perform at a level that could ensure these unrealistic expectations. This occurred because of a history of self esteem disturbances and an inability to excercise self controls or disciplined behavior.

Unrealistic goals to compensate for a low self esteem system.

Self contempt due to low accomplishment levels because of his parents setting unattainable levels. This contempt often turns to loathing in later addictive phases because of constant devaluation of the addictive person and act by intimates, peers and society at large. If he is a "closet addict," this self hatred can be an even more malignant causative factor in perpetuation of the addictive behavior.

Peer Pressure

A need to establish peer status and to be accepted.

A need to, but fear of or inability to identify with, compete with or hold one's own with peers and their performances, standards and appearances.

Excessive passivity permits intimidation by peer pressure and results in initiation and perpetration of addictive practices and entrance into addictive subcultures and/or milieus.

A need to cover up or deny to peers fears of excessive passivity/dependency, resulting in a reaction formation of excessive aggressivity which is reflected in exhibitionistic behavior that is expressed in the process.

A need for peer leadership which cannot be attained by any other means. A previous history of leadership, i.e., in social, academic, physical and creative areas, which is lost and is attempted to be regained by the process.

An inability to establish, identify and cope with prototype standards of gender/erotic roles or to cope with peer sexual practices.

Introduced to addiction by the formation of a one on one "closet" addictive peer collusion, not only as a way to enter the process but to sustain it without anxiety and split it off from establishment pressure.

Failures to measure up to proscribed standards of adequate aggressive, competitive, academic, social, athletic and erotic behavior considered appropriate to the majority of peers in the socio-economic class with which he and his family are identified.

Socio Economic Factors

An inability to establish any status with, identify with or stabilize oneself into a single socio-economic class.

Rapid, frequent and frustrating shifts upward or downward from one socio-economic class to another during significant periods of development or in the formative stages of one's life.

An inability to cope with major socio-economic and/or intellectual gaps between one's early socio-economic/intellectual background and current socio-economic/intellectual class.

An inability to comfortably identify with the new socio-economic class attained.

A total or partial blockage of the individual's ability to attain any social and/or economic mobility with attendant frustrations in acquiring the material, educational and career privileges of the classes above their own class, i.e., a denial of social-economic-career mobility where others are seen to easily acquire these privileges.

Extreme economic pressures with deprivation of material comfort or rewards when these were at one time experienced or attainable, but are currently frustrated.

A means of acquiring economic security to compensate for social inadequacies.

A need to identify with excessive materialistic value systems; that is, where material possession is put on a higher priority than the human relations by members of the person's own family and peer group.

Cultural Factors (Attitudes-Availibility-Media-Rituals)

Extensive, easy and at times the excessive availibility of the addictive agent and milieu.

An overt and covert propagandizing through all media (especially advertising) of the agents and the process.

An acceptance by powerful media (T.V., film, popular print) of the process as conflict solving.

A saturation by media of contradictory and polarized presentations of the functional (value) and dysfunctional (dangers) of the agent and process at the same time.

Periodic swings from excessive prohibition to excessive permissiveness of the process and agents with confusion reigning as to consistent reactions and actions from social and legal forces.

Discipline problems that result in lack of support and identification and in development of adequate superego (controls).

Absence of internal monitors of self control exhibited by parent so that none can be developed by the child.

Inability to delay gratification and a low level of tolerance for frustration as taught or exhibited by the parent.

Lack of learning from parents that rewards for consistent and ordered effort are the only means to success. Expectations of success despite disproportionate, inadequate or inappropriate effort.

Relationships are chaotic and/or unstable, or at varying stages of destruction (separation, divorce, uncharted "new" living arrangements).

A totally absent family in the literal, physical or psychological sense.

Child neglect in significant areas of need for approval, development of self esteem system, dealing with failure and frustration.

Marked swings from unrealistic praise to hypercritical behavior, producing inability for growth or development of self esteem or self control systems.

Imbalances in gender and erotic role playing of one or both parents. Weak, ineffectual, non-disciplining or absent father figure found to be the most commonly significamt contributing factor in family etiology.

Addictive models in one or several family members. The child can react as the *Addictive Complement,* in *collusion* or in *interlocking* mechanisms. He can adopt a fully different form of addiction as a means of consciously rejecting the common addictive practices in family members, i.e., there is identification with the addictive process, but not the specific addiction.

Frequent parental role reversal in areas where parent or other family members consciously or unconsciously manipulate, intimidate or exploit the child into parental role, i.e., to discipline, control, to take inappropriate and premature responsibilities for the family unit that rightfully should be the parent or another senior member's responsibility.

Inter-Intra Personal Interactions

Excessive, early *social isolation* within the family and peer group, often due to one or many of the above factors, which when combined result in a paucity of meaningful interpersonal relationships.

Due to early social isolations and disturbed interfamilial relationships, there is an inability to learn basic lessons of how to relate to others individually or to the established peer group.

Relating to others becomes more painful than gratifying.

Commercial support of the process (via products) regardless of psychological and physical dangers and current illegalities which are borne out by ambivalent and ambigious attitudes.

No standardized controls over social rituals so that the dangers of addictive agents can be easily monitored in the family, peer group or individual social unit.

A commercial (and at times corrupt) exploitation of vulnerable individuals by saturation centers of availability.

Symptoms

Predictable and repetitive psychic and somatic pain, i.e., anxiety, tension, panic, depression, somatic disturbances.

Excessive dependency, passivity and poorly or inappropriately handled agressivity.

Hypersensitivity to failure and rejection.

Unrealistic assessment of one's ego, i.e., excessively low or high self esteem.

Paranoid reactions, i.e., high degrees of suspiciousness, blaming others for insecurities, ineffectualness and failure.

Poor emotional control, i.e., impulsive behavior, marked mood swings, usually about which the individual has absent or low levels of awareness. Polarized passivity, aggression and hostility (unconscious and/or conscious) in which addictive agent or act becomes substitute.

Repressed or periodic highly explosive expression of emotions, i.e., the erotic, aggressive and hostile emotional life being those which are least in control.

Excessive preoccupation with the self (somatically and psychically) with extremely low levels of awareness of others, often related to physical and emotional detachment provided by the addictive agents.

Inability to achieve or sustain intimacy. Use of addictive agents to reduce psychic pain related to closeness. Significant periods of emotional alienation, detachment and isolation, despite surface gregarious social interaction.

Life style disturbances with an absence of a stabilized identity.

Time reversals (day into night or absence of awareness of time).

Poor reality testing and excessive fantasy life, particularly related to the addictive agent or practice.

Characterologic Defects

Defects that existed previously or were provoked by the process of familial, social and cultural disapproval of the addictive agent or act, such as:

Excessive dependence
Dishonesty
Lack of discipline
Unreliability—Irresponsibility
Lack of or
Manipulative controlling
Immaturity
Soft and hard core criminality (only where an illegal addictive agent or act is involved).
Passivity-Aggressivity
Demanding
Narcissistic (grandiose-exhibitionistic)
Insatiability
Impulsivity
Inability to delay gratification

Psychodynamics

Trigger Mechanisms

A trigger mechanism can be a psychological and/or physiological pain, conflict, pressure, crisis, interpersonal interaction or environmental stimulus of which the person is invariably initially unaware, that ultimately provokes the addictive process.

Trigger Mechanisms

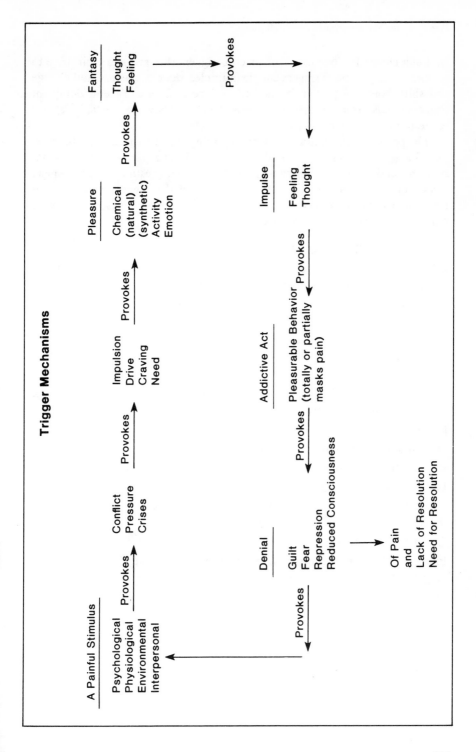

103

Each person has one major or several triggers that provoke their drive to engage in the process. Triggers can be multiple, occur in clusters, and change and shift from one period to another in a person's life. Several dominant triggers persist from the person's earliest years. They are predictable, and relate to family histories.

The process is circular and self-perpetuating because the original function for which the pleasure was used is not served. The partial reward is not sufficient and escalation (tolerance) and withdrawal (abstinence) phenomena can occur due to the absence of any resolution of the triggers which may or may not be out of that person's consciousness. The partial pleasurable reward removes awareness of pain provoked by the triggers.

The Major Trigger Mechanisms

Addictive models, agents, conducive settings, social, cultural and subcultural group forces (media) that promote addictiveness.

Availibility

Boredom

Isolation-Alienation-Lonliness

Anxiety-Depression

Pressure

Extreme life crises with excessive changes and traumas, i.e., at adolescence, marriage, mid-life.

Death of one or both parents

Dissolution of family (divorce, physical separation, etc.)

Rapid shifts in physical locales

Fatigue (overwork)

Addictive career environments and addictive career peer models

Rejection-Failure (work, economic, sexual, erotic)

Competition-Comparisons

Physical-Intellectual (constitutional) defects or physical endowments

Social Inferiorities

Hypercriticism

Sexual Dysfunctions

Disruption of separate gender/erotic identity formation

Money

Power

Psychosis (the addictive agent is used as self-medicant to establish homeostasis)

Common Interpersonal Mechanisms

Collusions—Direct or cross addictive identifications

Addictive complement

Interlocking addictions

Sado-masochistic interactions

Subcultural interactions (several or one-to-one)

Defense mechanisms:
  Denial
  Repression
  Sublimation
  Regression

It might well be said that the prevalent trigger mechanisms, interpersonal dynamics and forms of addictiveness that are most currently observed in a culture will tell you about that culture's Achilles heel. This will explain why so many people in that society are addictive. If that be so, one merely has to examine the conflicts, contradictions, hypocrisies and polarized excesses which occur most often in any one culture to determine *the* most significant triggers to addictive behavior that any member of that society is likely to experience. In ours I would say that the triggers are *hostility, acceptance, aggression, money, power* and *sexuality.* . . which, after all is said and done, might be said for any culture at any point in history. . . which is why addictiveness has been known to occur in almost every century and known culture.

Bibliography

1. Battegay, R. Muhlemann R. Zehnder, R. Comparative Investigation of Abuse of Alcohol, Drugs and Nicotine for a Representative Group of 4,082 men age 2.A *Comprehensive Psychiatry.*75 May-June Vol 16 (3) 247–254
2. Frosch, William Psychoanalytic Evaluation of Addiction and Habituation. A Report, *The Journal of the American Psychoalalytic Association* Vol 18, 1, 209–218 Jan 1970
3. Lester, David—Burksman, J. Herbert—Gandica, Alfonso—Narkunslic, Abraham The Addictive Personality *Psychology* May 76 Vol 13 (2) 53–57.
4. Rado S. (1933) The Psychoanalysis of Pharmacothemia (Drug Addiction). *Psychoanalytic quater.* 2:1.23
5. Savitt, R.A. (1963) Psychoanalytic Studies on Addiction: Ego Structure in Narcotic Addiction. *Psychoanalytic Quart.* 32:43.57.
6. Savitt, R.A. The Psychopathology of The Addiction Process: *Journal of the Hillside Hospital* Vol XVII: April-July, 1968:2:3.
7. Hatterer, L.J. "The Pleasure Addicts—Food, Sex, Drugs, Alcohol, Work, The Addictive Process," 1980. A.S. Barnes, New Jersey Cranbury.

Chapter 8

PATHOLOGY OR NORMALITY: A SOCIOLOGICAL VIEW OF COMPULSIVE GAMBLING

Jay Livingston, Ph.D.

Jay Livingston, Ph.D.

Dr. Livingston is currently teaching sociology at Montclair State College in New Jersey and received his B.A. from Brandeis University and his Ph.D. in Psychology and Social Relations from Harvard. He has taught in the Psychology Department at Princeton University and is the author of COMPULSIVE GAMBLERS.

Definitions or Labels

In discussing compulsive gamblers, one ought to begin with a definition of basic terms. Ideally, a definition of compulsive gambler would include all members of the category and exclude all non-members. No 'social gambler' would be included, no compulsive gambler would be left out. To attempt such a definition immediately raises two problems, one practical, the other theoretical. First, no actual definition I could compose would satisfy everyone; contradictory examples, actual or hypothetical, and borderline cases can be argued endlessly, and too often the effort evolves into a maze of qualifications. Perhaps more importantly, an either/or picture of gambling as compulsive *or* normal may distort the phenomenon, for it imposes a dichotomy upon what may be better thought of as a continuum. Notwithstanding the idea that all quantitative differences eventually become qualitative, to set the exact point between "social" and "compulsive" gambling will prove untenable. In my original study[1], I avoided the definitional problem by working with a sample of self-identified compulsive gamblers, men who at least once a week publicly announced, "I'm a compulsive gambler."

I will not, therefore, offer a comprehensive definition here; however, I will include one cautionary word *about* definitions. When we use a word, when we affix a name (e.g., apple) to something, we turn it into a member of some class. Until we make further specifications by using different words (e.g., Rome Beauty), all members of that class, i.e., all objects so named, are to be treated as interchangeable with each other.[2] We tend to focus on their similarities rather than their differences. The label also suggests as ideal type, an embodiment of all possible characteristics associated with that name. (The apple is that round, shiny red picture from our first Alphabet. "Drug addicts" are the young dope-fiend junkies lurking in the street, not fifty-year old physicians on Demerol. Alcoholics are skid-row winos or Days of Wine and Roses social nose-divers. The danger is that the caricature may influence our perceptions when we encounter real people who bear the label. Even social scientists close to the phenomenon can be affected by prior "knowledge" of these labels. Early in my research on gamblers, I remembered best the flashy Guys-and-Dolls types; somehow I did not see so clearly the men in faded plaid shirts and khaki work pants.)

This stereotyping may be inherent in the nature of language. Still, it seems to work most powerfully when the labels denote deviance. A deviant characteristic is *the* essential fact about the person so labeled. In the eyes of others, all aspects of the deviant's identity are spoiled.[3] We may be surprised that a "murderer" held a white collar job (or that he can even read and write fluently). "Cripples" find their stigma attached not merely to their damaged legs; people are capable of such observations as, "How strange that someone so pretty should be in a wheelchair."[4]

It would be a far too simplistic and limiting perspective to identify a person with particular symptoms of "deviance" as a compulsive gambler. Apparently, there are the common denominators in the compulsive gambler type, which need to be investigated further.

Personality and Culture

A sample of compulsive gamblers subjected to a battery of personality assessment devices, clinical interviews and the like would probably show some predictable similarities. A summary and synthesis of such personality research could be presented as the following composite picture.[5] The nucleus of the gambler's inner world is formed by three interlocked thematic elements: brains, money, and power. The "power" is not a direct, forceful kind, nor is it political in either the arm-twisting or organizing sense. It is rather like narcissism—being the focus of admiration. In logical sequence, the smartness and shrewdness lead to money, which in turn brings the adulation of others. (A favorite gamblers' fantasy involves showering upon appreciative others the material benefits of the big score—mink coats for wives, restaurants and other entertainment for peers, etc.) Of course, the three elements are a set, not a sequence, and the presence of any one element implies the other two. For example: if others admire me, I must be a smart guy, and therefore the big score must be just around the corner (Admiration→Brains→Money).[6]

As psychological, if not logical, corollaries to this core of feelings, a few other assumptions inform the gambler's thought. He generally approaches life in a highly competitive spirit. Life is a zero-sum game. If someone else loses, you gain. Other people are not to be trusted; those who trust others are the suckers who get taken. Gamblers seem to take an attitude of "basic mistrust,"[7] and greatly value unattachment and autonomy. A gambler may concoct a nearly impossible test of a friend's or wife's trustworthiness, and when the other person proves untrustworthy, the gambler sees this as justification for his further gambling. Even Gamblers Anonymous members caution against becoming too involved with other members, or especially, trusting others with money. Independence, autonomy, unattachment are made virtues. Gamblers prefer extreme geographic mobility, and this theme turns up not only in subtle forms on TAT protocols but in such mundane items as job preferences. Better to drive a cab than to work in a job where one is socially and geographically anchored, tied to a desk or a construction site, forced to work with co-workers, superiors or inferiors. Needless to say, most compulsive gamblers describe themselves as loners.

One final element in this brief sketch is self-control. Gamblers score quite high on measures of self-control and describe themselves as always keeping a tight rein on emotions. Particularly difficult is the problem of hostility.

Much aggression seems directed toward oneself and is seldom expressed overtly against others. Race tracks, casinos, and other gambling settings rarely witness the kinds of fights or even brawls we associate with bars and saloons. Drinkers who overindulge may become fawningly sentimental towards others or they may start throwing furniture. The gambler who has overindulged is unlikely to hit or even yell at anyone (except perhaps his wife). Instead gamblers become classic "injustice collectors" harboring a myriad of resentments.

The trouble with this personality assessment is not its accuracy. For the moment, let us accept its validity but consider instead the broader issue of how we shall think of personality. Our notion of pathology (a notion made nearly inescapable when we use psycho-analytic terms) leads us to look for harmful, foreign agencies within the organism. This sense of abnormality implicit in concepts like "abnormal psychology" and "psychopathology" obscures the great overlap between culture and personality. In the case of the compulsive gamblers, each of the salient personality characteristics can be seen quite easily as individual expressions of cultural values.

The descriptions of compulsive gamblers' personalities fit equally well the typical member of the urban working-class community.[8] Moreover, these traits markedly resemble the "focal concerns" Walter Miller has identified as the basis of lower-class culture: toughness, smartness, fate, autonomy, and excitement.[9] Miller estimates that this culture may reach as many as 60% of the American people, and Miller's severest critics argue not that he is wrong but that the same values apply to the solid middle classes as well, though their financial security makes "fate" less of a concern.[10] The same argument can be made for self-control, the ability not to show emotion, which has an important place among values at large in our society, in both the upper and lower strata. In sum, gambling—with its attendant virtues—occupies an honored place in our culture and is a regular feature of much peer-group activity.

These sociological concepts like "value" need not be thought of as mysterious forces. Cultural (or sub-cultural) values draw people towards certain kinds of behavior and away from others. Those who live up to these values win respect, approval, admiration, and affection from others; those who do not may meet with unpleasant reactions ranging from indifference to pity to hostility. These reactions—specific positive and negative sanctions—help form "identity"—that sense of who we are, how well we are doing, and what is rightfully due to us. Since from birth we have learned to take these identity cues from others, these shared values play a crucial part in even our most personal intimate emotions. In other words, social groups ("Society," if you will) delimit and shape the ways in which a person can feel good about himself.

The "gambling personality," then, is far from pathological; and gambling can provide a path toward achieving important values. Moreover, gambling as an activity—regardless of the outcome—affords the gambler both the intrinsic excitement of the play and the opportunity to display those virtues generally associated with "action."[11] The important thing is to stay in action. Or as the old gambling proverb puts it, "The next best thing to winning is losing."[12] In fact, a special admiration is accorded the man who can sustain a large loss or a long siege of bad luck without losing his composure. For a long time, therefore, compulsive gamblers can attribute any misery derived from gambling not to the quantity of their gambling but merely to the misfortune of their losses. Like any normal person, they prefer to see as financial what others might think of as moral or psychopathological. Needless to say, without financial problems, no gambler would ever consider the idea that there is something wrong with him.

If gambling is a valued activity, and if losses can be interpreted away, when does a compulsive gambler come to regard his gambling as a problem? Here a sociological answer should be particularly apt, for underlying psychodynamics run far too deep to change from day to day. But self-concept feeds on the continuing interaction with other people who confirm it. Most gamblers swear off gambling countless times. Usually these vows occur when events would disconfirm one's self-concept as a successful action man, e.g., after still another losing day, or when credit runs out and with it the chance to get even. But these are solitary moments, seldom reinforced by others, who continue to act towards the gambler in the usual way.

The true crunch comes when gambling and its losses prevent the compulsive gambler from sustaining other roles required to preserve an apparently successful identity. The inability to hold his job, maintain his family, or keep his wife can jar the gambler into a new view of his gambling. But even these crises effect only the gambler who is committed to solid-citizen values. For the young and single, who have never held a long-term job, only the loss of peer group ties might amount to the same kind of threat—and that only for those who are embedded in such a group. Even then, most gamblers can always find a group of kindred souls. Like the compulsive gambler who is winning, the man who feels no residual remorse over not living up to these values will not be heard from in the helping professions.

One further set of observations calls into question the usefulness of "personality" or psychopathology as the principle source of deviance. That is the marked similarity of personalities of different deviants. While I was doing my research on compulsive gamblers, I had occasion to read articles on alcoholics, embezzlers, check-forgers, etc. Often I would be struck by the applicability of much of this material to my own data, and I began to wonder whether all these persons who seemed to share a common psychology could have sought such diverse modes of expression. Or perhaps there was a simpler explanation based not on theories of personality but on the notion of how deviants must interact with their society.

While this hypothesis is still speculative and without much formal supporting evidence, it nevertheless seems reasonable. People who commit deviant acts, breaking social norms which they themselves believe in, are forced to adopt certain strategies of interaction. Some biographic information must be hidden, other items must be fabricated; some relationships become threatening, others serve as a kind of defense. Pressures mount, and the self becomes more and more vulnerable. For this kind of deviant, some of these pressures originate in the discrepancy between what he says he does and what he does, between his proclaimed identity and his actual condition (a deeply indebted gambler passing himself off as happily breaking even or winning). Other pressures have a more palpable reality—in the form of creditors or such social control agencies as police, courts, social workers, etc. Still others derive from fictions invented earlier to avoid one crisis but which must still be maintained. The deviant act, once a mild diversion or escape now appears as the only solution to these problems. But of course, it also becomes the source of further problems.

Can we not expect that people who live in these circumstances, regardless of the specific form of deviance, will begin to resemble each other in the way they see the world and themselves in it? They will share common perceptions, attitudes, and beliefs—in short, personality. For those with the same form of deviance, the correspondences should be even more detailed.

Can we assume, therefore, the priority of personality—even in the case of abnormal behavior. Those who must deal with these people first hand (friends, family, etc.) face strong pressures to locate the behavior—especially the abnormal behavior—in the person himself. Among clinicians, there is the strong temptation to believe that if we can clinically assess the personality of compulsive gamblers, we will have found the secret, predisposing causes of their problems. In contrast to this view, I am suggesting here that the personality revealed by these measures is as much a *result* of recent biographical events as it is a cause of them.

The question of culture or personality requires a choice of perspective, one we cannot resolve according to fact; it is a question of utility or aesthetics. Shall we see compulsive gamblers as being pushed from within by hidden forces, wracked by unconscious sources of guilt (e.g., for masturbation or Oedipal desires): or shall we see him as pulled from without by social values and the sanctions of other people?

Fantasies or Realities

William James once wrote that a person has as many social selves as he has social groups. Despite these multiple selves, we usually experience ourselves as whole, as individuals, not as a discontinuous set of discrete selves. We engage in completely contrary behaviors throughout our daily lives and do not feel schizophrenic. Understanding and loving at home, impersonal on the subway, pleasant but serious at work, jovial with friends, and so on; and in each case we are not self-consciously putting on an act. We are being our "true selves." Still, with any given setting and its people, only certain behaviors and emotions are appropriate; other selves must be kept out of sight. Most of us have learned to keep these various selves from interfering with each other. We have arranged our lives so that for each "audience" we never give the wrong performance. In fact, we are so adept at this kind of tact that we seldom feel that we are making any effort at it. Yet, to a certain extent, in any situation we are all impostors; obscuring what we deem unacceptable in ourselves.[13]

These social settings, besides tuning us in to appropriate behaviors and affect, serve as separate cognitive worlds, what James called "sub-universes." Depending on the situation and our role in it, we attend closely to some facts and disregard others. We interpret other people's behavior and our own not from a single point of view but with reference to situational demands. Of course, most of these worlds can be subsumed under "everyday reality,"[14] and one could argue, for example, that work world and home world do not conflict but merely represent different areas of this overall reality which we all agree on. [This is comparable to noting that aside from minor variations in accent we all speak English. However, we also know that within different settings and groups specialized languages develop when special meanings are attached to certain words (ball, strike, fair, foul), or when special words are used to redefine certain events (e.g., to label as "containing Watergate" what others would come to label as "obstruction of justice").]

Thus, it may be useful to view social life as "multiple realities,"[15] a landscape of many cognitive worlds. Some of these worlds overlap; others are more separate and may even conflict with each other. Often, each is associated with a particular time or place so that people will know which self to present and which cognitive framework to apply. A few people seem incapable of making the usual shifts of frame and carry a single divergent framework into all areas. Some of these people are said to have reached altered or higher states of awareness; others are called schizophrenics.

The perspective of multiple realities can be especially useful in thinking about compulsive gambling. Reformed or abstinent compulsive gamblers often say that when they were gambling they were "in another world," or "in a dream world." As the phrase implies, the gambler's thinking is altered, and the world looks different to him. But this thinking and the world in which it exists are not so irrational or abnormal as we might think. Gamblers ingest no drugs to impair their awareness, dull their thought, or induce hallucinations. They neither nod nor black out; they do not exhibit rage reactions.

I refer the reader elsewhere for full accounts of the cognitive aspects of the world of action.[16] It will suffice here to note that from the gambler's perspective, making another bet is usually a most rational action. As outsiders we might look at a gambler and see a man under some irrational compulsion, hooked on some fantasy, for how could someone freely choose to throw so much money to the tracks and bookies? Ironically, gamblers in action *do* see themselves as compelled to continue, but the compulsion comes not from internal, unconscious forces but from real, external agents.

To begin with, previous losses compel a gambler to make another bet. Even if the losses are small, they still constitute a threat to the self, for the gambler would see himself as a smart handicapper, a winner. A loss is a personal insult and must be avenged. Thus gamblers will speak of a horse or a team that "owes me money." Others want to "get even with" a bookie— and not just financially; they want revenge. On losing streaks, when losses seem to increase geometrically, threat comes in the form of unpaid bills, nagging wives, and persistent creditors. All of these exert immediate pressure on the gambler, and this threat—like threat in general— causes a narrowing of perspective. Long-range possibilities do not occur to him. The idea of quitting gambling and paying off debts gradually, if he thinks of it at all, is dismissed as unworkable. He needs money now to remove the threat. A few more dollars lost means nothing given his current debts; at the same time those few dollars might be parlayed into a big score. So why not continue gambling? If you perceive the problem as one of getting a lot of money quickly starting with a limited amount of capital, what solution short of crime is there but gambling?

Rationalizations or Reasons

Still, one might ask if it is reasonable for a man making $15,000 a year to bet several thousand on a ball game. The question itself reflects the difference in cognitive frames. Unlike the naive questioner, the gambler in action does not evaluate the bet in relation to his annual income, nor does he usually view the sum of his day-to-day activities as forming any clear pattern identifiable as compulsive gambling. His temporal perspective is far narrower. Today's bet is not a step further on an endless downward spiral, nor is it any evidence linking past and present pathology. More likely the gambler sees it as a reasonable response to his immediate situation. The $2000 bet today is not compared with the $400 rent or mortgage or any other mundane expense. Nor is the bet compared with the original $10 or $20 bet made months (or years) ago. Most significant in the gambler's frame of reference is the $1000 lost yesterday and the day before, the $2500 he thinks he can count on borrowing in a pinch, and the likelihood that the Celtics at home are 2 1/2 points better than the 76ers. The money and the action order this separate world, and it is a province with its own system of monetary values.

Compulsive gamblers occasionally call their gambling money "sacred," indicating that it would not serve as currency in the mundane world. "Action money" has its distinct meaning. Compulsive gamblers are not unique in their subjective valuation of money. Common valuations, like those of the gambler, fluctuate according to recent experience. A five-pound bag of sugar for $2 is a bargain if the price was $3 last week; but it is outrageous if last week's price was 89¢. And we make this calculation without considering the $7000 we may have just spent for a new car. There's "car money" and there's "sugar money." Similarly, for gamblers, there's "action money"; if you've been betting $200 a game of late, a $10 bet is nearly meaningless.

Each act of the compulsive gambler, therefore, can be rationalized with reference to his cognitive world. Both the decision to gamble (which is not given a great deal of thought) and the decision over the correct bet to make (which is given a great deal of thought) are products of rational processes. To name these ideas excuses or rationalizations is to dismiss the reality of the gambler's everyday world. This world, however, is not so easily denied as the idiosyncratic reality seen by schizophrenics or the "folie à deux (or more)" seen by various groups or cults of "kooks." It is a reality shared by thousands of people; more important, this reality is embodied in social and physical institutions—race tracks, bookies, loan sharks, betting information services, etc. Each time the gambler acts within these institutions and is responded to in the expected, typical way, his view of this world as objective reality is reinforced. Either it is a reality, or thousands of people are living a well-organized, orderly, collective insanity.

In the world of gamblers, gambling (and its various consequences) is no stigma requiring explanation. Not gambling would be considered an unusual action demanding an explanation. An argument that gambling is wrong or debilitating or ultimately ruinous would be dismissed as a mere excuse, a cover for lack of nerve. The difference between reasons and rationalizations lies in one's choice of realities. One man's reason is another man's rationalization.

The compulsive gambler shuttles back and forth between realities. A bad experience at the track may cause him to question the validity of his actions. The debts and desperation form flaws[17] in the gambling reality—occasions where this reality becomes unmanageable, tempting him to quit that world. But the nongambling world has equally serious flaws—particularly the gap between the sums one can earn in that world and those the gambler needs to pay off his debts so as to live a normal, middle-class life. He may experience in the nongambling world the discrepancy between the happiness this world promises and his own feeling of being frustrated, bored, or trapped.

Compulsions or Bad Habits

I would like to offer one more observation on the cognitive world the gambler lives in. Gamblers refuse to consider certain aspects of their lives, and gambling groups and settings reinforce this selective inattention. A straight psychopathology perspective would view these blind spots as part of the neurosis. One could cite the example already mentioned that gamblers avoid any broad temporal perspective on their gambling; they ignore both long-range antecedents and consequences of their behavior. One might view this as "repression" or some other aspect of the pathology. The gambler, or some part of his psyche, forces such untoward ideas into the unconscious. On the other hand, we can look at this cognitive frame as the outcome of normal processes—namely the routinization of some aspect of life. Compulsive gamblers gamble regularly, and when gambling becomes part of everyday life, a gambler can do it routinely, i.e., without thinking about such external questions as whether or not to do it at all. These more or less ultimate questions remain out of consciousness not because one cannot think of them, but because one does not think of them.

Such a perspective is not necessarily abnormal. We all must routinize our lives in order to make them livable. A psychotherapist does not begin each day questioning the ultimate utility of his life or the validity of the theoretical constructs which he uses implicitly in doing his work. Instead he must focus upon more immediate matters (such as, what do I hear Patient X saying?). Fortunately, people seldom ask *why* he does therapy or what in his psyche compels him to go to work today. Those decisions are not really made; they are matters of routine. One has learned them so well that they have become habitual. Thus, a compulsive gambler who has tried to quit says, "One day, I found myself down at the track"; or another, "It was the only thing I knew. I always knew how to go to the track." And when asked about the previous resolutions to quit, a gambler explains, "You don't think about that."

This begins to sound almost like a smoker who quits and the next afternoon finds himself halfway through a cigarette; or the fingernail biter who absent-mindedly starts chewing away again. These are bad habits. A worker promises that tomorrow he will ask for a raise; a wife tells herself that tonight she will start talking divorce. Yet once they are in the old routine situations, the ideas evaporate. Are these people the victims of compulsion? Or is it habit? There are important differences, between compulsive gambling and other habits. First, the immediate consequences can be more serious. And second, an entire material and cognitive world exists to sustain people who would indulge this habit.

Notes

1. Jay Livingston, *Compulsive Gamblers,* Harper and Row, 1974.
2. These views derive chiefly from Roger Brown, "How Shall a Thing Be Called?" *Psychological Review,* 65, pp. 14–22, 1958.
3. Erving Goffman, *Stigma,* Englewood-Cliffs, N.J.: Prentice-Hall, 1963.
4. Fred Davis, "Deviance Disavowal," *Social Problems,* 9, pp. 120–132, 1961.
5. For a fuller picture and review of the literature, see Livingston, op. cit., chapters 1–2.
6. This clustering of ideas suggests a factor analysis. To my knowledge, none has been done along these lines, but I offer the idea for further research.
7. The phrase, obviously, suggests Erikson's "basic trust," but I do not wish to imply that the whole syndrome be traced back to difficulties occurring in the oral stage.
8. A good description can be found in Herbert Gans, *The Urban Villagers,* Free Press, 1962.
9. Walter Miller, "Lower Class Culture as a Generating Milieu of Gang Delinquency," *Journal of Social Issues,* 14, pp. 5–19, 1958.
10. William Ryan, *Blaming the Victim,* Random House,
11. For a full description of "action" virtues, see Erving Goffman, "Where the Action Is," in *Interaction Ritual,* Garden City, N.Y.: Doubleday, 1967.
12. Nowadays, this chestnut is often attributed to Jimmy "the Greek" Snyder, but I suspect that it goes back to much earlier sources.
13. Erving Goffman, *The Presentation of Self in Everyday Life,* Garden City, N.Y.: Doubleday, 1959.
14. This is essentially the view taken in Peter Berger and Tomas Luckman, *The Social Construction of Reality,* Garden City, N.Y.: Doubleday, 1966, but I am arguing here that "everyday reality" is not the cognitive monolith which their view implies.
15. The phrase "multiple realities" is taken from Alfred Schutz (for example, see Collected papers: I, The Problem of Social Reality, The Hague, Martinus, Nijhoff, first published 1953), but my concept of these realities has them as more diverse. Schutz posits only a handful of realities—everyday reality, the religious reality, the scientific reality, etc.
16. Livingston, op. cit., Irving Zola, "Observations on Gambling in a Lower-Class Setting, *Social Problems,* 10, 1963, Marvin Scott, The Racing *Game,* Chicago, Ill.: Aldine, 1968, Robert D. Herman, "Gambling as Work," in Herman, ed. *Gambling,* Harper and Row, 1967.
17. On the notion of reality flaws, see H. Taylor Buckner, *Deviance, Reality, and Change,* Random House, 1971, (pp. 116ff.).

Chapter 9

DON JUANISM

Irving Solomon, Ph.D.

Irving Solomon, Ph.D.

Dr. Solomon is a Diplomate in Clinical Psychology; a graduate of Yeshiva University where he received his Ph.D. in Clinical Psychology. He is a graduate of the Adelphi University Postdoctoral Program in Psychotherapy. Adjunct Clinical Associate Professor of Social Work in the Social Work Doctoral Program of Adelphi University. He is the author of AN INTRODUCTION TO PSYCHOLODYN-AMICS AND PSYCHOTHERAPY and is in private practice.

At the onset, I would like to cite an excerpt from a letter written by Van Gogh, that passionate, deeply insightful genius painter to his brother Theo, which I feel succinctly conveys the main component of a mature love object relationship. "In every love there are many different loves . . . the principal thing is to continue and persevere; he who wants variety must remain faithful. And he who wants to know many women must stick to one and the same." (Van Gogh, V. 1958, p. 552)

In this paper I want to clarify and deepen the understanding of Don Juanism, and interrelate my clinical experience with psychoanalytic theory. In particular, I wish to delineate the relationship between Don Juanism, depression and entitlement, thus far not dealt with in the literature.

Entitlement (Solomon, I. and Leven, S., 1975) is the narcissistic assumption or conviction that one is special, and therefore has the right to treat, or be treated by others in a privileged manner because of the way he once was (suffering or pampered), the way he still is (suffering or pampered), or the way he will be (suffering or unusual or eminent). Many other clinicians have discussed entitlement beginning with Freud's (1916) observation that an individual can arrogate to himself certain rights. For instance, as an outgrowth of unjust childhood suffering, one may develop the conviction that he can abuse others without their objecting. On this basis one may feel that he is special—different from his fellow men.

In her last book, Horney (1950), under the heading of "neurotic claims" detailed aspects of entitlement and indicated how a person might feel entitled to special attention, deference, and consideration by others. She did not treat entitlement, however, from a psychoanalytic meta psychological framework. Murray (1964, coined the term entitlement in describing individuals who want to be loved and expect all things to come to them. Most recently Leven (1969) has written of narcissistic entitlements, giving as one example the husband who feels entitled to a wife who never gets upset.

With regard to Don Juanism, I have observed that individuals who have Don Juanism attributes manifest the following entitlements, that is, convictions held without any self-criticality or hesitancy:

1. Look out for yourself when you relate to a woman.
2. Never let a woman rule you or be on a par with you.
3. Passion but no deep entanglements.
4. Have women love you but set up the relationship so that they chronically have a lingering doubt that you are fully committed to them.
5. Exploit and hurt women subtly and be cut off from their hurt.
6. Search for endless peak experiences even if it means temporarily leaving a "loved" woman for another.
7. Seek the perfect woman or amalgamate the perfect woman out of many women, the female for all seasons.

8. Establish that basically women are all alike similar to the faithless bad mother.
9. Don't love with total committment for love may reduce one's self, causing intrapsychic death or the object's demise.

Since entitlements have a central narcissistic component, that is, the conviction of specialness or perfection, Kohut's (1971) discussion of the narcissistic personality is relevant here. He conceptualizes the grandiose self which is a replacement of primary narcissism and the establishment of a grandiose and exhibitionistic image of the self. The terms "grandiose" and "exhibitionistic" may cover a wide range of behavior, including the Don Juan's compulsive sexual exploits. The Don Juan's entitlements stem from his grandiose self, in Kohut's sense, and serve to counteract the danger of self-depletion, self-fragmentation and depression.

To clarify and concretize our understanding of Don Juanism, I will present a case history of my patient, Malcolm, who manifests some Don Juan propensities, correlated with a fictionalized biography of James Bond, known affectionately to his fans as "double-o-seven." In response to those critics who might consider a case discussion of a fictionalized biography of a fictional character as frivolous, I reply that the dynamics of Don Juanism appear so prototypically and valuably transparent in "double-o-seven" as to fairly cry out for psychoanalytic presentation. I might add in passing that my patient, Malcolm, has made gratifying progress in therapy. He now has a more mature love relationship with his wife and is more committed to her. He no longer is indiscriminate in his choice of women and looks for deeper, more meaningful relationships.

A Review of the Literature

A number of clinicians (Kuiper, 1975, Freud, 1910, Rank, 1922, Klein & Riviere 1937, and Robbins, 1956) have observed that the Don Juan patient has a compulsive urge to look for women and establish a sexual relationship with them. There are different ideas as to what are the main dynamic considerations behind Don Juanism. Kuiper (1972), as well as Robbins (1956), postulate that unconscious castration anxieties and the oedipal wish underlie Don Juanism, as well as the need to rescue women to be mother substitutes. Rank (1922) agrees with Freud, stressing the idea that many women are needed as they represent the irreplaceable mother. Supporting Freud, Fenichel (1933) expands the dynamics beyond the oedipus complex to include the compulsive wish to increase self-esteem and gain repeated forgiveness. Klein and Riviere (1937) introduce the element of excessive, unrealistic wishes. They see the Don Juan as greedily searching for the perfect woman, then rejecting her as she inevitably fails to live up to his perfectionistic standards.

Differing with those who espouse an oedipal complex is Lample-de-groot (1946), who considers the Don Juan's compulsive search as a replacement not of the oedipal mother, but as a yearning to obtain the degraded, preoedipal mother.

Other analysts (Kuiper 1972, Steke 1921, Wittels, 1938) have pointed out the repressed homosexual component in Don Juanism. Kuiper, for instance, indicates that the Don Juan indentifies with the woman gratifying his passive needs, but wards off homosexual impulses by reactive heterosexuality. Wittels (1938) focuses on the characterological use the Don Juan makes of his feminine identification. He states that the individual with Don Juan propensities has a sensitive, refined taste in clothes, can readily empathize with women and consequently captivate them.

The Don Juan's secret hostility toward women is noted by Kuiper (1972), Klein and Riviere (1937), Wittels, (1938) and Lample-de-groot (1946). The Don Juan individual expresses his anger towards women by not accepting a lasting relationship (Kuiper, 1972, Riviere & Klein, 1937, Wettels, 1938 and Lample-de-groat, 1946). This animosity toward women is revealed through his unfaithfulness, triumphant rejections, sadism, discontent and disdain. Freud (1910) observes that the Don Juan has a need to repay the oedipal mother by giving her a child. Out of guilt at rejecting the oedipal mother or being rejected by her, he wants forgiveness. In a sense, the Don Juan's rejection of the woman is his reparative attempt to preserve her from his hatred (Klein and Riviere, 1937). According to Wittels (1938), the Don Juan succeeds so well in making reparation to his victims that they frequently forgive him and he rarely comes for treatment.

Robbins (1956) appears to be the only analyst who suggests a specific technique in treating the Don Juan patient. He notes that the Don Juan wants to be the "good boy," and can be quite manipulative. He desires continual reassurance that each hour is a "good" one and may seek to inveigle the analyst into revealing his own personal life. Robbins does not explain the basis for the Don Juan's intrusiveness and need for consentual validation. I feel it is due to the Don Juan's wish to project out his badness onto the analyst and to confirm that he has succeeded in this process by hearing about some discord in the analyst's life. I disagree with Robbins' (1956) suggestion that the Don Juan patient be treated coldly as a way of penetrating his defenses and avoiding manipulation. I view this suggestion as probably based on counter transference, and the apprehension that the Don Juan patient will sadistically penetrate the analyst.

Robbins himself (1956) describes how his patient became manicy at one point during treatment, breaking the hospital rules. I theorize that the therapist's austere detachment led to anxious fantasies of abandonment, triggering off depressive features and initiated the patient's manic attempt to triumph over and control the external object, the analyst, and the persecuting internal objects, the interjected sadistically treating parents.

In summary, the literature reveals the following dynamic elements in Don Juanism in varying degrees and mixtures:

1. Oedipal and pre-oedipal fantasies
2. Homosexual urges and feminine identification
3. Compulsive, reactive heterosexuality
4. Idealistic images of the "good" mother
5. Sadistic subtle and not so subtle disdain toward women
6. A need to rescue and reparative wishes
7. Manipulative and controlling features

James Bond: an Illustration of Don Juanism

To comprehend the Don Juanism of James Bond it is necessary to give a brief version of his fictionalized life (Pearson, J. 1973) with a special emphasis on his relationships with women. James Bond's father was an engineer and was responsible for dismantling the German industrial empire of Alfred Krupp and Sons. His mother was Swiss. According to James, the men in his family tend toward depression. The Bonds believed in guilt, scrupulous attention to money matters and "the need for every man to prove himself."

Andrew, James' father, had one arm, the other lost in the war. His mother, Monique was high spirited and frivolous and had little in common with her husband.

James worshiped his mother. The more she despaired of him the more he idealized her. Although she had affairs and was wildly extravagant, James regarded her as a female paragon. According to James he "loved his father, but could not speak to him of anything that mattered, worshiped his mother, but could not forgive her for rejecting him." (Pearson, J. 1973, p. 31)

James was a sturdy boy and enjoyed fighting. He also loved eating and was considered a greedy child. For a period of time he was extremely fat. Even today he orders double portions of everything. Another aspect of his boyhood was the continual travel of the Bonds. They moved from England, to Egypt into Germany to France, to Russia. James was left pretty much on his own as his mother was usually preoccupied with another admirer. It was in Cairo, in fact, that James first noticed his mother's affairs. When he asked his mother what she was doing with a strange man in a hotel, she became enraged, insisted she had been at home and confined James to his room for defiance. "This was, as Bond says wryly, his first real lesson in the female heart." (Pearson, J. 1973 p. 33) In France James fell in love for the first time with a butcher's daughter, "a sloe-eyed, well-developed girl of twelve, who deceived him for an older boy who had a bicycle." (Pearson, J. 1973 p. 33)

While in Russia, Bond's mother experienced the tension of the purge of anti-communists; this coupled with repeated separation from her husband precipitated a paranoid episode. When his mother left the sanitorium, his parents attempted to renew their love for each other. It was on a mountain climbing trip, perhaps the same mountains where they had first met, that they suffered a fatal accident. We should note that it was Henry, his older brother who displayed his sorrow. James amazed all by his self-possession. He had almost a premonition the last time that he saw his parents that he would not see them again. He recalls his father's last words, an injunction and entitlement that we shall see play a vital role in his Don Juanism, "you must look after yourself, laddie. If you don't there's no one else that will." There is the possibility that his mother had attempted suicide and James' father may have died along with his wife as he tried to rescue her. What is important for our purpose is that James believes that, "she could not face leaving her husband or returning to him." (Pearson, J. 1973 p. 40).

James fancied women and became involved with a maid at the college. For this episode he was disciplined by the college dean and thrown out of Eton. He was perpetually on the alert for girls and his eyes would automatically follow their plump bottoms. The vision of female pulchritude seemed to serve as a delightful relaxation. James could be quite charming with women of every age. In addition, to be doing nothing was quite upsetting to him. He was likened by one former girlfriend to the character of Nora in Ibsen's Doll House—always waiting for something exciting to turn up. It did. His wallet was stolen by a woman with whom he had just had sex and a new affair began when the beautious hotel female manager arrived. He learned from her all manner of ways to make love. He was totally obsessed with her; and she with him. She evidently had advanced sexual taste for on occasion she invited James to see her making love to a former lover. Though he seemed to tolerate this she had carried on other affairs unbeknownst to him and stirred up by this knowledge and patriotism, he wined, dined, loved, and killed her in this manner; after flattering her, he pressed his foot to the accelerator and she and the car plummeted down the mountain to her death. Her last words were "Darling, I do hate being thirty. It's so old. I can't bear being old." His reply was "you never will be" as he hit the gas pedal. He cooly took away from this incident the following injunction and from our point of view another entitlement. "Never let a woman rule you. Total disaster if you do." (Pearson, J. 1973, p. 60) There followed numerous sexual adventures with unusually attractive women. Some he "loved" in his words because there was passion and anonymity and no entanglements. Almost all had unusual names "Honeychile Ryder, Pussy Galore, almost all were wealthy or married.

Bond remained resolutely single and involved with women who were very similar to each other (recall the quote from Van Gogh) fairly young, beautiful, married or divorced. They enjoyed sex as much as he did and adhered strictly to his basic rule, "pleasure but no extraneous demands, sentimentality, but no sentiment, passion, but no come back from the world outside. Bond secretly preferred them to leave shortly after making love. (Since they generally had husbands, they invariably did). (Pearson, J. 1973, p. 162)

Paradoxically, though, James enjoyed family life. He loved to play with children, tell them stories or perform magic tricks for their amusement. He also admired faithful wives, perhaps the only women he truly admired. He adherred to one basic rule in his relationship with women-"no entanglements." He made sure that they understood each other. There was to be no jealousy or possessiveness. Thus he was able to carry out affairs simultaneously with three married women. Such was his gift for rationalization that he justified being with one of the women by feeling it was good for her marriage, that he was fulfilling a need that her husband could not meet. He defined love as a "mixture of tenderness and lust." Vulnerable women most attracted him. He had a positive instinct for female lame ducks. His protectiveness would become aroused. He dreaded being bored by a woman and felt most comfortable when he could be a teacher and the woman a dedicated pupil. The only woman who left him was a woman called Tiffany. She ended the relationship because, as she put it, "We have enjoyed ourselves, and I shall be always grateful. But the truth is that you don't need a wife but I need a husband. When we first met you told me that you were married to a man called M (the head of British Intelligence). I think I know now what you meant." (Pearson, J. 1973 p. 259)

Bond was married once and on his honeymoon his arch enemy, Blofield managed to kill his wife, Tracy. As before, James felt no deep sorrow, no intense need for vengeance. He described his feelings in this manner, "she was dead and that was that and, of course, I thought that I had killed her. You see, so many women I had loved had died." (Pearson, J. 1973, p. 314) His last relationship, with a woman called Honeychile ends when Bond goes off to another adventure and she is moved to say, "Well, that's that," as she turned her back to the Rolls, "the bastard's gone." (Pearson, J. 1973, p. 333)

The Don Juan Personality

Women gravitate toward the Don Juan. He listens politely and empathically. He may exhude an aloofness, a fascination. He promises excitement to a woman and above all else her complete fulfillment as a woman. Why then view the Don Juan as a tormentor of women? Because while treating women in a gentlemanly fashion, he slowly shrivels them. Professing concern and sometimes love he places his needs, his wishes above theirs. There comes a time when he presents women with an irrevocable status quo, namely their acceptance of his partial committment to them or the termination of the relationship. He says in effect, "Love me, gnawing frustration and all, or leave me."

In accordance with their frustration of females, I have found that Don Juans have massive rage toward women. Malcolm, my patient with some Don Juan tendencies, despised and loathed his mother's domination and control of his father and himself. He hated her contempt for his father and her fostering devisiveness between himself and his siblings. Similarly, James Bond must have experienced extreme pre-oedipal anxiety, animosity and envy when he found his mother with a lover. Her blatant denial of his reality perception probably served further to intensify his disgust and rancor towards women. His next experience with the butcher's daughter plus his mother's separation from him due to her psychotic episode must have also enhanced his distrust and depression. The final "straw" of course, was his parents' death. His mother's rejection of him filled him with a poisonous self-rejection. He then had to project out this self-rejection into external objects; he shattered the spurning internal mother, projected outward his animosity and fragmented his links to women, or their links to other men, thus he broke up the internalized pre-oedipal parents and the external pre-oedipal parents as well.

My patient, Malcolm, an individual with some Don Juan proclivities, illustrates quite well the existence of unneutralized anger directed toward women and their perception of this trait. In both individual and group therapy Malcolm had begun to recognize and come to terms with his sadistic tendencies and all its ramifications. In group a woman told him that he was attractive, but she sensed an underlying cruelty. Another member noted that when Malcolm heard a sadistic sexual fantasy he seemed to become unusually responsive or excited. One woman presented a dream in which she portrayed him as a bloodthirsty savage. Malcolm himself recalled that toward the end of his affair his girlfriend told him that she did not wish him to call her again as he was too "cruel." In an individual session he remembered that whenever he played with children, they inevitably would get hurt. I interpreted at this juncture that he had resentment toward others for enjoying themselves so that when he gave to a woman or played with children he may have thought, "Why should they enjoy or receive the love that I couldn't!" By hurting them he duplicated his mother's subtle sadistic treatment of him. He confirmed this interpretation by remembering how his mother tantilized him and left him painfully misunderstood. He then cancelled out this insight by retreating into a cerebral query concerning the effectiveness of psychoanalysis. I understood his resistance of intellectualization as his way of saying "Look, you are not that potent so that I'm not the only defective, hurt one, you are too." With regard to the narcissistic personality, Kernberg (1974) observes that they need to devaluate whatever they receive. Nothing is ever quite good enough and this prevents the self from experiencing envy. Malcolm in a way was protecting me from destruction by his anger by devaluating me as a faithful-faithless mother (Schwartz 1973). He was yearning for a loving relationship, and an idealized therapy that would not be impaired by his hatred or depression.

James Bond handled his depression by functioning on a level of frozen detachment. He had obtained a narcissistic tranquility (Ostow, M. 1969). He lived by the entitlement "to myself I am enough." He decided he didn't really need anybody and fed himself as he had wished his mother to feed him, greedily, with food and with women. His father's caution shortly before his death that he look out for himself validated his entitlement to exploit women. Inducing a narcissistic tranquility and a sense of a grandiose self enabled James to retain the enduring conviction that he could hurt women and remain unaffected by their hurt. He emotionally abandoned them before they left him.

The Kleinian framework (Segal, H, 1964) suggests that the Don Juan feels his demands would impoverish a woman and anticipating guilt, believes he will be persecuted by her. He regresses to the paranoid-schizoid position wherein he fragments or splits the external objects (women), introjects them as persecuting objects which in turn shatter the internal maternal introjects. His depression compels him to seek in a manic way for outside stimuli that he will approach as reparations leaving each woman to become the departing "bastard," the James Bond, the kind of man he would have liked his father to have been. He may reason, as a "bastard," unlike his father, "I'm alive, powerful and can make amends to the next woman."

James Bond prototypically depicts how the Don Juan equates women as a relaxing tranquilizer similar to a drug. Women evoke in the Don Juan a sense of increased physical stamina, recalling the feeding mother who "poisonously" filled him, and, in a sense, the depriving mother who took his appetite away. (Berman, L. 1964). Women become mere deliverers of supplies. Affairs are initiated to overcome a lack of closeness with a false sense of closeness.

Don Juans have a readiness to tolerate a variety of sexual liasons, although unresolved negative oedipal impulses with homosexual concomitants are shown in their preference for married women and their attraction to primal scene, "menage a tois" experiences. With regard to themselves, they probably look for a woman's betrayal of them and are terribly shaken by such an occurrence. I suggest that they prefer to do the abandoning, and resent what seems to be another man's competitive, triumphant victory over them. A woman's more total committment to another man may represent the mother's deceitful oedipal rejection of them. James, for instance, ruthlessly destroyed one woman for such a betrayal.

Bond, like most Don Juans, yearns for a specific idealistic relationship, no entanglements, no deep involvement. They want a duplication of their mother's relationship to them, with a mother they perceived as floating in a nether world, somewhat with you and somewhat not. Regressing to the paranoid-schizoid position, the individual with Don Juan proclivities splits the internal and external maternal object. Mothers are idealized as all good and are eagerly sought after, whereas the bad mothers are rejected or delicately calibrated away. The Don Juan may have identified with his mother, who, (Kohut, H. 1971), with a disconcerting detachment from her son, focused on peripheral issues. Similarly, the Don Juan veers away from his love object towards tangential issues. James, for instance, was quite capable of perplexing women regarding his and their motives. He is considerably helped in this mystifying process by being so quietly articulate and so strongly in control of his feelings. He has his focus on problem solving and appears able to justify all his actions on a practical basis. Although giving women the apparent freedom to decide their fate in relation to him he usually has unerringly calculated their probable response to any of his behaviors. One group member, for example, character-ized Malcolm as a supreme puppeteer, masterfully pulling strings on all women.

The man with Don Juan tendencies is challenged by the woman who is married and unhappy, perhaps, but not unfaithful. He is compulsively driven to prove her unfaithful and by so doing establishing that basically women are all alike, as the faithless, bad mother. By identifying with the "bad," self-loving mother, and seducing women, then leaving them, he establishes that women lack genuine self-esteem and are phoney (Hart, H.H. 1958). He also fulfills the mother's disappointed destiny, her rivalry with men as he breaks the link between vulnerable women and their husbands or other male rivals.

Vulnerable women are attractive when they increase the Don Juan's self-esteem by rescuing them, and their neediness establishes them as non-threat-ening. In addition, to be needed by another offers a powerful potential repar-ation and relief of guilt and depression. But love for the Don Juan does not engender more love within him; it creates the fear of death, the psychological extinction of the self due to maternal envelopment or death of the "loved" object through being abandoned. As Bond states, "You see, so many women I had loved died. . . . " He, therefore, feels entitled not to love for he feels that his committed love will reduce his self and the self of others. He so fears the potential destructiveness of deep love that he delimits his love life, mis-takenly equating quantity of "love" with "quality." In this connection, Kern-berg's (1974) discussion of the different levels of idealization in his paper, "Mature Love: Prerequisits and Characteristics," is relevant. He delineates three levels, the first one being the most primitive, characteristic of borderline personality organizations and associated with splitting mechanisms. This level does not usually lead to a capacity for remaining in love. The second level of idealization, the "depressive" position (i.e., the Don Juan's position in my opinion) leads to a capacity for mourning and concern. Realistic idealization can occur and empathy for the partner is present. Kernberg, I think, credits this level of idealization with more empathy than is truly here. Perhaps, he means empathy with erratic compassion. Nonetheless, a stable love relationship can exist though largely stormy, conflict ridden and unsatisfactory. The last, the mature level of idealization, is accomplished toward the end of adolescence or in young adulthood, based on a stable sexual identity and a realistic awareness of the love object. Mature idealization, the final state, entails the final state, entails a compassionate concern for the significant needs and predilections of the loved one.

To illustrate Don Juan tendencies toward the obtainment of the immature idealization, I shall return to my patient, Malcolm. He had decided to go on a vacation without his wife. Before going away he had verbalized to the group that he hoped to meet a woman who would contribute toward making his vacation a most memorable one. This idealized fantasy of the exciting, nourishing, good mother was tarnished by the subsequent reality of not meeting any woman with whom he could establish an intimacy. Instead, he remained in his hotel room alone, despondent and forlorn. Finally, on a grey day he drove to the airport in the drizzling rain and took the first plane home. The group received his woeful story with a puzzled silence. One member volunteered that she had felt Malcolm as being far away during his narration. Another added that his story sounded rehearsed and flat. I, too, experienced him as removed and non-spontaneous. He responded defensively, "sure it sounds rehearsed because I've already told it to my wife." The group responded to his protestations by their asserting that they felt he was running away, that he did not seem to be willing to work on himself. Another interrupted to say that she felt that Malcolm was settling for his wife and that no deeply feeling wife truly liked to be settled for as second best. At this point another patient softly said, "Is that all there is, you know what Peggy Lee sings. I'm sitting here and as Malcolm spoke that song kept going through my mind, "Is that all there is?" The group was endeavoring to demonstrate to Malcolm that he was still running away from himself by trying to use women as distractions, his grudging conditional settling for his wife, his discounting of one of life's greatest joys, the deep total committment to a woman; all in his pursuit of the spector of the idealized woman. In essence, the group was saying that the compulsive search for the "perfect" woman with whom he could blissfully fuse was acting as an introjected, persecuting ideal leading to chronic depression and gnawing emptiness.

References

1. Berman L. (1964), The Role of Amphetamine in a Case of Hysteria, J. of the American Psychoanalytic Association, 20
2. Fenichel, O., (1933), An outline of Clinical Psychoanalysis, Psycho-analytic Quarterly, Vol. 2
3. Freud, S., (1910), A Special Type of Object Choice in Collected Papers, Vol IV London Hogarth Press
4. Freud, S. (1916) Some Character Types Met within Psychoanalytic Work. Collected Papers, Vol IV, London: Hogarth Press.
5. Hart, H.H. (1958) Maternal Narcissism and the Oedipus Complex, International Journal of Psychoanalysis, 39
6. Horney, K., (1950), Neurosis and Human Growth, New York: Norton, 1950
7. Kernberg, O., (1974), Mature Love: Prerequisites and Characteristics, Journal of the American Psychoanalytic Association, 22
8. Klein, M. and Riviere, J., (1964) Love, Hate and Reparation, New York: W.W. Norton & Co.
9. Kohut, H., (1971) The Analysis of the Self, Monograph No. 4, New York: International Universities Press, Inc.
10. Kuiper, P.C., (1972) The Neuroses, New York: International Universities Press, Inc.
11. Lample-de-groot (1946), The Preoedipal Phase of Development of the Male Child in Pre-Stude Child, Vol. 2
12. Leven, S., (1969) Further Comments on a Common Type of Marital Incompatability Journal of the American Psychoanalytic Association, 17
13. Levin, S., (1978) Internal mechanisms that Support the Acting Out of Destructive Impulses, *Int. Rev. Psycho-Anal., 5*, 55–60.
14. Murray, J.M., (1964) Narcissism and the Ego Ideal. Journal of the American Psychoanalytic Association, 12
15. Ostow, M. (1967), The Syndrome of Narcissistic Tranquility. International Journal of Psychoanalysis, 48
16. Pearson, J. (1973) James Bond: The Authorized Biography of 007, New York: Pyramid Books
17. Rank, O., (1922) Die Don Juan, Gestalt, Imago, Vol 8
18. Robbins, L.L. (1956) A Contribution to the Psychological Understanding of the Character of Don Juan, Menninger Clinic Bulletin, Vol. 20
19. Schwartz, L. (1973) Technique and Prognosis in the Treatment of Narcisstic Personality Disorders., Journal of American Psychoanalytic Association, 21
20. Segal, H., (1964) Introduction to the Work of Melanie Klein, New York, Basic Books
21. Smith, S. (1977) The Golden Fantasy: A Regressive Reaction to Separation Anxiety, *Int. J. Psycho-Anal., 58*, 311–324.
22. Solomon, I., and Leven S., (1975) Entitlement. Psychotherapy: Theory, Research and Practice, Vol. 12, No. 3.
23. Stekel, W. (1921) Stuerungen des Triebu Affekticgens: Bd II
24. Van Gogh, V. (1958) The Complete Letters of Vincent Van Gogh, Vols. I, II, New York Graphic Society
25. Wittels, F., (1938) The Position of the Psychopath in the Psychoanalytic System, Int. J.P.A. 19

THE COMFORT OF LONELINESS, DEPRESSION AND SELF-DESTRUCTIVENESS AND ITS RELATION TO EGO-AUTONOMY

Theodore Saretsky, Ph.D.

Theodore Saretsky, Ph.D.

Dr. Saretsky is Clinical Associate Professor and Supervisor of Psychotherapy in the Postdoctoral Program in Psychotherapy at the Institute of Advanced Psychological Studies of Adelphi University, Director of Group Therapy, East Plains Mental Health Clinic and is in private practice.

I once went to the theatre to see the musical, "Jacques Brel is Alive and Well and Living in Paris," and met there someone that I knew who told me that he had seen the play 25 times since the death of his wife. I couldn't understand how anyone could sit through the same play so many times, but besides that, I wondered why this man would be so morbidly attracted to words and music that were so bittersweet, cynical, and dysphoric. I forgot the incident until a few weeks later when a patient was describing his interest in Bette Middler. "I go to see her every chance I get and every single time I get depressed, but I love it. She represents something raw, primal, screaming, ranting, fuck it how I look. She magnifies her flaws; she's gut. I want to swallow her up and be her or at least be part of her life. She has power; I want to share some of that." Several days later another patient was describing how a close friend told her something very cruel and cutting. The patient was very hurt but when the friend apologized the next day, the patient was vaguely disappointed. "I don't know why but I hated to have to surrender my bad feelings. Just because she was making up to me made me feel I no longer had the right to be upset." Still another patient had described the following fantasy: "I wish there was a cause I felt really strongly about. If I was the last Jewish soldier between the Arabs and Tel Aviv and I knew I was going to die for a purpose, then I think I could die with a smile on my face." These individuals are all struggling to preserve their sense of ego identity. They could all be described as schizoid types. Their rich and active fantasy lives and desperate searching for moving inner experiences are viewed here as defenses against the growing depersonalization of the self of everyday life. Their inner sense of apathy, emptiness, and withdrawal, together with the absence of genuine emotional rapport with the outside world leads them to the increased fear of regression, decompensation and finally dying in the absolute sense of non-existence.

I had occasion at some later date to speak to the acquaintance that I had originally met at Jacques Brel. This highly intelligent and articulate individual who is presently in analysis and who's probably the least schizoid of the people I have mentioned, surprised me with his explanation of why he attended a play so religiously. "My wife died two years ago in June. Since then the world seems flat and empty. I'm afraid to look at anything or touch anything because then if I couldn't feel anything, I'd feel even more mechanical. Maybe you don't know what it's like to feel hollow inside. Every so often I say to myself, 'I am me', but it doesn't feel like me—everything just seems so surfacy and superficial."

This conversation disturbed me and over the next few months I started developing a somewhat different perspective with the various patients that I was treating. I began to become more aware that the usual constellations of depression, anxiety and guilt, frequently cover over pathological formations of a more schizoid nature. The proliferation of articles in the literature recently (Giovachinni, 1972; Kernberg, 1967; Kohut, 1966) concerning the feasibility of working with borderline and schizoid personalities reflect simultaneous awakenings on the part of many analysts that these patients may represent one of the largest diagnostic entities that we are presently treating; and a recognition that modifications in technique and shifts in theoretical orientation may be necessary in order to more effectively treat these people. In light of these implications, I have chosen this paper to be an elaboration of a few key hypotheses concerning schizoid phenomena and methods I have found useful in dealing with the emerging resistance and transference problems in therapy.*

It is generally agreed that the fundamental schizoid fear is an almost claustrophobic reaction to close relationships (Giovachinni, 1972). This fear can manifest itself through the dread of "being smothered," "possessed," "dominated," "absorbed," or even "making a commitment to something." Many writers (Guntrip, 1968; Fairburn, 1952a, Winnicott, 1965a) have suggested that the basis for this anxiety originates in the parasitic symbiosis experiences in the mother-child interaction. The specificity of early separation problems is unique for each person; however several predominant trends can be detected in the case of individuals who grew up along schizoid lines of development.

These people began their lives in an environment that was extremely intrusive and impinging. The availability of cherishing, validation and love were unduly contingent upon the irrational values and expectations of parental figures who had great difficulty seeing their children in anything but ego-extension terms. There is a serious lack of respect for the integrity and individuality of the child. I would hypothesize that such normal acts as self-assertion, the keeping of secrets, and the wish for privacy gravely threatened the parents because these capacities all represent ego-autonomy and apartness. Behavior that ordinarily would be construed as depicting progressive mastery and growth (being exploratory, putting fingers in the mouth, shouting, touching things) in the eyes of the average parent would be seen by these parents as defiant and bad. Pierce and Newton (1963) have speculated that the malevolent parents' need for manipulation and aggressive control is associated with a reactivation of ambivalent, unresolved symbiotic ties with their own parents. It is further suggested that the parenting figure has an unconscious stake in promoting the fear of disorganization, pathological dependency and a gradual loss of self in the child. The child comes to feel that not even slight divergences of opinion can be expressed, unless the parent can be convinced

---

*The term "schizoid" refers to a broad range of clinical symptomology reflecting early development failure. It is consistent with Harry Guntrip's conception of schizoid phenomena and what are commonly called "borderline conditions."

that it is acceptable. The rich secret life that the child develops retains an unreal quality because it can be exposed only in sporadic and fragmented form to contemporaries. The net result is that the validating love object and reality tester is the very same person who originally fostered the unwholesome dependency.

With enough reinforcement, this arrangement can create a very tenuous and tentative feeling in the child. On the one hand, the child must repudiate many basic aspects of his own being when feeling engulfed by the parental need-gratification system. This dissociation and subsequent splitting of feelings outside of consciousness leads to a relatively stable but sometimes terrifying level of adjustment within the nexus of the parent-child interaction. Patients have a difficult time describing the accompanying feeling state because most often it's very frightening and pushed way out of consciousness but through dreams and intensive analysis we sometimes do get a hint at what might actually be going on. A slow, steady deterioration of the "vital self" is sensed. This "secret essence" (Reik, 1952) represents the core being, the "living, breathing me." When this central structure is co-opted and coerced into capitulation, nothing else is left. The total experience must be very close to primitive myths concerning the feeling of death and entering the great void beyond. On the other hand, when this degree of disruptive regression threatens to occur, patients will resort to any method that will preserve some shred of personal identity. What we usually think of as "craziness," is very likely a compromise formation that balances the need for closeness and the fear of it. By accepting the stigma and symptomatology as the identified patient, the schizoid individual takes the onus off the parents and in return is able to establish some distance and keep some part of himself alive for another day.

Following are several clinical illustrations to illuminate these conceptual formulations.

One patient was a very unhappy 30-year-old man who entered treatment because of an inability to find a satisfactory sexual role. At various times, he participated in heterosexual, homosexual and bisexual relationships but acted as though he could never find more than fleeting pleasure in any of them. Some additional features of this case was the patient's addiction to a wide assortment of hard drugs, his compulsion to pluck hairs from his face, and a generally wasted life that involved clowning around, titillating friends by singing in falsetto, impersonating female entertainers—all followed by periods of deep depression.

What I remember most about this man was how quickly he developed a precipitously positive, idealized transference. Whereas four or five previous therapists never made a dent on him, with me many of his original complaints rapidly cleared up, he reported feedback from his friends that indicated significant changes in the way that he carried himself, and he kept repeating every session how he's got to be himself to be happy. Every chance he got, he would conscientiously report advances or slippages that occurred in terms of being true to himself and behaving the way he really felt. I regarded this whole scene with some astonishment and felt I was observing somebody who was engaged in a very subtle but cruel bargain with the devil. The patient seemed to be feeding me things to cure him of, almost generating pathology that was so obviously gross in terms of the patient's actual capacity to curb his behavior that it was a relatively easy thing to reduce the early presenting symptomatology. Among other things, the patient would describe slave–like masochistic adorations for mean, exploitative men. After about two interpretations, these "chronic patterns" magically changed. The patient reported he was going to look for meaningful relationships. The patient would describe extremely childlike dependencies on both his parents (e.g., having his father get up in the middle of the night to change his tire, having them pay for his car insurance; calling them up at the slightest hint of illness). Again, these seemingly ingrained habits seemed to change after only a few interpretations, with no real working through or any kind of in-depth understanding. One last point: despite his masochistic tendencies, this man found his most deeply satisfying relationship in homosexual arrangements. He was never able to go public and to really accept this part of himself, however. He resisted joining homosexual organizations, didn't let fellow workers who were themselves homosexuals know about himself and kept this a secret from his parents. With me, he tried very hard to disgust me, to present the raunchiest, seediest aspects of homosexuality in such a way as to try to shock me. By providing me with this garbage to sift through and "satisfy my needs to save him from this sordid existence," it was my impression after a time that the patient was acting as though he was willing to surrender this part of his behavior so long as I didn't take his homosexuality away from him. The only problem was that he was fooling himself. I had no intention of infringing on his homosexuality. It was his own inability to live with it and enjoy it that made him feel that he had to pretend that it was getting him into these awful messes. The patient was unconsciously behaving as though if I cured him of enough pathology I would let him and his secret enjoyment of homosexuality alone.

Eventually in treatment, we got to the meaning of the "plucking of hairs" symptom. The patient understood these hairs represented "wild hairs"; that is, real, growing parts of himself that were not supposed to be noticed. If the patient removed them (castrated himself) before anybody became aware of them, then the patient had the fantasy that he might seem damaged and perhaps even crazy but his basic capacity for life, change, and growth would be preserved. The self mutilation that the plucking represented and which was acted out in so many other ways by this man was ultimately seen as a ploy to distract the superego and its externalized representation from ever realizing that life was throbbing under the surface, for he feared that if this was ever discovered, he would surely be destroyed once and for all. This was all beautifully summarized in a fantasy he described, "You remember during World War II? The minesweepers would chase the submarines. The submarines would shoot oil slicks, garbage and pieces of debris out through the torpedo tubes and up to the surface. When the pursuers would sight this debris, they would think they sank the sub and they would go away. The submarine would wait until nightfall and slowly slip away."

The next patient I will discuss was a woman in her mid-thirties who was obsessed with the idea that something terrible was going to happen to her nine-year-old son. Early in treatment she described a dream where she imagined that her son was her inner lining. "Everything he does I watch like a hawk. Every move, every hurt, every possible pitfall, I anticipate. I know it's nuts but I can't help it." This woman had a mother who "did everything for her child. My mother told me very directly what kind of person I should be—good-natured, outgoing and smart. She always exaggerated how much she loved me and was always telling me who I was and what I was feeling. Once in a while, I would tell her I was unhappy and she would say, 'spare me your hurt; things aren't as bad as you're making them; be happy—it's the best way,' " This woman learned two main lessons from this exposure: (1) that the mother really didn't love her or at best, that this love was very conditional and (2) the kind of response that was expected had to be false and other-oriented. The anger and despair that was aroused could rarely be expressed because even a small degree of unhappy behavior was viewed as extremely disappointing. The relationship with the son was interpreted as a reenactment of the early symbiotic tie with the mother. The manifestations of hate that took the guise of love through possessiveness, surveillance and apprehension were then undone by sugar coatings of love, demonstrativeness and suffocating affection. The net result was a child who was rapidly developing disturbing symptoms and of a mother who was acting out another version of the very kind of mother she despised.

Very early in treatment, I pointed out some of the more obvious parallels. After a short while, the patient's response was to agree that the primary problem was herself and not the son. She kept prefacing this insight with the statement, "I'm not trying to please you—it's just that I now know that if I help myself, I'll help my son." I suggested that this all sounded very good except that she seemed more concerned with giving the correct response rather than voicing her own real fears and concerns that persisted regarding the son. The patient then became very agitated and confused. It soon became apparent that if the patient was stripped of the characterological ingratiating attempts at fusion in the sense of identifying with the line of thinking that the therapist approved of, she floundered and didn't know what to say. "I don't know what to say. Anything I think of sounds like a lie. Do you mean that if I don't try to please there's hardly anything else for me?"

Several months later, this same woman was describing some positive changes that she had undergone. "I have a sense of relief with my son—he stopped blinking and I'm less hovering with him, I'm buying more clothes, keeping the house nice, and I cut my hair. The only thing I'm not doing well is with my weight. I eat for relief. Sometimes I think I like to be heavy. It gives me a more comfortable feeling. When I'm thinner, I feel empty; I feel something's missing."

Within the personality organizations of these two patients their internalized object relationships are subject to a significant amount of "splitting." "Splitting" is the process of actively dichotomizing feelings towards early love objects so as to idealize certain positive qualities and to deny or repress negative ones. The mothers of these patients are both insistently loving. They actively offer tokens of unconditional, indiscriminate availability and act very hurt and angry if their need to be needed is thwarted. The degree of selfishness, aggression and the potential for destructiveness is great, as the child is utterly confused by the mixed signals. The result in both cases is a character structure consisting of shallow friendliness and pseudo-submission, covering over an emotional detachment, which combine to seal off an extreme amount of primitive anger. The patients were sometimes able to express this anger toward their mothers and could argue with them at times, but were at a loss for words as to why they were practically choking with paroxysms of rage at what they considered to be basically "good Jewish mothers, just like their friends had."

It is my clinical impression that most of the patients of the schizoid variety that I have noted to inflict pain on themselves, feel as though something is lacking if they don't have problems and are highly creative masochists. I offer a two-fold hypothesis to account for this phenomena: (1) There is the explanation that I have already gone into, namely that deeply felt hurt may reflect the only thing these patients are able to call their own. Although the schizoid patient is capable of distinguishing between internal experience and external perception and his reality testing is largely preserved, this capacity is lost during emotional moments which cause regressive episodes. There is a confusion at these times between what is occurring "inside" and what is taking place "outside." The patient, by causing his own pain, can at least partially regulate and control what is taking place, thereby distinguishing between himself and outside events. This very costly resurrection of ego boundaries is worth the price if the patient believes that it defends him against going crazy. In effect, pain or depression can temporarily stabilize a lost sense of identity and halt a terrifying cycle of pathological projective and introjective processes. (2) Another possibility is that the chronic generation of self-induced pain is a highly symbolic attempt to reestablish a fantasy relationship with the idealized "loving" mother. In an overdetermined way, the patient acts out the internalized experience of underlying hate that the parent originally manifested, passively offers himself as a damaged object to be "loved," transformed and experimented with to gratify the parents' narcissism, and unconsciously demonstrates an original truth—that the earliest need-satisfactions occurred in a climate of hidden sadism and resulting ego injury. In a very condensed fashion, the individual can be expressing his own distorted beliefs concerning the necessary conditions for love. From this point of view, deepening the pain experience is seen as a triggering mechanism designed to revive early paradisical fantasies, separated from early experiences of harm and resulting ego injury.

These theoretical speculations contain implications for treatment. My experience with schizoid patients suggests the presence of a strong, latent, negative transference covered over by an emotionally shallow therapeutic relationship. Because of this condition, it is easy for the analyst to be deceived by surface changes and reports of improvement that are more apparent than real. A key requisite for broadening the observing ego and solidifying a true therapeutic alliance is to constantly work at preventing the development of insoluble transference-countertransference binds. To repeat what was stated earlier, schizoid patients seem to offer the therapist superficial parts of themselves to rescue, rehabilitate and approve of, thereby perpetuating the myth of the idealized, giving-loving parent. The purpose of this maneuver is to protect the inner self against the dread of control and fusion. During the course of treatment, after first establishing an early positive supportive relationship, the therapist should strive to reveal and interpret every evidence of manifest and latent negative transference. The rationale behind this is to repeatedly demonstrate to the patient that he is primarily engaged in gratifying the therapist's supposed need for dominance and that by taking this passive-submissive role, he secures his feelings of frustration, emptiness, and anger. The acting out of the transference by attempting to please the analyst, is highlighted as the main resistance to further change. A simplified summary statement here would be "don't blame me for what you're doing to yourself." For example, if a patient is jealous but deals with it as though it's a problem to be worked on and conquered and he dependently requests that I help in overcoming this shortcoming, I tell him that it must make him very angry if he feels he has to ask to be cured of a perfectly normal feeling. In cases like the patient mentioned earlier who basically preferred his homosexual orientation, I suggest that it must be a terrible thing to have to degrade perfectly enjoyable aspects of homosexuality by feeling obliged to emphasize only the lurid details and masochistic aspects of his adventures. I remind him that I can pay for my own entertainment.

In regard to the specific countertransferential elements operating in working with schizoid defenses, I think that most analysts would agree that treating this "neurosis of failure" (Racker, 1968) is extremely frustrating. In spite of repeated "correct" interpretations and a good deal of energy expenditure, the persistence of the patient's illness derides, controls and dominates the analyst's best efforts. Many of these patients come to us after having already humbled several previous analysts. A common occurrence is for the analyst to react to the challenge by becoming very active. A combination of the patient's passivity, frightening regressive tendencies, masochism and despair drive many analysts to play the Messiah and strive to save the patient from himself. It is precisely the early recognition of these situations and the analyst's grasp of the vicious cycle that could easily be reenacted that is of decisive importance to the entire future course of treatment. It is so easy for the analyst who is acting out his own grandiose narcissistic needs to be trapped by the patient's hidden resistances. The analyst begins to feel anxious at the possibility of failure and can become quite angry with the patient for making him aware that he had been living in a fools' paradise. If this anger is repressed and translates itself in the disguised form of precipitating attempts to restructure the patient's life, an over-concern with the reduction of presenting complaints, a tendency to "give a lot to the patient," and an unconscious pacification of the patient's transference needs, then a very dangerous repetition of the past is set in motion. In this way, the analyst is drawn into a self-centered, omnipotent compensation for his bruised ego, the patient is unconsciously encouraged to surrender his autonomy to protect the analyst's insecurity, and the crucial early mother-child interaction is blurred over and acted out instead of being worked through. A precious opportunity is lost for cultivating more genuine object-relationships. The analyst who has resolved his own narcissistic tendencies will have a higher capacity for tolerating frustration, will be less likely to get bogged down in untenable countertransferential traps, and will be able to selectively focus, within the transference, on the patient's pathological defenses.

Summary

To summarize this paper, it is the author's point of view that schizoid and borderline patients cling to misery and inflict pain on themselves in order to symbolically separate themselves from an introjected enveloping narcissistic mother. The suggested psychotherapeutic strategy is to slowly bring out the patient's underlying negative transference that is experienced as a reaction to a historical need to surrender a part of himself to gratify the imagined needs of the therapist-mother. The personal security of the therapist and his ability to handle his own narcissism in curbing countertransferential attitudes is suggested as an important element in determining the treatment prognosis in these cases.

Bibliography

1. Eliezer, D.: Psychic Energy and Mechanisms of Defense, *The Psychoanalytic Study of the Child,* 18, 511–540, 1963, International Universities Press, New York.
2. Peller, L.: Libidinal Phases, Ego Development, and Play, *The Psychoanalytic Study of the Child,* 9: 178–198, 1954, International Universities Press, New York.
3. Winnicott, D.: Mind and Its Relation to the Psyche-Soma, *Brit. J. Med. Psychol.,* 27, 112–126, 1954.

Chapter 11

SOCIAL, BEHAVIORAL AND ADJUSTMENT FACTORS IN OBESITY

David L. Snow, Ph.D.

David L. Snow, Ph.D.

Dr. Snow received his Ph.D. in Clinical Psychology from the University of Washington in 1969 and completed two years of postdoctoral training in the Department of Psychiatry, University of Colorado Medical Center. He is currently an Associate Professor in the Department of Psychiatry and Child Study Center at Yale University School of Medicine.

Obesity represents one of the most serious public health problems of the present time. It is estimated that 20 to 40 per cent of the population in the United States is obese (Stuart and Davis, 1972). Among adolescents, it has been reported that 15 to 20 per cent of this age group is overweight (Wilson, Farber, Kimbrough and Wilson, 1969). The relationship between excess weight and increased mortality and medical difficulties makes evident the importance of understanding and controlling this particular condition. The mortality rate for obese individuals between the ages of 20 and 64 years is 50 per cent greater than for normal weight men and women (Mayer, 1953). In addition, for many medical disorders, the presence of obesity adversely influences the prognosis of the disease and leads to marked increases in mortality (Kaplan and Kaplan, 1957).

Obesity results from an imbalance between caloric intake and energy expenditure. By definition, it is a condition in which the body contains an abnormally large amount of adipose tissue or in which a disproportionate amount of body weight is represented by fat deposits. Recent investigations have indicated that early development of fat cells predisposes an individual to becoming overweight. Since the number of fat cells is probably fixed after adolescence, the age of onset of obesity is an important distinction. Van Itallie and Campbell (1972) have written that those who become overweight as adults (growth onset obesity) appear to have enlarged fat cells without a corresponding increase in adipose tissue cellularity. On the other hand, those whose adiposity develops in infancy or early adolescence demonstrate a significant increase in the number of fat cells (hyperplasia). Such an increase in the number of cells can result from overfeeding during critical periods of development. Later attempts to modify food intake and/or energy output can result in the reduction of fat deposits, but the number of fat cells remains basically unchanged making maintenance of weight loss more difficult. The developmental focus is important since most overweight individuals show a history of the early onset of obesity. Abraham and Nordsieck (1960), in a longitudinal study, found that the vast majority of overweight children become overweight adults. In addition, Eid (1970) reported that infants who gained weight rapidly in the first six months were likely to be obese by six to eight years of age, and Huenemann (1974) concluded that the first six months of life may be a critical period for obesity development. Certainly, early patterns of feeding, activity, and associated learned eating behaviors appear to be critical in the development of obesity.

A determination of the etiology of obesity, however, has proven extraordinarily complex. The possible role of genetic, metabolic, social, psychological and behavioral factors have been investigated from a variety of theoretical positions. Even given the possible influence of biological factors, certain investigators have stressed the role of nonphysiological factors in the development and maintenance of obesity, and the predominant importance of such variables in the majority of cases of obesity. Sheldon (1970), for example, has stated that if certain metabolic abnormalities were responsible for causing obesity, one would expect that these disorders would be evident after weight reduction. This is generally not the case. In addition, these same metabolic abnormalities can be produced by overfeeding normal individuals which suggests they result from rather than cause obesity. Much attention has been paid to the possible role of hypothalamic abnormalities in causing obesity (Mayer, 1953; Schachter, 1971). Again, however, amount of body fat can lead to behavioral disorders similar to those produced by damage to the hypothalamus. Nisbett and Gurwitz (1970) have shown that the eating behavior of overweight infants is quite similar to that of rats made obese by ventromedial hypothalamic damage.

The purpose of the present paper is to review the social, behavioral, and adjustment factors that have been studied in relation to the problem of obesity. First, certain socio-demographic variables will be reviewed that have been found to strongly influence the prevalence patterns of obesity and which may have an important role in the development and maintenance of this condition. Second, behavioral patterns characteristic of obese individuals will be discussed from the standpoint of four theoretical positions: the stimulus-binding hypothesis, the deficit-in-response-inhibition hypothesis, the psychosomatic concept of obesity, and the role of inactivity. Although these views are not necessarily incompatible, different emphases are placed on the variables important to understanding the behavior of overweight individuals. Third, studies of psychological and personality correlates of obesity will be reviewed to determine whether characteristic patterns of adjustment or personality have been identified for obese as compared to normal-weight individuals. In conclusion, implications will be drawn from the analysis of the above factors to indicate possible methods for the treatment and control of obesity.

Social Factors

A number of socio-demographic variables are significantly related to the prevalence of obesity demonstrating the importance of social influence factors. Several investigators have demonstrated a marked relationship between social class and obesity in adults. Moore, Stunkard and Srole (1962), using data from the Midtown Manhattan Study, found that the prevalence of obesity was 7 times higher among women reared in the lowest social class as compared to those reared in the highest social class. The social class measure was based on the status of the respondent's father when the respondent was entering adulthood, and therefore served as an antecedent measure of social influence. Thirty per cent of the women in the lowest category were obese as compared to only 4% in the highest category. A similar relationship was found for men although to a lesser extent. Employing a measure of the individual's own socioeconomic status, comparable findings have been reported in two subsequent investigations (Goldblatt, Moore and Stunkard, 1965; Silverstone, Gordon and Stunkard, 1969). In addition, in a study of college students, presumably of relatively higher socioeconomic status, only 2.4% of the sample was found to be obese (Pargman, 1969).

The influence of social class on obesity also has been examined in relation to school age children (Stunkard, d'Aquili, Fox and Filion, 1972). Class differences were shown to emerge at an early age. Obesity was significantly more prevalent in lower-class than upper-class girls with nine times greater prevalence by age six years. Similar but less striking differences were found between lower and upper class boys. Moreover, the pattern of thinness among girls was found to be significantly more characteristic of the upper-class group. At the same time, with increasing age, the prevalence of obesity was shown to increase at a more rapid rate among lower-class girls.

Goldblatt, Moore and Stunkard (1965) have analyzed the relationship between a number of other social factors and the prevalence of obesity. Social mobility was shown to affect this relationship in women but not in men. Social mobility was derived by comparing the individual's own socioeconomic status with that of her parents. Downwardly mobile females were more often obese (22%) than upwardly mobile females (12%). The significance of acculturation is shown further by analysis of the number of generations one's family has lived in the United States, an important factor for both men and women. Obesity was far more prevalent among individuals of first generation as compared to fourth generation families. Even controlling for socioeconomic status (which was positively related to generation), the inverse relationship between obesity and generation in the United States remained significant.

The authors suggest two processes to account for the demonstrated relationships between the various social factors and obesity. First, a selection process may operate in any status-conferring situation so that preferential choice occurs in relation to thinner women. Second, a process of acculturation may occur so that an individual's adult weight is in part due to important social and family influences during childhood. Some evidence is found for this process in the relationship between obesity and socioeconomic status of origin.

Further support was derived by examining the relationship between obesity and ethnicity. In this same study, a much lower prevalence of obesity was found in females of British descent (9%) as compared to those of Italian descent (27%). It has been shown that the preferred diet of Italian-Americans contains a higher proportion of fat content than that of the average American diet (Childs, 1933; Stout, Morrow, Brandt and Wolf, 1964). The reported dieting habits of Czech families (Joffe, 1943) also might account for the very high prevalence of obesity among lower-class Czechs (Goldblatt, *et al.*, 1965). In addition, certain beliefs regarding obesity in children as a protection against illness, and an insurance for recovery when ill, also may serve as an important social influence favoring obesity in certain groups (Joffe, 1943).

The study of the relationship between various social factors and the prevalence of obesity makes evident the role of family and cultural influences in determining whether a person becomes overweight. The results of these influences are apparent at an early age and may affect the nutritional and eating practices existing during critical periods for obesity development. Stunkard and Burt (1967) have reported that the odds against an obese child becoming a normal-weight adult are more than 4 to 1 at age 12 and increase to 28 to 1 if the individual continues to be overweight by the end of adolescence. The greater effect of these variables on women, and the resulting higher prevalence of obesity among women than men, may be due to differences in work and activity level, the closer association to tasks related to food preparation, and the normally higher proportion of fat cells in women than men. Whatever genetic or biochemical determinants may operate, the development of obesity is influenced significantly by nutritional practices and eating patterns that may occur most frequently in particular social or ethnic groups, by the value placed on being overweight, by economic conditions that may affect the nature of a family's diet, and by one's response to perceived expectations of his social milieu.

Behavioral Factors

A variety of experimental and nonlaboratory investigations have revealed certain characteristic patterns of behavior in obese as compared to nonobese individuals. In these analyses, the primary focus is on determining the variables and conditions that differentially influence behavior related to food intake and energy expenditure. The reported behavioral observations will be discussed as they relate to particular theoretical considerations.

Stimulus-Binding Hypothesis

Schachter (1967) has hypothesized that obese individuals are, to a great extent, under external control and are relatively insensitive to internal cues related to bodily state or hunger. In this sense, the eating behavior of the obese is basically unrelated to internal, visceral state, and is determined by external, food-relevant cues. On the other hand, the eating behavior of normal-weight individuals is determined by an interaction of internal and external cues.

Bruch (1964) has theorized that obese individuals have difficulty identifying emotions and other internal states correctly, and have feelings of being influenced from the outside. Further evidence has accumulated substantiating this general lack of responsiveness to internal state. Obese subjects show little correspondence between the state of gastric motility and self-reports of hunger, while there is relatively close correspondence for the nonobese (Stunkard and Koch, 1964). While the pattern of gastric motility does not differ for obese and normal-weight subjects, the obese are as likely to report hunger in the absence of gastric motility as in its presence and as likely to deny hunger when the stomach is contracting as when it is not. Therefore, the obese are less responsive to internal physiological cues indicative of hunger or satiety. However, obese subjects can learn to recognize more accurately their gastric contractions under conditions of reinforcement (Griggs and Stunkard, 1964). This effect argues against the possibility of faulty neural mechanisms.

Schachter, Goldman and Gordon (1968) have reported that the amount eaten by obese subjects is not affected by conditions of fear arousal or food deprivation, while normal-weight subjects eat more when calm than when frightened and more when food deprived than when sated. In addition, obese individuals show a deficiency in satiation response to sucrose (Cabanac and Duclaux, 1970), and in general may take longer to recognize the point of satiety (Linton, Conley, Kuechenmeister and McClusky, 1972).

Various external cues have been assessed as to their effects in determining the behavior of obese subjects. The obese are more responsive to changes in taste which typically is viewed as an external or peripheral stimulus. Nisbett (1968) found responsiveness to taste positively related to weight while responsiveness to deprivation was inversely related to weight. In this particular study, overweight subjects ate more than normal-weight subjects if the food was rated as tasting good but showed no difference if not liked. Price and Grinker (1973) found that obese subjects are more responsive than normals to their preference functions, and that the more overweight are more responsive than the less overweight. Contrary to previous results, no differences were found in relation to food deprivation. More often, obese subjects drink or eat less food than normals if rated as bad or bland in taste (Decke, 1971). Obese individuals eat considerably less than normals when restricted to a bland, unappetizing diet (Hashim and Van Itallie, 1965), and will choose more often than normal-weight individuals not to eat institutional food (Goldman, Jaffa and Schachter, 1968).

The obese are more affected by the manipulation of time. Schachter and Gross (1968) found that obese subjects ate four times as much in a condition in which they believed it was after when it was actually before dinner time as in the condition where they believed it was before and it was actually after dinner time. Moreover, they have less difficulty fasting if in surroundings that minimize or eliminate external, food-relevant cues, while normals do not show a similar effect (Goldman, Jaffa and Schachter, 1968). In the observation of supermarket shopping behavior, Nisbett and Kanouse (1969) reported that normal-weight individuals bought more if food deprived than if they had recently eaten, while the obese actually bought more if they had recently eaten. Also, the nonobese spent more time shopping than the obese if deprived and less time if they had recently eaten. Finally, it has been shown, in non-food related experiments, that the obese are more field dependent (Karp and Pardes, 1965) and are more persuasible than nonobese individuals (Glass, Lavin, Henchy, Gordon, Mayhew and Donohoe, 1969). Both findings are further indications of greater susceptibility to the influence of external cues.

Considerable evidence has accumulated, then, which suggests that the eating behavior of obese individuals is under external, rather than internal, control. In view of these findings, Schachter (1971) has characterized the obese as stimulus-bound. In the presence of food-relevant cues, the obese are more likely to eat and to eat more than normals, while in the absence of such cues, they are less likely to eat or to complain about hunger. Schachter further contends that this stimulus-binding effect is not limited only to food-relevant cues but is a general characteristic of the obese. As an extension to his original hypothesis, he states: ". . . any stimulus, above a given intensity level, is more likely to evoke an appropriate response from an obese than from a normal subject (1971, pp. 137–138)."

Several findings lend support to this contention. Obese subjects recall more words or objects than normals from slides exposed for brief periods, and respond more rapidly and make fewer errors in tasks measuring complex reaction time but show no difference from normals for simple reaction time (Schachter, 1971). While better at proof-reading when undistracted, their performance is more seriously disrupted by distracting stimuli so that, under conditions of extreme distraction, their performance is significantly worse than that of normal-weight subjects (Rodin, 1970). Johnson (1974), in studying instrumental food-directed performance, found that the behavior of obese subjects varied as a function of cue prominence, while that of normal subjects was relatively unaffected. Schachter (1971) has reported additional evidence indicating that the obese eat more than normals when the food cue is salient and less when it is remote. Finally, the obese tend to respond more strongly to positive and negative affective stimuli (Pliner, Meyer and Blankstein, 1974). From these findings, it does appear that obese individuals demonstrate a generally heightened responsiveness to external stimuli. In addition, the variable of stimulus prominence seems to play an important role in determining whether the obese are more or less reactive than normal-weight individuals in eating as well as in non-food related situations.

Deficit-In-Response-Inhibition Hypothesis

Singh (1975) has criticized the stimulus-binding hypothesis for failing to explain adequately certain eating habits, primarily the termination of eating behavior in obese individuals, and for not taking into account the role of response habits in determining the behavior of the obese. She proposes that the behavior of obese individuals is controlled mainly by response tendencies, and that they will respond longer than normal-weight individuals in those situations in which an ongoing response is to be terminated. Furthermore, she states:

> Stimulus-bound behavior in obese subjects would be evident only in those situations where external cues and response tendencies are compatible. If cues and response tendencies are incompatible as exemplified by negative transfer of training or reversal-learning situations, the behavior of obese subjects would be controlled by existing response tendencies (p. 221).

Three experiments were employed to study the behavior of obese subjects in situations in which the external stimulus and response tendency were incompatible. It was found that the obese ate less when the required response for obtaining food was incompatible with induced response tendencies. Moreover, on a timing task, obese subjects did worse than normals if given prior interfering training, but performed better if no training was given. Finally, the obese demonstrated greater problem-solving rigidity than normal subjects after being given training creating a mental set, while there was no difference in the performance of obese and normal subjects in the absence of such training. These results give support to the hypothesis that the behavior of obese individuals is more affected than that of normal individuals by existing response tendencies, and that the primary disorder is one involving a deficit in response inhibition.

Singh suggests that it is possible to integrate the stimulus-binding and deficit-in-response-inhibition hypotheses. An understanding of the behavior patterns of obese individuals can be derived through an examination of the interactions of external stimuli and response tendencies and their roles in regulating behavior. Stimulus bound behavior will be most evident in stimulus-response-compatible situations, while the behavior of the obese will be most determined by response habits in stimulus-response-incompatible situations.

Disorders in the regulatory functions of the hypothalamus have been introduced as possible explanations for the observed behavior in both lines of investigation. Schachter (1971) compared the findings related to behavior of obese humans and of rats made obese by lesions to the ventromedial hypothalamus. He found striking parallels and proposed that obesity may have a physiological locus in this area of the hypothalamus. However, whether disruption in regulatory mechanisms leading to overresponsiveness to external cues and deficit in response inhibition is caused primarily by damage to the hypothalamus or by increasing the amount of body fat remains unclear. If the latter plays a more central role, then weight loss may be effective in correcting abnormalities in regulatory functions, but a learned orientation to external rather than internal cues and certain established response patterns would remain unchanged. In fact, Nisbett (1968) found that the eating behavior of normal-weight subjects with a history of being overweight was more similar to that of obese subjects. Therefore, modification in patterns of orientation and response would be important not only to losing weight but to maintaining weight loss.

The Psychosomatic Concept of Obesity

The psychosomatic concept of obesity holds that overeating is due to emotional disturbances which lead to abnormal increases in food intake (Kaplan and Kaplan, 1957). A disturbance in appetite is seen as the crucial factor in most cases of obesity, with appetite viewed as a learned phenomenon under the influence of psychic and emotional factors that affect normal regulatory mechanisms. The desire for food is highly conditionable, and this conditioning process has its neurological basis in the hypothalamus. Cognitive and affective cues as well as sensory stimuli can affect the hypothalamus. Therefore, hunger can be evoked by factors such as fear, anxiety and loneliness if such reactions have in the past been associated with hunger. It is assumed that eating serves to reduce such feelings of emotional distress and becomes a means of coping with psychological difficulties.

For the most part, tests of the psychosomatic concept have not offered substantiation for this theory of obesity. McKenna (1972) found that overweight subjects ate more in a condition of high than low-anxiety, while normal-weight subjects ate less under high- than low-anxiety conditions. However, he failed to find support for the prediction that eating serves to reduce anxiety. Abramson and Wunderlich (1972) studied eating behavior in control, interpersonal anxiety and objective fear situations. No significant differences in food consumption were found for the obese subjects. While the obese were more reactive to anxiety-provoking stimuli (also reported by Pliner, *et al.,* 1974), there was no evidence that eating represented a means of coping with this anxiety. Meyer and Pudel (1972) found a tendency toward hyperphagia in obese subjects under conditions of stress. However, the effects of the experimental treatments in producing frustration or anxiety were not measured independently. This leaves open the possibility that the stress situations involved primarily the introduction of additional external stimuli which may have differentially affected the responses of obese subjects. Finally, a number of studies reported earlier in this paper (Cabanac and Duclaux, 1970; Linton, *et al.,* 1972; Schachter, *et al.,* 1968; Schachter and Gross, 1968; Stunkard and Koch, 1964) provide evidence that the obese are less responsive than normal-weight individuals to conditions of internal state. In general, then, the psychosomatic concept of obesity appears highly questionable as a basis for understanding the behavior of overweight individuals.

The Role of Inactivity

Most research has placed greatest emphasis on the role of overeating, and factors that affect eating behavior, as most significant in producing an imbalance between caloric intake and energy expenditure. Based on the preceding analysis, these conditions have obvious importance to the problem of overweight. However, a surplus of calories available for fat synthesis also can result through reduced caloric output. Mayer (1971) has cited evidence indicating that although appetite will increase with energy expenditure, it is not reduced proportionately when physical activity is reduced below a minimal level thus producing an imbalance due to lowered activity in relation to food intake. At the same time, short periods of activity are not followed by increases in normal caloric intake. Again, the total absence of such activity leads to the accumulation of weight.

Several investigations involving obese children and adolescents (Bullen, Monello, Cohen and Mayer, 1963; Johnson, Burke and Mayer, 1956; Stefanik, Heald and Mayer, 1959; Wilkes, 1960) have shown the obese groups to be abnormally inactive. Moreover, in some comparisons, the caloric intake of the obese was not higher and in many cases was lower than that of the nonobese. Therefore, many obese individuals can be characterized by inactivity rather than overeating. For adolescents, abnormally low activity is as frequent a behavioral observation as abnormally high food intake (Bullen, *et al.,* 1963). Mayer (1971), utilizing time motion studies, demonstrated that when performing sports, obese girls exercise far less vigorously, and engage in activity only a fraction of the time spent by the nonobese. To what extent activity level plays a part in the etiology of obesity is not clear, but early patterns of inactivity, if perpetuated, would certainly make more likely the accumulation of excess calories and weight. In any case, the role of inactivity is a necessary consideration in developing an overall view of the relationship between behavior and obesity.

Adjustment Factors

Attempts to determine characteristic adjustment patterns of overweight individuals have been varied and inconsistent. Methods employed have included clinical interviews, projective and objective personality assessment, and descriptive and problem-oriented checklists. Adequate steps often have not been taken to control for possible confounding variables, such as age of onset of obesity and social class, and some investigations even lack nonobese comparison samples. Studies have focused primarily on obesity in adults, with greater emphasis on females, and on pre-adolescent and adolescent female groups. The interest in females stems from the greater prevalence of obesity among women than men, and because, within our social context, obese women are open to greater social disfavor, ridicule and rejection. Although there has been no direct comparison, it has been assumed that adjustment in adolescent and adult females is more seriously disrupted by these factors.

The search for a distinctive personality structure in obese adults has not proven productive. However, there are some indications of the type of adjustment difficulties experienced more frequently by obese than nonobese individuals. In comparison to a normative sample, obese adults demonstrated lower need for achievement, poorer personal adjustment, and fewer preferences for group association and other activities related to affiliation (Wunderlich, Johnson and Ball, 1973). Controlling for socioeconomic status and age, Moore, *et al.* (1962) compared obese and nonobese groups on eight psychological scores and a psychiatric evaluation of symptomatology. The obese group showed significantly greater rigidity, immaturity and suspicion. Seltzer (1946), in a study of college males, concluded that any bodily disproportion was related to less stable and less well integrated personalities. Levitt and Fellner (1965) compared three subgroups of obese women: psychogenic, mixed and metabolic. The psychogenic group showed greater elevations on 10 of 13 MMPI scales lending support to the notion of personality differences among subgroups of the obese. Two studies involving superobese adults (Atkinson and Ringuette, 1967; Fink, Gettesfeld and Glickman, 1962) revealed psychiatric diagnoses in the vast majority of cases with depressive reactions a common feature. However, there was no distinctive or consistent diagnostic pattern or presenting problem. Body image disturbances have been noted in some obese primarily related to early onset of obesity, presence of neurosis and negative parental evaluation of the obesity (Stunkard and Mendelson, 1961). Perception of body size is an important aspect of body image. Glucksman and Hirsch (1969) reported that obese subjects increasingly overestimated body size during and following weight loss. While reduced, they perceived themselves as if no weight had been lost, and consistently overestimated the size of other external stimuli.

In contrast to the above findings, some authors have failed to demonstrate differences in the adjustment of obese as compared to nonobese groups. Weinberg, Mendelson and Stunkard (1961) utilized a wide range of psychological tests and found no differences between overweight and normal-weight men. Similar results were reported in a study of college women (Friedman, 1959). The only distinction was that obese women were less objective in thinking and more hypersensitive. The writer interpreted this latter finding as due to the obese woman being open to social disfavor, and such pressure fosters hypersensitivity. Finally, in a comparison of normal, moderately overweight and superobese, lower-class women, no differences were found among the groups in gross psychiatric disturbance (Holland, Masling and Copley, 1970). It was suggested that obesity may not result in the same social disfavor in lower-class as middle-class populations.

For overweight adults, it appears that no consistent pattern of adjustment difficulties has been identified. Two points seem most important. A careful analysis of the adjustment of obese adults must focus on particular subgroups, since factors such as sex, social class, degree of obesity and age of onset of obesity account for differences in whether certain psychological difficulties are likely to develop. In addition, it may be that many of the problems in adjustment that are observed in the obese are a result of the pressures and social disfavor that occur in a culture which adhers to narrowly defined standards of attractiveness.

Studies of pre-adolescent and adolescent females more consistently show patterns of psychological and social difficulties (Carrera, 1967; Snow and Held, 1973). Werkman and Greenberg (1967) compared obese adolescent girls at a medically oriented camp for overweight individuals with normal-weight girls at an ordinary summer camp on a number of personality and interest measures. The obese group showed greater narcissism, impulse control difficulties, social anxiety, behavioral immaturity and depression. They concluded that obesity appears to be consistently associated with personality difficulties of a serious nature. Feiner (1954) studied certain aspects of the perception of parental figures and sexual identification of an obese adolescent female group. The obesity group exhibited greater dependency on parents, especially mothers, and greater aggression toward fathers than did the normal-weight group. In a comparison of obese and non-obese female adolescents from a medical clinic population, Held and Snow (1972) found that the obese group scored significantly higher on a problem checklist and five scales of the MMPI. The difficulties of the obese group were characterized by feelings of depression, alienation and low self-worth. In addition, they tended to be mistrustful and nonconforming and to exhibit problems in impulse control.

Although problems can develop at an earlier age, it appears that the obese adolescent female faces special difficulties. The importance of peer group acceptance, emerging sexuality, and the growing emphasis placed on hetero-sexual relationships create a multitude of pressures and anxieties even if one is not obese. Even pre-adolescent obese girls have been found to engage very little in social activity (Wilkes, 1960). The pattern for younger children is different. Though obese children show a more negative self-concept (Sallade, 1973), there are no differences in social adjustment, or in other areas of emotional adjustment, and the obese children are not rated differently as a group from the non-obese on a sociometric instrument. It is possible, then, that pre-adolescence and adolescence are critical periods for the development of psychological and social difficulties in the obese female.

Implications for Intervention and Treatment

An attempt to broadly address the problem of obesity must involve an emphasis on early intervention and prevention. Although many have indicated the need for such efforts, too few resources are directed toward the development of preventive programs. Most research has focused on the study of obesity in adults and on the application of a wide variety of treatment approaches to adult obesity. The need to develop effective treatment interventions for this population is clear, but the extensive nature of this condition argues for the establishment of programs to alter those patterns basic to obesity development. Too often the problem is viewed as only within the individual, while it is evident that family and socio-cultural factors greatly influence the early onset of obesity and the establishment of patterns of behavior related to eating and activity.

The focal point for a program in early intervention and public health education might best be provided through the public school system. Seltzer and Mayer (1970) reported encouraging results from a school-based, weight control program. Emphasis was placed on increased daily physical activity and nutrition education, as well as the provision of continuous support to the children in their efforts to lose weight. The major thrust of the program was on the establishment of daily habits of physical activity and proper food intake. The authors stressed several reasons for the location of such a program in the schools. It provides access to the largest number of children and places the issue in the context of education. Continuous supervision and support is available, and it can be integrated into regular school activities at low cost. In addition to this rationale, the school can serve as a base from which to direct efforts toward parent groups and families, particularly those groups at high risk for obesity development. The involvement of parents is essential in order to provide information regarding dietary practices and the relationship between overeating and increased mortality rates and disease. Whatever settings might be utilized for this type of program (child care centers, nursery schools, etc.), or whatever professional groups can direct increased attention to this matter in their work with families and children (pediatricians, nutritionists, public health workers, etc.), the emphasis on early intervention remains most important.

The results of traditional forms of outpatient treatment for obesity have been poor. At the same time, although obese individuals are able to lose considerable weight when hospitalized, this weight loss is usually not maintained during subsequent periods. The analysis of behavioral and adjustment factors related to obesity, and the results of certain therapeutic interventions, suggest the possible effectiveness of integrating behavioral and group therapy approaches in the treatment of obesity. Since environmental stimuli and basic response tendencies play a significant role in determining the eating behavior of obese individuals, attempts to directly modify situaticnal variables and response patterns seem most indicated as methods to effect weight loss.

In contrast to previous treatment results, the outcomes of research studies employing external reinforcement, self-reinforcement or a combination of these two behavior modification procedures have demonstrated considerable success in producing weight changes (Harris, 1969; Harris and Bruner, 1971; Jeffrey, 1974; Mann, 1972; Pennick, Filion, Fox and Stunkard, 1971; Stuart, 1967; Wollersheim, 1970). Utilizing the behavioral approach, certain methods are applied to the management of behavior related to eating. First, emphasis is placed on training in reinforcement principles and the involvement of the individual in the careful assessment and documentation of his eating behavior. Such an analysis provides a means to identify those conditions under which eating is likely to occur and those stimuli controlling eating behavior. In addition, this process allows the individual to begin to learn that he is in control of his own behavior. Second, attempts are made to minimize or eliminate external or situational cues related to eating (e.g., eating only in one designated place in the home, reducing the amount of food purchased or prepared, and not pairing eating behavior with any other activities which might elicit eating with the occurrence of the other behavior). Third, training is provided to modify basic response patterns (e.g., slowing the rate of eating and interrupting the meal for a predetermined period of time). And fourth, criteria are established for the application of reinforcement for efforts to modify weight or for designated degrees of weight loss. Reinforcement is provided by the therapist, by the individual through self-reinforcement, and/ or by some member of the individual's social environment. The involvement of other members of one's social milieu to support changes in behavior may be essential to the occurrence and maintenance of weight loss. In a recent study, Jeffrey (1974) reported that, although external- and self-reinforcement procedures both produced significant weight loss, the self-control procedures were most effective in the maintenance of weight loss. He also found that the self-control treatment led to changes on an internal-external control measure toward greater internality. Utilizing self-reinforcement approaches, then, may be important to altering the observed external orientation in obese individuals.

Along with the procedures outlined above, the need to provide dieting and nutritional instruction and to modify the activity level of the individual is often emphasized. Although further replication of the reported effectiveness of behavior modification methods is required to delineate the most essential elements of the treatment process and to assess outcome on a longer-term basis, the application of behavior therapy approaches to the control of obesity seems promising.

The adjustment difficulties experienced by many obese individuals indicates the need to consider broader therapeutic interventions than only programs to effect the reduction of weight. Additional treatment involvement should not be applied indiscriminately assuming unitary need, but should be based on careful individual assessment. Given the social and interpersonal nature of the difficulties often associated with the problem of obesity, and which may result from being overweight, group psychotherapy can serve as an important adjunct to behavioral approaches directed specifically at weight reduction. Many obese individuals demonstrate considerable social anxiety and a pattern of limited social interaction. They are often mistrustful and suspicious of others and hypersensitive to their reactions. These responses may be due, in large part, to a previous history of felt rejection and ridicule which also produce feelings of low self-esteem. Group therapy provides the opportunity for the development of positive interpersonal experiences and offers a social structure in which the issues of trust and acceptance can receive major attention (Snow and Held, 1973). In this way, the group becomes a transitional experience in promoting feelings of increased self-worth and the development of more satisfying interpersonal relationships. In addition, the process of both support and confrontation within the group is very useful to altering the sense of limited internal control and the related general feelings of powerlessness and depression. Members are helpful in identifying activities and interactions in which individuals can be successful and can gain a greater sense of self-effectiveness. They are able to confront others' attitudes of being unable to control various aspects of their life situations, and to support the perceptions that outcomes are a function of their own behavior and decisions. Obviously, this process is important to individuals' attempts to lose weight and to gain control over their eating behavior. In general, group psychotherapy is viewed as a useful and necessary treatment intervention for many overweight individuals, and one which can be integrated with more specific behavioral approaches to the control of obesity.

References

1. Abraham, S. and Nordsieck, M. Relationship of excess weight in children and adults. *Public Health Report,* 1969, *75,* 263–273.
2. Abrahamson, E.E. Behavioral approaches to weight control: an updated review. *Behavioral Research and Therapy,* 1977, *15,* 355–363.
3. Abrahamson, E.E. and Wunderlich, R.A. Anxiety, fear and eating: a test of the psychosomatic concept of obesity. *Journal of Abnormal Psychology,* 1972, *79,* 317–321.
4. Ashwell, M. and North, W.R.S. The prevalence of obesity in working populations in London. *Proceedings of the Nutrition Society,* 1977, *36,* 109A.

5. Atkinson, R.M. and Rinquette, E.L. A survey of biographical and psychological features in extraordinary fatness. *Psychosomatic Medicine,* 1967, *29,* 121–133.

6. Bruch, H. Psychological aspects of overeating and obesity. *Psychosomatics,* 1964, *5,* 269–274.

7. Bullen, B.A., Monello, L.F., Cohen, H., and Mayer, J. Attitudes towards physical activity, food and family in obese and nonobese adolescent girls. *American Journal of Clinical Nutrition,* 1963, *12,* 1–11.

8. Cabanac, M. and Duclaux, R. Obesity: absence of satiety aversion to sucrose. *Science,* 1970, *168,* 496–497.

9. Carrera, F. Obesity in adolescence. *Psychosomatics,* 1967, *8,* 342–349.

10. Childs, A. Some dietary studies of Poles, Mexicans, Italians and Negroes. *Child Health Bulletin,* 1933, *9,* 84–91.

11. Coates, T.J. and Thoresen, C.E. Treating obesity in children and adolescents: a review. *American Journal of Public Health,* 1978, *68,* 143–151.

12. Decke, E. Effects of taste on the eating behavior of obese and normal persons. Cited in S. Schachter, *Emotion, obesity, and crime.* New York: Academic Press, 1971.

13. Eid, E.E. Follow-up study of physical growth of children who had excessive weight gain in first six months of life. *British Medical Journal,* 1970, *2,* 74–76.

14. Elman, D., Schroeder, H.E. and Schwartz, M.F. Reciprocal social influence of obese and normal-weight persons. *Journal of Abnormal Psychology,* 1977, *86,* 408–413.

15. Feiner, A.H. A study of certain aspects of the perception of parental figures and sexual identifications of an obese adolescent female group. Unpublished doctoral dissertation, New York University, 1954.

16. Fink, G., Gettesfeld, H. and Glickman, L. The superobese patient. *Journal of Hillside Hospital,* 1962, *11,* 97–119.

17. Friedman, J. Weight problems and psychological factors. *Journal of Consulting Psychology,* 1959, *23,* 524–527.

18. Glass, D.C., Lavin, D.E., Henchy, T., Gordon, A., Mayhew, P. and Donohoe, P. Obesity and persuasibility. *Journal of Personality,* 1969, *37,* 407–414.

19. Glucksman, M.L. and Hirsch, J. The response of obese patients to weight reduction. III. The perception of body size. *Psychosomatic Medicine,* 1969, *31,* 1–7.

20. Goldblatt, P.B., Moore, M.E. and Stunkard, A.J. Social factors in obesity. *Journal of the American Medical Association,* 1965, *192,* 1039–1044.

21. Goldman, R., Jaffa, M. and Schachter, S. Yom Kippur, Air France, dormitory food, and the eating behavior of obese and normal persons. *Journal of Personality and Social Psychology,* 1968, *10,* 117–123.

22. Griggs, R.C. and Stunkard, A.J. The interpretation of gastric motility: II. Sensitivity and bias in the perception of gastric motility. *Archives of General Psychiatry,* 1964, *11,* 82–89.

23. Harris, M.B. Self-directed program for weight control—a pilot study. *Journal of Abnormal Psychology,* 1969, *74,* 263–270.

24. Harris, M.B. and Bruner, C.G. A comparison of a self-control and a contract procedure for weight control. *Behavior Research and Therapy,* 1971, *9,* 347–354.

25. Hashim, S. and Van Itallie, T. Studies in normal and obese subjects with a monitored food-dispensing device. *Annals of the New York Academy of Sciences,* 1965, *131,* 654–661.

26. Held, M.L. and Snow, D.L. MMPI, internal-external control, and problem checklist scores of obese adolescent females. *Journal of Clinical Psychology,* 1972, *28,* 523–525.

27. Holland, J., Masling, J. and Copley, D. Mental illness in lower class normal, obese and hyperobese women. *Psychosomatic Medicine*, 1970, *32*, 351–357.
28. Huenemann, R.L. Environmental factors associated with preschool obesity. *Journal of the American Dietetic Association*, 1974, *64*, 480–487.
29. Jeffrey, D.B. A comparison of the effects of external control and self-control on the modification and maintenance of weight. *Journal of Abnormal Psychology*, 1974, *83*, 404–410.
30. Joffe, N.F. Food habits of selected subcultures in United States. *Bulletin of the National Research Council*, 1943, *108*, 97–103.
31. Johnson, W.G. Effect of cue prominence and subject weight on human food-directed performance. *Journal of Personality and Social Psychology*, 1974, *29*, 843–848.
32. Johnson, M.L., Burke, B.S. and Mayer, J. Relative importance of inactivity and overeating in the energy balance of obese high school girls. *American Journal of Clinical Nutrition*, 1956, *4*, 37–44.
33. Kaplan, H.I. and Kaplan, H.S. The psychosomatic concept of obesity. *Journal of Nervous and Mental Disease*, 1957, *125*, 181–189.
34. Karp, S.A. and Pardes, H. Psychological differentiation (field dependence) in obese women. *Psychosomatic Medicine*, 1965, *27*, 238–244.
35. LeBow, M.D., Goldberg, P.S. and Collins, A. Eating behavior of overweight and nonoverweight persons in the natural environment. *Journal of Consulting and Clinical Psychology*, 1977, *45*, 1204–1205.
36. Leon, G.R. and Roth, L. Obesity: psychological causes, correlations, and speculations. *Psychological Bulletin*, 1977, *84*, 117–139.
37. Levitt, H. and Fellner, C. MMPI profiles of three obesity subgroups. *Journal of Consulting Psychology*, 1965, *29*, 91.
38. Linton, P.H., Conley, M., Kuechenmeister, C. and McClusky, H. Satiety and obesity. *The American Journal of Clinical Nutrition*, 1972, *25*, 368–370.
39. Mann, R.A. The behavior-therapeutic use of contingency contracting to control an adult behavior problem: weight control. *Journal of Applied Behavior Analysis*, 1972, *5*, 99–109.
40. Mayer, J. Genetic, traumatic, and environmental factors in the etiology of obesity. *Physiological Reviews*, 1953, *33*, 472–508.
41. Mayer, J. Overweight. Englewood Cliffs, N.J.: Prentice-Hall, 1971.
42. McKenna, R.J. Some effects of anxiety level and food cues on the eating behavior of obese and normal subjects: a comparison of the Schachterian and psychosomatic conceptions. *Journal of Personality and Social Psychology*, 1972, *22*, 311–319.
43. Meyer, J.E. and Pudel, V. Experimental studies on food-intake in obese and normal weight subjects. *Journal of Psychosomatic Research*, 1972, *16*, 305–308.
44. Meyer, J.E. and Pudel, V.E. Experimental feeding in man: a behavioral approach to obesity. *Psychosomatic Medicine*, 1977, *39*, 153–157.
45. Moore, M.E., Stunkard, A. and Srole, L. Obesity, social class and mental illness. *Journal of the American Medical Association*, 1962, *181*, 962–966.
46. Nisbett, R.E. Taste, deprivation, and weight determinants of eating behavior. *Journal of Personality and Social Psychology*, 1968, *10*, 107–116.
47. Nisbett, R.E. and Gurwitz, S.B. Weight, sex, and the eating behavior of human newborns. *Journal of Comparative and Physiological Psychology*, 1970, *73*, 245–253.
48. Nisbett, R.E. and Kanouse, D.E. Obesity, food deprivation, and supermarket shopping behavior. *Journal of Personality and Social Psychology*, 1969, *12*, 289–294.

49. Oken, B., Hartz, A., Biefer, E. and Rimm, A.A. Relation between socioeconomic status and obesity changes in 9046 women. *Preventive Medicine*, 1977, *6*, 447–453.
50. Pargman, D. The incidence of obesity among college students. *Journal of School Health*, 1969, *39*, 621–627.
51. Penick, S.B., Filion, R., Fox, S. and Stunkard, A.J. Behavior modification in the treatment of obesity. *Psychosomatic Medicine*, 1971, *33*, 49–55.
52. Pisacano, J.C., Lichter, H., Ritter, J. and Siegal, A.P. An attempt at prevention of obesity in infancy. *Pediatrics*, 1978, *61*, 360–364.
53. Pliner, P., Meyer, P. and Blankstein, K. Responsiveness to affective stimuli by obese and normal individuals. *Journal of Abnormal Psychology*, 1974, *83*, 74–80.
54. Price, J.M. and Grinker, J. Effects of degree of obesity, food deprivation, and palatability on eating behavior of humans. *Journal of Comparative and Physiological Psychology*, 1973, *85*, 265–271.
55. Rodin, J. Effects of distraction on performance of obese and normal subjects. Unpublished doctoral dissertation, Columbia University, 1970.
56. Rodin, J. and Slochower, J. Externality in the nonobese: effects of environmental responsiveness on weight. *Journal of Personality and Social Psychology*, 1976, *33*, 338–344.
57. Sallade, J. A comparison of the psychological adjustment of obese vs. nonobese children. *Journal of Psychosomatic Research*, 1973, *17*, 89–96.
58. Schachter, S. Cognitive effects on bodily functioning: studies of obesity and eating. In D.C. Glass (Ed.), *Neurophysiology and Emotion*. New York: Rockefeller University Press and Russell Sage Foundation, 1967.
59. Schachter, S. Some extraordinary facts about obese humans and rats. *American Psychologist*, 1971, *26*, 129–144.
60. Schachter, S., Goldman, R. and Gordon, A. Effects of fear, food deprivation, and obesity on eating. *Journal of Personality and Social Psychology*, 1968, *10*, 91–97.
61. Schachter, S. and Gross, L.P. Manipulated time and eating behavior. *Journal of Personality and Social Psychology*, 1968, *10*, 98–106.
62. Seltzer, C.C. Bodily disproportion and dominant personality traits. *Psychosomatic Medicine*, 1946, *8*, 75–97.
63. Seltzer, C.C. and Mayer, J. An effective weight control program in a public school system. *American Journal of Public Health*, 1970, *60*, 679–689.
64. Sheldon, J. Obesity: some current views regarding its aetiology. *Postgraduate Medical Journal*, 1970, *46*, 613–617.
65. Silverstone, J.T., Gordon, K. and Stunkard, A.J. Social factors in obesity in London. *Practitioner*, 1969, *202*, 682–688.
66. Singh, D. Role of response habits and cognitive factors in determination of behavior of obese humans. *Journal of Personality and Social Psychology*, 1973, *27*, 220–238.
67. Snow, D.L. and Held, M.L. Group psychotherapy with obese adolescent females. *Adolescence*, 1973, *8*, 407–414.
68. Stefanik, P.A., Heald, F.P. and Mayer, J. Caloric intake in relation to energy output of obese and non-obese adolescent boys. *American Journal of Clinical Nutrition*, 1959, *7*, 55–62.
69. Stout, C., Morrow, J., Brandt, E. and Wolf, S. Unusually low incidence of death from myocardial infarction: study of Italian American Community in Pennsylvania. *Journal of the American Medical Association*, 1964, *188*, 845–849.
70. Stuart, R.B. Behavioral control of overeating. *Behaviour Research and Therapy*, 1967, *5*, 357–365.

71. Stuart, R.B. and Davis, B. *Slim chance in a fat world.* Champaign, Ill.: Research Press, 1972.
72. Stunkard, A.J. and Burt, V. Obesity and the body image: II. Age at onset of disturbances in the body image. *American Journal of Psychiatry,* 1967, *123,* 1443–1447.
73. Stunkard, A., d'Aquilli, E., Fox, S. and Filion, R. Influence of social class on obesity and thinness in children. *Journal of the American Medical Association,* 1972, *221,* 579–584.
74. Stunkard, A. and Koch, C. The interpretation of gastric motility: I. Apparent bias in the reports of hunger by obese persons. *Archives of General Psychiatry,* 1964, *11,* 74–82.
75. Stunkard, A.J. and Mendelson, M. Disturbances in body image of some obese persons. *Journal of the American Dietetic Association,* 1961, *38,* 328–331.
76. Van Itallie, T.B. and Campbell, R.G. Multidisciplinary approach to the problem of obesity. *Journal of the American Dietetic Association,* 1972, *61,* 385–390.
77. Weinberg, N., Mendelson, M. and Stunkard, A. Failure to find distinctive personality features in group of obese men. *American Journal of Psychiatry,* 1961, *117,* 1035–1037.
78. Werkman, S.L. and Greenberg, E.S. Personality and interest patterns in obese adolescent girls. *Psychosomatic Medicine,* 1967, *24,* 72–80.
79. Wilkes, E.T. A survey of three hundred obese girls. *Archives of Pediatrics,* 1960, *77,* 441–451.
80. Wilson, N.L., Farber, S.M., Kimbrough, L.D. and Wilson, R.H.L. The development and perpetuation of obesity. An overview. In N.L. Wilson (Ed.), *Obesity.* Philadelphia: F.A. Davis Company, 1969.
81. Wollersheim, J.P. Effectiveness of group therapy based upon learning principles in the treatment of overweight women. *Journal of Abnormal Psychology,* 1970, *76,* 462–474.
82. Wunderlich, R.A., Johnson, W.G. and Ball, M.F. Some personality correlates of obese persons. *Psychological Reports,* 1973, *32,* 1267–1277.

Chapter 12

ADDICTION AS RESISTANCE IN THE AVOIDANCE
OF DEPRESSION

Martin N. Fisher, Ph.D.

Martin N. Fisher, Ph.D.

Dr. Fisher is presently an Associate Professor
at the Institute of Advanced Psychological
Studies of Adelphi University; a psychoanalyst
in private practice in New York City. He
earned his doctorate from New York University and obtained his certificate in individual
psychoanalysis and in group psychoanalysis
from the Postdoctoral Program in Psychotherapy of the Institute of Advanced Psychological
Studies, at Adelphi University. He is a diplomate in clinical psychology.

The position taken in this paper is that a necessary and unavoidable condition of being human is to experience some degree of anaclitic depression. This contention is based on a thesis that a requirement for birth, and subsequent socialization, means that the infant must experience and continually reexperience a partial loss of the primary source of love and life creating massive anxiety. What immediately follows, then, is a depressive reaction, intended to avoid the anxiety and maintain some semblance of equilibrium. Freud pointed out that the prototype of anxiety has its roots in the "act of birth." (1966). He said that

> We believe that it is in the act of birth that there comes about the combination of unpleasurable feelings, impulses of discharge and bodily sensations which has become the prototype of the effects of a mortal danger and has ever since been repeated by us as the state of anxiety. . . . We shall also recognize it as highly relevant that this first state of anxiety arose out of separation from the mother. It is, of course, our conviction that the disposition to repeat the first state of anxiety has been so thoroughly incorporated into the organism through a countless series of generations that a single individual cannot escape the effect of anxiety . . . (p. 397).

O. Rank used "The Trauma of Birth" (1952) as the central thesis of his early work in formulating a theory of neurosis. It was so essential and critical that Rank speculated that every human being needs many years in attempting to overcome this very first intensive trauma in any way approximating normalcy. In subsequent formulations, Rank constructed an early precursor to the later writings of existential psychoanalysts, which in effect hypothesized a "life-death struggle." The implications were found in the child's leaving of the womb (and moving toward autonomous functioning) and the attendant fear (anxiety) of living. The alternative is represented by moving psychically back to the womb, away from life, and the attendant fear (anxiety) of union and psychic death. The struggle is never fully accomplished and psychological renegotiation is intrinsic to human behavior.

The thesis that follows, then, is that this unavoidable experience of anxiety initiated the attempt to master it; and the automatic and unavoidable result to avoid or master the anxiety through depression. This led me to review the literature on depression, and it became quite evident that the earliest roots of depression involve the experience of loss. Salzman (1970) sums up this notion best when he writes,

> Some of our earlier psychological theories emphasized the element of "loss" in depression. While the loss was characterized as an object to which one had ambivalent feelings, others viewed it as the loss of love for an object, person, value, standard or ideal. In other words this reaction seems to occur following a loss or the apprehension of a possible loss of something or someone that is viewed as necessary and irreplaceable for the continued functioning of the individual. . . . Depression, therefore, occurs as a neurotic maladaptive response in which the individual attempts to force the return of the lost object or value. (pp. 111–112).

Using the above as a working model, depression then appears to be an unavoidable reaction which has a profound impact on the creation of character of *humans* as *humans*. While it is assumed that there is a very wide potential range of depressive feelings, from "normal" to pathological, I nevertheless view it (depression) as a universal phenomenon.

A brief review of the evolution of thinking about depression may be helpful in illuminating the position I take in this paper. Fenichel (1945) in elaborating the orthodox psychoanalytic position suggests that preoedipal experiences of abandonment and loneliness contain the origins of primary depression. He refers to Karl Abraham to suggest that the etiological prerequisite for the development of later psychotic depressions stems from loss. It was Abraham's notion that depression occurs when a severe injury to the infantile narcissism takes place through a combination of disappointments in love. The great disappointment in the love object takes place long before the Oedipus wishes are successfully overcome. The repeated psychical experience of this original disappointment (in the pre-Oedipal mother) in later life becomes the precipitating event for depression.

A conceptualization in keeping with the orthodox psychoanalytic position was pursued by Melanie Klein and the English school. The explanations are consistent but the emphasis on the very early infantile interaction with the mothering one takes on added emphasis. Joan Riviere, in her essay on Hate, Greed, and Aggression (1937) contends that ". . . psychoanalysis can trace this anxiety of dependence back through countless situations to the very early one *experienced by us all in babyhood*—that of the child at the breast. . . ." (italics mine) (p. 8).

A further examination of the position of M. Klein is made by R.E. Money—Kyrle in the Introduction to New Directions in Psychoanalysis (1955). Two principals introduced and enlarged by Klein are central to her theoretical and applied work.

> The first of these results from the infant's unintegrated, and violently conflicting, attitudes to the vital objects of his world, particularly his mother's breasts. Both because her breasts are sometimes gratifying and sometimes frustrating and because the child's own impulses are projected into it, or felt to come from, these objects, they are themselves felt to be sometimes good and loving, sometimes bad and dangerous. And since he also "introjects" or incorporates them in phantasy, he feels himself to be possessed as well as surrounded by alternately protective and persecutory objects. The persecutory anxiety which always arises in this period retards and often temporarily disrupts the 'gradual' integration of his ego. In short, the early stage is characterized by what Melanie Klein has appropriately named the paranoid-schizoid position.

This first stage is inevitably followed by the infant's attempts at the increasing integration of these very early impulses. What the infant comes to perceive is that these gratifying objects which are felt as necessary and loved are at one and the same time also aspects of frustrating objects he hates and destroys in fantasy. As this dichotomous experience moves to some level of psychic awareness the infant begins to experience concern for these objects and thus to experience depression. The child finds this depressive position so painful that he begins to search for ways in which to avoid the depressive feelings. His choice is either to regress to the prior persecutory position or to adopt what Klein called a manic defense in which guilt is denied. Most critically, what emerges is the intense and unavoidable experience of ambivalence which then leads to anxiety and results in depression.

In an essay entitled "A Psychoanalytic Concept of the Origin of Depression" Scott wrote that depression frequently occurs early in the first six months of life. Further, he suggests that the capacity for reality testing during this same period are exceedingly questionable. The source of this early form of depression is the feeling which emerges . . . "first out of the realization that it is the same self that can both love and hate, and secondly, out of the realization that the ego can both hate and love the same object, and thirdly, out of the realization that the same object or person can be both gratifying or frustrating or can appear to be loving or hating." (p. 42)

One further view of the Kleinian position takes account of the very primitive and therefore powerful impact of the infants polar potential for adjustment. Klein felt that the two possibilities available to the infant to resolve the love/hate dilemma of the "mothering" one were the paranoid or the depressive position. Guntrip explains the choice in the following way

> In the choice of the paranoid position the infant assumes a relationship with an object but feels simultaneously persecuted by this object. In the second choice, which is referred to as the depressive position, the child has overcome these persecutory difficulties and can, as a result, move more fully into a whole-object relationship. The result of this move, however, leads now to guilt and depression as the child simultaneously discovers that he can hurt the very objects he has become capable of loving. In this context it is the quality of the ego experience, in terms of object-relations, of the infant with the preoedipal mother. This formulation leads to a construct in which a theory of object-relational positions takes place. The infant has to reach, and therefore adjust to, his emotional and interpersonal development with his mother and this psychic trip sets the stage for all future relationships.

Finally, to allow for some rapprochement in seemingly divergent theoretical positions, M. Boss (1963) in a discussion of the early infant-mother relationship wrote from an existential view . . .

> . . . we are well advised to remember one of Freud's observations which he described with the (theoretically inadequate) concept of "oral fixation." This psychoanalytic concept justifiably refers to the time when the infant's relationships toward his world consisted almost exclusively of sucking, in both the physical and psychic sense, at this time, *when the childs existence was inseparably bound to his mother, a fundamental rupture of the basic trust in this*

relationship must have taken place. Here, as always, it is by no means clear in a given case whether the disturbance is due to an exaggerated sensitivity and excessive love requirement on the part of the child, or whether it stems from a lack of love on the part of the people who took care of him, or whether both factors are to blame. At any rate, it is the disturbance—by too severe a frustration—of this basic way of existing in an intimate infant-mother relationship which inhibits further development and is responsible for the existential guilt that eventually develops. For this reason, all depressive patients in therapy (whether their illnesses are the so-called reactive or the so-called endogenous type) show a tremendous desire to make up for what they missed during infancy in regard to the sucking infant-mother relationship . . . (italics mine) (pp. 210–211).

The notion of the importance of the mother-child relationship is further elaborated by Roy Schafer in a recent paper he wrote in reformulating his notion on resistance (1973). He advances the idea that Freud overvalued the concept that resistance has as its prototype the authority of the father in the oedipal situation. Schafer suggests,

. . . Freud did not teach us to appreciate the fundamental developmental importance of the infant's prolonged helplessness and of the early danger situations corresponding to this helplessness, *especially of the loss of the love object and loss of love . . .* the prospect of being abandoned by her (mother) physically and emotionally, really or in fantasy, *never loses its painful if not terrifying aspect . . .* anxiety over losing the mother or her love threatens to undermine the boy's and the girl's very sense of worth or right to exist. . . . If we think of the analysand as defying the archaic mother's authority too, we will think as well of the growing importance to the child of differentiating himself from his mother. . . . By dint of these strivings the child establishes and maintain's differentiation and wards off its wishing to merge with the mother through incorporation as well as the mother's seductions to merge and her devouring approaches. (1973).

I want to strongly emphasize that the critical and overriding issue I take in this paper is that depression is a *universal phenomenon* and not a clinical category suffered by a select few humans.

It is now important to turn to a second notion in order to understand a theory of addiction. I am referring to the psychodynamic problem of resistance. Resistance, as a phenomenon, became apparent in the early work of Freud. Attention was paid to resistance as a necessary and intrinsic issue to be confronted in psychoanalysis. Freud's last statement on resistance is found in Lecture XIX of the Introductory Lectures on Psychoanalysis. Freud explained "Resistances . . . should not be one-sidely condemned. They include so much of the most important material from the patient's past and bring it back in so convincing a fashion that they become some of the best supports of the analysis if a skillful analyst knows how to give them the right turn. Nevertheless, it remains a remarkable fact that this material is always in the service of the resistance to begin with and brings to the fore a facade that is *hostile to the treatment*. (italics mine) (p. 291).

In the above model, Freud implies that the patient's resistance is to the process of psychoanalysis and/or the psychoanalyst and results in the patient's unconscious avoidance of these external forces.

Another view of resistance, more consistent with my own, is expressed by the existantial psychoanalyst Bugental. In his book, "The Search for Authenticity," Bugental contends that ". . . the resistance is the shield the patient erects to forestall the feared confrontation with the reality of his being in the world. (Thus, the therapist who thinks of the resistance as a warding off of his own efforts misses the point and confuses the patient). The therapist's task is to help the patient rediscover the conflict within himself that gave rise to the resistance and other defensive and constrictive maneuvers . . ." (p. 43). In truth then, the patient resists not the therapist and/or therapy but the dread of discovering himself. As Bugental said, "Resistance is the name that we give to the general defensive wall the patient puts between himself and the threats that he finds linked to being authentic. Resistance is (simply) anti-authenticity." We have moved, then, away from the psychoanalyst's couch into the wider and real life experience in the world.

The existential model of resistance implies threat. Simply stated, it represents the threat of non-being. The resistance then, is man's constant effort to avoid the pain of feeling, thinking, or reexperiencing non-being. There seems little doubt that the prototype for this potential non-being lies in the early traumatic feelings of potential non-being that each separation repeatedly aroused in the infant.

A further extension of the existential view is that humans seek to avoid anxiety; the anxiety of freedom. Freedom represents a world of increased contingencies. An increase in contingencies represents more possibility of failure, rejection, loss of self-esteem, etc. More pointedly, however, this same acceptance of freedom brings the reality of ultimate non-being painfully into awareness.

Authenticity represents the antithesis of resistance. Bugental suggests that the authentic person is first, broadly aware of himself, his interpersonal relationships, and all dimensions of his real world. Secondly, the authentic person accepts the fact that life represents choices, that he goes forth to meet these choices, and that decisions are the very stuff of life. And third, the authentic person assumes full responsibility for approaching these contingencies, making decisions, and accepting full responsibility for his acts.

Rank had pointed out that . . . "living is a fearful process because it inevitably entails separations which simultaneously precipitate uncertainty as to what will happen, requires the person to assume greater and greater responsibility for himself, and render him ever more alone and lonely." (Maddi,

1972) (p. 57) He further speculated that since this experience of living arouses so much fear, avoidance may be the defensive response. However the avoidance of life involves a repudiation of life and this can only be accomplished by killing one's self, psychically or physically.

This response is implicit in addiction. Broadly viewed, addictive behavior is the essence of avoidance, the shrinking of choice and chance-taking, and in general a shrinking of the intra-psychic and interpersonal world. Again, authenticity requires a life of increased contingencies; a life of addictive behavior encourages decreased chance-taking.

E. Singer (1965) suggested a similar notion in discussing psychological "health." He says . . .

". . . psychological well-being is synonymous with psychological aliveness; . . . this aliveness shows itself most potently in effortful activity; and that activity, paradoxically both requires and reflects itself in openness to stimulation—internal or external, intellectual, physical or emotional. Evaluating a person's psychological well-being, therefore, revolves around the assessment of his availability and openness to experience. Such openness cannot exist unless the person is ready to experience the unforeseen, the odd, the new, even the fantastic, and shows the willingness to be surprised. Inability to stand surprise thus becomes one of the common denominators of emotional illness. . . ."

The critical comments for me are availability and openness to experience. This openness must be accompanied by the individual's capacity to entertain surprise.

The idea that is most salient is the issue of universality. It is my contention that the resistance we see in patients is merely one example of an ongoing ever-present potentiality as a function of being human. We see, then, that avoidance behavior in everyday interpersonal and intra-psychic activities is the prototype of resistance in psychoanalysis. As in all defensive behavior, the individual strives to avoid the real conflict and prefers instead to engage in another form of maladaptive behavior which feels less threatening. The adopted behavior becomes repetitious and its choice made outside of awareness to the issue at hand. In the present case, the painful issue is the early traumatic separation which initiated the anxiety, led to depression and the individual's adoption of behavior which is in the service of avoiding the pain of the remembered early experience of this separation.

This brings the present discussion to the issue at hand; addiction. The conclusion that emerges from the prior discussion is that addiction, in general, is a profound attempt to avoid these depressive feelings which are a constant source of psychic pain. If I follow this line of thinking, it raises the idea that the degree of addiction should be far more wide-spread than is now evident. In fact, however, it is true that there exists in the world far more addiction (and addictive behavior) than we commonly acknowledge or recognize. The problem is that in the context of addictions, most people tend to think in terms of drugs, alcohol, tobacco, etc. In truth, the fact is that a whole symphony of behaviors can be and are addictions. Included in such a list could be found sexual behavior, marriage, work, therapy, etc. The critical common element, of course, is the degree of compulsion, repetitiveness, and lack of awareness with which the individual is functioning.

Putney and Putney (1966) attempted to outline the vagaries of love and marriage. They contend that individuals project on to others qualities they desire in themselves and fall in love, as it were, with these projected ideals. In effect they contend that . . .

> The demonstration that love is not caused by unique qualities of the beloved is as simple as noting that a constant cannot explain a variable. John may not love Mary, may come to love Mary, and may cease to love Mary—all while Mary remains unchanged. Clearly, it is something within the lover which causes him to love, and that something is the *desire to recapture alienated self-potential* . . . (italics mine) (p. 113).

In a previous paper (1975) this writer discussed an idea in which the individual denies a variety of feelings and ideas which have the potential to evoke rejection from others. In effect, all of those ideas and feelings which lead to guilt and subsequent threat of loss of love were suppressed and then repressed because they diminished anxiety. In this case, again the threatened loss has the prototypical nucleus of the anaclitic relationship and the dread of its loss. In this way, then, love and/or marriage may be easily seen as behavior intended to gain this lost love-object and the avoidance of depression.

At a recent symposium held at Adelphi University a paper by Ruth Fox was read. The symposium was called "The Neurosis of our Time: Acting Out." Dr. Fox described her findings after having worked with four thousand alcoholic patients. In the book compiled of these proceedings she points out . . .

> A battery of psychological tests done on three hundred consecutive private patients showed gross disturbance in each case. Although not conforming to any one personality type these patients showed markedly similar character traits. Characteristic of them all was *low frustration tolerance and an inability to endure anxiety or tension. All showed depression, with emotional withdrawal,* a sense of *isolation, extremely low self-esteem, sensitiveness,* and a *masochistic type of self-punishing behavior.* Dependency strivings were very marked, frustration of which led to *depression* or *hostility and rage.* (italics mine) (p. 220)

Fox (1973) makes an interesting observation in the reference cited earlier. She found that adults who received the "normal" amount of love and discipline in childhood were far less apt to become addicted, whereas adults from broken homes or ambivalent parenting homes were far more likely to be alcoholics.

Leon Wurmser (1974) has worked for the last nine years with a large number of narcotics addicts in intensive, mostly psychoanalytically oriented psychotherapy and at the same time was in charge of three drug abuse treatment programs. He made a number of observations about drug addicts, but for our purposes the following is noted.

> All the patients described feelings of loneliness, emptiness, *and depression,* of meaninglessness and pervasive boredom preceding drug use and following withdrawal. In all of them, very intense feelings of murderous rage and vengefulness; or of profound shame, embarrassment, and almost paranoid shyness or of hurt, *rejection, and abandonment were discovered* during psychotherapy. . . . Others said it helped them *not to think of depression* (italics mine) (p. 832).

Wurmser points out in this same article that among the unconscious motivations which exist in addition to oral gratification is the profound need to replace a lost love object. He describes the way drug addicts relate to their drugs and drug paraphernalia with what he described as loving tenderness as though they were love partners. Wurmser contends that "the very term, drug dependency, reminds us of what we are dealing with, namely an *archaic passive dependency* on an all-giving sempiternal, though narcisstically perceived . . . object, as is evidenced by the single-minded devotedness and frenzy of the chase after the beloved, in the incorporative greed, the masturbatory and orgiastic aspects of the use, and in the mixture of ecstatic idealization and depreciation vis-a-vis the drug." (pp. 837–8).

In a collection of essays on drugs in our society, O.S. Ray comments on his work with cigarette smokers and alcoholics (1972). He finds that smoking represents the need for oral stimulation. He notes that in addition to the smoking habit, the smoker consumes greater amounts of alcohol and coffee and that in infancy, smokers evidenced more thumbsucking. Most interesting for our purposes, however, is Roy's finding that the longer a smoker was found to be breast-fed, the less he smoked. Further, the longer he was breast-fed, the easier it was for him to stop smoking.

In discussing the alcoholic, Ray uses descriptive terms such as "low frustration tolerance" "impulsivity" "hostility" and "isolated." All suggest the infantile and primitive potential in human behavior. More pointedly, however, he says that many studies have shown that an intense conflict exists between wanting to be independent but overriding fear and clinging to dependence. Here again, it is easy to infer the same conflict in infancy and the attendant feelings about giving up the breast.

Erikson (1963) urged that weaning of the infant not be abrupt in order to avoid a feeling of basic mistrust in the child. He hypothesizes that . . . "a drastic loss of accustomed mother love without proper substitution at this time can lead . . . to acute infantile depression or to a mild but chronic state of mourning which may give a depressive undertone to the whole remainder of life. But *even under the most favorable circumstances,* this stage leaves a residue of a primary sense of evil and doom and of *a universal nostalgia for a lost paradise.*" (italics mine) (p. 80).

The issue, then, for a theory of addiction, is how to understand its basic referents. The position taken here is that all of mankind is located on some continuum of mild-to-severe depression having its roots in the anxiety attendant on the early separation with "mother." A lifetime is spent in one way or another to avoid the pain of this depression.

If we look at the repetitious and out-of-control nature of the addictions it is easily seen that the addictions are, in their very essence, repetition compulsions in the truest sense. And, as with repetition compulsions generally, they represent early learned forms of avoiding anxiety, albeit self-destructive in their own right. And, unfortunately, many repetition compulsions become ego syntonic (i.e., Don Juanism, eating, etc.) and are, as a result, exceedingly difficult to treat. Anyone familiar with treating addicts has testified to this fact. As with all neurotic behavior, anxiety is a necessary ingredient to change. Acting out diminishes anxiety and avoids the painful confrontation that is necessary for change.

The addictive behavior, as a form of acting-out, maintains some equilibrium, avoids the depression which masks the anxiety, and as a result, prevents change. It can be seen, then, that removal of the addictive behavior must first take place. This will always be followed by anxiety, often severe, followed by depression, most certainly severe, and the ultimate confrontation with the fear of abandonment and death. Fortunately or unfortunately, only when such a confrontation takes place can some semblance of peace be possible.

There is an obvious difference between the chemical addictions such as drugs, alcohol, and tobacco, and less toxic addictions such as behavioral addictions. In any addictive behavior, the avoidance of depression through the resistance of addictive acts is anti-authentic. The psychoanalytic position requires, in my view, a climate of basic trust between analyst and anaysand. In such a relationship, there is the pull toward intimate relatedness, encouraged by the absence of rejection or fear of loss; the rejection having as its primitive paradigm the loss of the preoedipal mother. In the context of the intimate relatedness of a psychotherapeutic shared-experience (Wolstein, 1971) the patient is encouraged to authentic behavior and finds the courage to accept and live, temporarily, with his depression. The awareness that addictive behavior is a form of resistance guards against the consciousness of this painful state. Addictive behaviors are common defenses as resistance and depression appear to be universal phenomena in the human experience.

References

1. Beck, A.T.: *Depression*. Philadelphia, University of Pennsylvania Press, 1967.
2. Boss, M.: *Psychoanalysis and Daseinsanalysis*. New York, Basic Books, 1963.
3. Bugental, J.F.T.: *The Search for Authenticity*. New York, Holt, Rinehart, and Winston, 1965.
4. Erikson, E.: *Childhood and Society*. New York, W.W. Norton, 1963.
5. Fenichel, O.: *The Psychoanalytic Theory of Neurosis*. New York, W.W. Norton, 1945.
6. Fox, R.: Overall treatment of the alcoholic. In D.S. Milman and G.D. Goldman (Eds.), *The Neurosis of Our Time: Acting Out*. Springfield, C.C. Thomas, 1973.
7. Freud, S.: Resistance and repression. In *The Complete Introductory Lectures on Psychoanalysis*. New York, W.W. Norton, 1966.
8. Klein, M.; Heimann, P.; and Money-Kyrle, R.E.: *New Directions in Psychoanalysis*. New York, Basic Books, 1955.
9. Klein, M.; and Riviere, J.: *Love, Hate and Reparation*. New York, W.W. Norton, 1964.
10. Money-Kyrle, R.E.: Introduction to *New Directions in Psychoanalysis*. New York, Basic Books, 1955.
11. Putney, S.; and Putney, G.J.: *The Adjusted American: Normal Neuroses in the Individual and Society*. New York, Harper & Row, 1964.
12. Rank, O.: *The Trauma of Birth*. New York, R. Brunner, 1952.
13. Ray, O.S.: *Drugs, Society, and Human Behavior*. St. Louis, C.V. Mosby, 1972.
14. Salzman, L.: Depression: a clinical review. In J.H. Masserman (Ed.), *Depression: Theories and therapies in Science and Psychoanalysis*, Vol. XVII. New York, Grune & Stratton, 1970.
15. Schafer, R.: The idea of resistance. *International Journal of Psychoanalysis*, Vol. 54:259, 1973.
16. Scott, W.C.M.: A psychoanalytic concept of the origin of depression. In M. Klein, P. Hermann, and R.E. Money-Kyrle (Eds.) *New Directions in Psychoanalysis*. New York, Basic Books, 1955.
17. Singer, E.: *Key Concepts in Psychotherapy*. New York, Basic Books, 1970.
18. Wolstein, B.: *Human Psyche in Psychoanalysis. The Development of Three Models of Psychoanalytic Therapy*. Springfield, C.C. Thomas, 1971.
19. Wurmser, L.: Psychoanalytic considerations of the etiology of compulsive drug use. *Journal of the American Psychoanalytic Association*, Vol. 22:820, 1974.

Part III

Treatments of Addiction

In this section, viable methods for the treatment of addiction are suggested. The approaches originate from a dynamic understanding of the symptomology of addiction, and are both traditional and innovative attempts to work with the most relevant causes of this behavior to thus alleviate the addiction. Leon Brill begins, discussing the history of views concerning drug abuse. He cites reasons for the numerous obstacles that have hindered the successful treatment of addicted patients. He shows how an overemphasis was once placed upon the particular drugs abused resulting in the formation of stereotypes that did not explain, but condemned, the addict. The increasing prevalence of alcohol and barbituate use, and the problems ensuing were, over the years, dealt with in better perspective.

In *The Treatment of Drug Abuse: Evolution of a Perspective,* Leon Brill stresses the importance of understanding the diversity of the patient population in working towards the development of programs which consider socio-cultural factors. He does espouse the possibility of treatment methods which involve the entire reorganization of the patient's personality structure. He suggests the addition of legal enforcements of treatment and the availability of a treatment center for a co-ordination of different treatments, and to determine the suitability of a particular treatment process for a specific patient.

In *An Environmental and Therapeutic Approach to Breaking the Smoking Habit,* Drs. Stricker, Goldman and Nemon describe an innovative project in which participants undertook to stop their smoking, a habit most resistant to modification. The program took place on a cruise, where the special environmental setting played a significant role in the conditioning. Their results showed a percentage of success unmatched by other programs aimed to deal with smoking, and reaffirmed certain existing theories about smoking, and the nature of smoking as a symptom was also examined in this article. As the altering of the personality through manipulation of the inner and outer environment seemed to be the most effective factor related to the project's success, a course of treatment is proposed, incorporating this finding.

Dr. Gerald Berenson observes the family structure as a system in which the addict is a member. He uses family theory as a method to achieve impact upon the already existing dynamics in the family structure, usually dynamics that have prevailed and been transmitted through generations. As the addiction has become incorporated into the family system, the system must be affected if addiction is to be relieved. As the family system of patterns that exist will continue to influence the addicted person, he asserts that the problem cannot be solely worked at an individual, intrapsychic level. The inner purpose of the addiction needs to be understood according to this perspective, and Dr. Berenson demonstrates a case experience to illustrate the effectiveness of the mode of intervention his theory indicates.

The Treatment of Smoking Habituation and Selective Drug Dependency and Abuse with Hypnotherapy, by Milton V. Kline, is a study of the value of hypnosis as a method to replace the addiction symptom, that has developed as a response to the patients inability to handle external pressures, with relaxation. This article suggests a desensitizing hypnotherapeutic approach, enabling the patient to manage his anxiety, rather than be overcome by the feeling of tension experienced. The inducement of hypnosis, and gradually, self-hypnosis, intercedes this reaction, aiming to establish a psychophysiological homeostasis in the individual.

The effectiveness of Transcendental Meditation to displace stress symptoms mentally, is analyzed through an evaluation of results obtained by testing, in the final chapter by Dr. Margaretta K. Bowers and Michael Grossman, *The Transcendental Meditation (T.M.) Program: Self-Actualization As Treatment for Drug Abuse.* The practice of T.M. is seen to be an alternative amelioration of the symptoms of anxiety and stress-related symptoms. It is reported to be highly successful as a method that finally becomes integrated as a coping mechanism for the individual, alleviating the block to growth that the experience of stress necessitates. The physiological changes that accompany the experience of this procedure are examined, as well as their relation to the dynamics of sleep. The benefits of the technique are substantial, and are suggested to be sufficient to replace dependency upon external substances such as drugs. T.M. is examined in this chapter in conjunction with other therapies in the treatment of extreme addictive behavior.

Chapter 13

THE TREATMENT OF DRUG ABUSE: EVOLUTION OF A PERSPECTIVE

Leon Brill, M.S.S.

Leon Brill, M.S.S.

Leon Brill is a certified psychologist and certified social worker who has specialized in problems of drug abuse. His training includes an M.S.S. from Columbia University, advanced credits from Yeshiva University and a Certificate in Applied Psychoanalysis from the William Alanson White Institute of Psychiatry as well as additional training in psychoanalysis. He served as Director of Program Planning for the NYS ODAS and as Director of the Division of Drug Rehabilitation for the state of Massachusetts. He is currently involved in private practice, consultation, and writing. He has authored or co-authored nine books and a large number of articles and monographs.

A psychoanalytic perspective of drug addiction began to be understood and developed in the thirties, forties and fifties, evolving from the experience of analysts with European addicts, most of whom were barbituate addicts and alcoholics in Europe, often in psychiatric hospitals; analysts such as Ernst Simmel at his Berlin Sanitarium and Sandor Rado. During this time, the primary drugs with which American society was concerned were heroin, *the* "bad" drug; and marijuana, which was legally defined as a narcotic, and viewed as addictive and as leading inevitably to heroin and cocaine use. There was far less public concern about other drugs such as barbiturates, amphetamines and alcohol, which are understood today as far more serious in terms of their physical effects on the body as well as the number of users involved. (Brill, 1977)

Psychoanalytic theorizing linked drug addiction with the "impulse neuroses," "perversions," "compulsion neuroses," "character disorders"; and, at times with the manic-depressive cycle. Drug addicts were uniformly viewed as persons with oral-narcissistic fixations manifested as a result of their inadequate psychosexual development. Fenichel surmised that "Addicts are fixated to a passive-narcissistic aim and are interested solely in getting their gratification. . . . Objects are nothing to them, but deliverers of supplies. . . . They are "persons who have a disposition to react to the effects of alcohol, morphine or other drugs in a specific way; namely . . . to satisfy the archaic oral longing, which is sexual longing, the need for security and the need for the maintenance for self-esteem simultaneously. . . . The premorbid personality therefore is the decisive factor. For them . . . it means . . . the fulfillment of a deep and primitive desire more urgently felt . . . than are sexual or instinctual longings by normal persons. . . . The genital organization breaks up and an extraordinary regression begins. The various points of fixation determine which fields of infantile sexuality—oedipus complex, masturbation conflicts, and especially pregenital impulses come to the fore; in the end, the libido remains in the form of an "amorphous erotic tension energy" without "differential characteristics or forms of organization." (Fenichel, 1945).

He added that, "The drug is felt as food and warmth. . . . Persons of this kind react to situations that create the need for sedation or stimulation differently from others. They are intolerant of tension. They cannot endure pain, frustration, situations of waiting. . . . All other strivings become gradually more and more replaced by the "pharmacotoxic longing. . . . The tendency towards such a development, rooted in oral dependence on outer supplies is the essence of drug addiction. All other features are incidental." And, "Impulsive behavior and drug addiction can be utilized as a means for attaining the same end: the provision of the needed narcissistic supplies. . . . Addictions and impulse neuroses, insofar as they still are able to achieve their end, are suitable for evading depressions." (Fenichel, 1945. Ibid.)

More explicit descriptions of the etiological factors were also attempted. According to Simmel, the use of drugs at first represents genital masturbation accompanied by appropriate fantasies; later, conflicts at deeper levels of development emerge, extending back to the oral stage. This corresponds to the gradual regressive disintegration of sexuality. The organs may also represent introjected objects, this being in accordance with an oral regression.

Simmel theorized "The identity of the decisive conflict explains the relation between drug addiction and the manic-depressive states." He designated the elation due to drugs as "artificial mania." In the final states of their illness, drug addicts live in objectless states, alternating between elation and "morning after" depression, a cycle corresponding to the alternation of hunger and satisfaction in the psychically undifferentiated infant. (Sandor, 1933).

Simmel undertook to develop a typology of alcoholics, distinguishing between social drinkers, reactive drinkers, neurotic alcoholics and sporadic spree abusers. In treatment, he suggested ancillary approaches such as occupational therapy in hospitals, environmental manipulation and the AA, whose principles he found very close to psychoanalytic thinking (Simmel, 1933). Knight and others described oral fixations and frustrations which resulted in a turning away from the frustrating mother to the father, as expressions of repressed homosexual tendencies. The unconscious impulses in alcoholics were, therefore, typically, not only oral, but also homosexual in nature (Cited in Fenichel, 1945). Gross suggested that in the addict, there is a dysfunction of the superego and of other identifications. (Ibid).

Sandor Rado's adaptational approach postulated a "tense depression" as the basic emotional state relieved by opiate intoxication, and tended to universalize all types of drug craving as variants of one single disease, "Pharmacothymia," a characteristic mental or emotional dependency on drugs. Rado found that addicts responded to frustration in life with this depression, marked by painful tension simultaneous with a high degree of intolerance to pain, a "condition remarkably improved by alcohol" (drugs). However, the improvement was invariably followed by the rapid return of the tense depression and a renewed craving for elation. (Meisalas and Brill, 1974). Most theorists today no longer use this idea of the equivalent of a manic-depressive cycle, but rather stress the underlay of depression. (Rado, 1933).

Regarding the therapeutic approach to be undertaken, Simmel suggested the following:

> "There is still much contention over the psychoanalytic therapy of persons with morbid impulses or addictions. An understanding of the mechanisms involved makes it plain that in principle such patients are amenable to psychoanalytic treatment, but that from a practical point of view there are particular problems to be overcome. Not only is the symptom itself pleasurable, so that the cases offer the analyst the same difficulties as do perversions, but besides, the pregenital, narcissistic constitution of the patients make it neces-

sary to work back to the deepest layers, and the intolerance of tension neces- sitates modifications of technique. It is, however, generally agreed that psychoanalytic treatment should be tried whenever possible. If the pre-morbid disposition of an addict is allowed to remain unchanged after a withdrawal cure, it will soon induce the patient to return to the use of the drug. It is not the chemical effect of the drug that must be combated but the morbid wish to be drunkenly euphoric (Sandor, 1933).

"The best time to begin an analysis is obviously during or immediately after withdrawal. But it is not to be expected that the patient will remain abstinent throughout analysis. If he has an opportunity he will probably use the drug again whenever the resistance in his analysis predominates. This is the reason why addicts are to be analyzed in institutions rather than as ambulatory patients" (Sandor, 1933).

While current approaches to the treatment of drug-dependent persons are drawn from this early psychoanalytic thinking, it became apparent during the 50's and 60's that the traditional approaches of psychoanalysis were minimally effective, and forced institutionalization for this purpose was not justified. This new thinking derived from at least three broad areas of understanding: (1) issues related to addicts themselves; (2) problems emanating from the methods of psychoanalysis; and (3) issues related to the "state of art"—that is, the incomplete understanding about drugs prevailing at the time. These areas will be considered seriatim in the succeeding section, followed by a discussion of current approaches.

A. Issues Related to Addicts Themselves

1. Because so many confirmed addicts tend to use acting-out behavior as a means of coping with their underlying depression and anxiety, it proved generally impossible for them to relate to fixed schedules and time-limited sessions such as psychoanalysis employed.

2. The drug user's need to escape insight and release of feeling ran counter to the processes of insight therapy. The more therapists probed, the more anxiety was engendered and the faster patients tended to run.

3. There were additional problems, such as developing trust to authority figures and relinquishing or lowering the defenses and the coping mechanisms being used.

4. Most addicts were engaged in the "hustling syndrome"; i.e., they re- sorted to illegal or, at best, borderline activities to maintain their supply of drugs and support their habit. Their "street junkie" life-style, the problems of maintaining a continuous heroin supply and the perennial recurrence of crises and emergencies led to their acute need for help at different times—as when their supply of drugs or funds ran out; or when legal, detoxification or

medical problems occurred—all resulting in a crisis-filled existence. Therapists needed to relate to them in the midst of these crises and hope gradually to engage them in sustained treatment.

5. As indicated, addicts frequently resorted to criminal activities to support their habit. Since the possession of heroin and the implements of use were in themselves illegal, addicts were often involved with the law and psychoanalysts were reluctant to intervene in such situations.

6. Most addicts consumed all their money purchasing illegal heroin and did not have the funds to pay for treatment unless their parents were willing to subsidize them.

7. Drug addiction was only later understood to be a chronic relapsing condition, with many ups and downs, "vicissitudes" and acting-out and relapse to be expected along the way. It was difficult for therapists to relate to such turmoil and crisis; or to tolerate the excessive dependency, insatiable demands and severe testing-out behavior.

8. Because addicts already had a "pharmacologic" solution which they used to insulate themselves against an awareness of their problems and feelings, they did not seek help voluntarily or even feel a need for it as long as their supply was available. Only after a period of years, as their use became increasingly dysfunctional or maladaptive, might they begin to seek a way out. The early years might be a "honeymoon period"—with far less storm and stress. In therapy the battle lines were often drawn early, therefore, between addict and therapist: the addict's "hidden agenda" was to remain on drugs at all costs, and the therapist's to get him off by all means. Therapists, for the most part, also insisted on total immediate abstinence, a goal impossible for most addicts to achieve.

9. "Character disorders" has been the diagnosis used most often to categorize heroin addicts. Their acting-out provided immediate gratification of need and satisfied their impulsivity. It was therefore closer to, and augmented the id rather than the defensive functions; i.e., it was "ego-syntonic" rather than dystonic. Many addicts, whether they had such patterns before use or developed them afterwards, were described as manipulative individuals who had learned to "con" their parents and, subsequently, society in the service of their own impulsive needs. In any case, the stereotype was long accepted that all addicts are manipulative. Therapists were fearful of being exposed to such conning, to be used, "ripped off" and forced to do things against their better judgement—or at times being caught up in the patient's illegal activities, or driven to provide drugs, etc. (Nyswander et al, 1958)

10. Because of the severe dependency of many addicts, treatment became a terrible drain on the therapists' patience. It was difficult to remain tolerant and objective in the face of the patient's continuous testing of limits, acting-out and challenge, which drained the therapists' endurance and patience.

11. Since most addicts in the 50's and 60's came from minority groups, therapists found it difficult to relate to their special problems and socio-cultural patterns. Classic psychoanalytic techniques were derived from a middle-class European framework and needed to be adapted to the special needs and socio-cultural contexts of blacks, Puerto Ricans, Chicanos and lower-class individuals generally, including whites.

12. More than insight, addicts frequently required help with concrete or tangible needs, including legal intervention in the courts, medical care, detox-ification, financial and housing assistance, family problems and others (Brill and Meiselas, 1973). If they were further along in treatment, then vocational guidance and employment, the advancement of educational levels, and related services were indicated. Most therapists were not geared to provide such services.

13. Because every addiction has a physical basis, there was frequent need for medical care and tie-in with hospitals to deal with overdoses, detoxification, medical illnesses such as hepatitis, abscesses, infections, endocarditis and other traumae associated with chronic use.

14. Because any addiction is a chronic relapsing condition, many of the patients frequently came in under the influence of drugs and were caught up in new crises. Most therapists found it difficult to relate to them in the midst of their use and crises.

B. Problems Emanating from Psychoanalysis

1. As mentioned, psychoanalysts dealt with addicts according to their established techniques, which required that they come in regularly at fixed times, lie down on the couch, acknowledge a problem, assume a dependent role and be labelled "sick"; then release emotion and develop insight, antici-pate the effects of their behavior better, curb their 'acting-out and give up all drug use. Most therapists had fixed stereotypes about addicts, fears about being robbed, assaulted, or else conned for medication. They were also con-cerned that addicts coming to their office would contaminate other patients not on drugs. (Nyswander et al, 1958).

2. Many therapists had unrealistic goals for patients, anticipating exten-sive personality reorganization. Actually, most patients were not capable of such personality changes or probing into the unconscious, or developing in-sight, remaining unresponsive to such approaches and terminating treatment. (Brill, 1972). Our current understanding stresses the factor of the diversity of the patient population; that there is variability in the responses to be expected and the goals to be pursued. This coincides with the addict dictum "Different strokes for different folks." It includes the likelihood that many addicts may never be able to achieve a completely drug-free existence and

may need to be maintained on a drug such as methadone indefinitely, if not forever. (Brill and Lieberman, 1972).

3. Most therapists found it difficult to understand the distinct socio-cultural problems of minority and lower-class groups in treatment. As Hollingshead and Redlich and others have described, there was a tendency to dismiss such patients by offering them institutionalization or medication instead of talking with them as with middle-class patients. This resulted in the need to rely on intermediaries such as para-professionals or ex-addicts as bridges between treating persons and clients. Eventually this "ex-addict mystique" diminished, as treatment personnel learned to relate more directly to their clients and involve them in treatment in terms of Karl Menninger's "treatment contract." This entails clients being viewed as "consumers," whose inputs in determining the content and conditions of treatment, as well as the goals to be sought, are crucial.

The need for such special socio-cultural understanding is significant if we are to expand the concept of community mental health and community medicine, determine such issues as the principles governing the delivery of health services, the role played by aides and other health workers in augmenting treatment, the effects of culture on the demand for services, and the uses made of them once they are provided. Still further, the concept of extending the role of health professionals beyond the curative function to social and preventive ones is no longer novel.

4. The psychoanalytic literature tended to describe drug users as if they were all alike, had exactly the same kinds of family constellations, and the same uniform traits such as self-defeating impulses, weak egos, rigid, archaic superegos, oral fixations, narcissism, poor frustration tolerance, intolerance of pain, etc. (Brill, 1972). The fathers were depicted as inconsequential persons, and the mothers as seductive and devouring. If these traits were ever valid, it would most likely have been for street addicts of the early 50's. The heroin population tended to become more and more diversified in the 60's and 70's, incorporating large numbers of white middle-class youngsters as well. Sheppard, Smith, et. al., at the Haight-Ashbury Free Clinic in San Francisco distinguished among at least three different groups of heroin users ten years ago: old addicts, transitional addicts and new addicts (Brill, 1977). We are also aware of the special case of Vietnam heroin addicts (Robins, 1974). Beyond this, the proliferation to other drugs and the better understanding of alcohol as a drug—probably our number one problem—have exacerbated the problem.

5. For many decades, therapists were fixated on exclusively psychological parameters as the primary and sole determinants of the drug problem. There has been increased understanding that the psychological dimensions are only part of the many reasons why a person becomes dysfunctionally involved with

drugs. In the case of heroin, for example, we would need to take into account such elements as socio-cultural factors, "differential association," that is, the kinds of motivations and associations which lead a person to become a delinquent, drug addict or "square" person; conditioning factors, including operant and instrumental conditioning which reinforce use, and others (Brill, 1977). We would also need to consider the special problems of minorities and disadvantaged groups in ghetto areas, where problems of living and the lack of opportunity are overwhelming; and the problem of alienation among middle-class youth as described by Kenneth Keniston (Keniston, 1964). Beyond this, we would need to include physiological, pharmacological, epidemiological and legal factors as well as the availability of the drug. These numerous dimensions support Freud's dictum that the etiological factors in any problem are multi-faceted and overdetermined. Any effort to minimize this multiplicity of factors and the diversity of drug abusers prevailing will lead to gross oversimplification and stereotyping of the problem—as indeed happened in the 50's and 60's, and still today.

C. "State of the Art" Issues

1. Still other problems resulted from the inability to draw from a wide-ranging experience and to develop a rational perspective on drug problems. For whatever reasons, American society was, for many decades, fixated on heroin as the villain drug; largely no doubt, because of its association with crime. This, in turn, was confounded by the social definition of heroin as a criminal problem, which proved to be a self-fulfilling prophecy. Along with the obsession with heroin, was a lack of concern about other, more serious drugs—such as barbiturates, amphetamines, alcohol and tobacco. This lack of concern was reflected in the failure of the Federal Government and states to regulate the prescription of barbiturates and amphetamines effectively until as late as the mid-sixties—when the Federal Government finally enacted the comprehensive Federal Drug Abuse Control Act. Alcohol was not viewed as a drug though from nine to thirteen million individuals were dysfunctionally involved with it.

2. The question of goals was also grossly misunderstood. The therapeutic emphasis on reorganization of personality, impressed a need to have users off heroin at all costs, often without consideration as to how the individual would function without drugs (Brill, 1977, 2). There was ignorance concerning withdrawal since it was felt that once a patient was off drugs he would be able to remain off. It was quickly learned, through follow-up studies and agency experience, that heroin addiction was a chronic relapsing condition, with recidivism and continued involvement with drugs to be anticipated over a period of many years (*Community Crime Prevention,* Chapter 4, 1973).

3. Many stereotypes prevailed about "*the*" addict's inability to be located, reached and treated (Duval et al, 1963).

4. There was also a tendency to see all drug use as "bad," without understanding that many drugs are, in fact, adaptive and help people function better. Even heroin was not clearly recognized to be the tranquilizer and anti-depressant it is. In the 50's and 60's, it became clearer that many individuals could live and function better with the aid of tranquilizers and anti-depressant drugs (Brill, 1977). This helped pave the way for a more rational perspective on drug use and the subsequent enlistment of methadone stabilization as a mode of treatment.

5. There was increasing awareness that many addicts are "recalcitrants"; i.e., they do not come into treatment of their own accord. Some structuring of services was therefore required to engage and retain them in treatment. What this meant was that some form of coercion was called for—hopefully to be used as "rational authority" and not as punishment (Meiselas and Brill, 1974; Brill and Lieberman, 1973). Most treatment personnel had not worked with such authority or controls; and, in fact, tended to react against the use of any kind of compulsion in treatment. They could not therefore relate to court agencies with responsibility for the client—such as Probation and Parole; and, indeed, tended to be protective of the client and withhold information from these agencies—a frustrating situation for the latter in view of their legal responsibility.

6. Still another dimension was the fact that many patients could not function stably in the community and required a period of residential treatment before they could be returned to the community.

7. In sum, the "state of the art" did not permit any adequate understanding of the basic parameters we understand better today: namely, the chronic relapsing aspect, the need for varied approaches, for relative, often limited goals and the many aspects cited earlier (Brill, 1977, 2). There is still no clear perception of how to evaluate progress in treatment or assess the impact and efficacy of different variables and treatment inputs. We have nevertheless accumulated considerable knowledge and experience over the years. What remains is to bring together the weight of the best thinking and use it more coordinatedly than before in treatment and prevention (Brill, 1977; *Community Crime Prevention,* Chapter 4, 1973).

III.

Looking back from the vantage point of several decades of experience and a better understanding of the treatment issues, what can we now say about drug use?

A. The Factor of Diversity

As indicated, the former stereotyping about "the heroin addict" has given way to a better understanding of the factor of diversity; that is, that drug users comprise a wide range of individuals from varying class, ethnic and geographic backgrounds; with varying psychological and social needs, and, in many cases with no problem at all; and with different degrees of involvement with different kinds of drugs and the "addiction system" (Brill, 1977, 1; Brill, 1977, 2).

B.

We are moving away from the former tendency to focus on the "terminal cases"; that is, the tertiary stage of chronic addiction in the sense of the confirmed street junkie or chronic alcoholic—as if they constituted the entire population. The fact is that the overwhelming majority of drug users are only minimally involved or else discontinue use entirely after a short period of experimentation. The best estimates of confirmed heroin addicts in the country have ranged between 250,000 and 400,000. This number has declined in recent years and been replaced by emerging polydrug use patterns (Brill, 1977).

To elucidate further the range of drug users, the following typology has been developed:

1. *Experimental users*—Drugs play no special or regular role in the experimental user's life. Use is episodic and reflects a desire to see what the drugs are like, or test their effect on other activities ordinarily experienced without drugs.

2. *Social recreational users*—Drugs are associated with social or recreational activities in which this type of user would take part whether or not drugs were present. Little or no time and effort are devoted to seeking out drugs or making connections to obtain them. The pattern of drug use is occasional and situationally controlled.

3. *"Seekers"*—Drugs play a significant role in the seeker's life. Time is dedicated to seeking them out or making connections to obtain them. The seeker cannot enjoy or cope with some situations without drugs. Use of drugs may range from irregular to regular, controlled, or heavy daily use, although the individual may still remain functional and able to meet primary social and physical needs.

4. *"Self-medicating users"*—The self-medicator uses legally distributed tranquilizers or stimulants. While this type of use may have beneficial characteristics, it also can become a habitual way of responding to boredom, loneliness, frustration, and stress. The precise incidence of such chemical coping is unknown, but existing data suggest that it is extensive. It is necessary

to learn more about the situations and experiences that move the self-medicator to dysfunctional use. At present, it is only assumed that some type of emotional difficulty or problem underlies such use.

Both self-medicators and seekers may be attempting to deal with anxiety, depression, or other problems; and may often use drugs as a kind of self-therapy, among other reasons.

5. *Dysfunctional drug users*—Drugs begin to dominate the life of the drug user and interfere with essential areas of living. The process of securing and using them may engage the entire life of the individual (Brill et. al., 1963, Simmel, 1949).

C. Focus on Person ("Drugs are a People Thing")

Until very recently, the primary focus was on the *drug* as if it were the culprit, with no real examination of the *person* using the drug and the role it was playing in his life. Emphasis is now placed more appropriately on the drug user and the circumstances under which the drug is taken. This underlines the point that dysfunctional involvement with drugs depends more upon the *person* than the *drug,* since any changes in mood, behavior, or emotion will be experienced as pleasurable or alarming, depending on his/her psychological or social needs. If a person is stable, he/she can engage in drug experimentation or social-recreational use without more serious involvement (Brill, 1977).

D.

Still another point relates to the fact that no single program can meet the needs of all drug users. As a result of the converging experience with ex-addict-directed therapeutic communities in the late 50's and 60's, with methadone and narcotic antagonists, starting in the mid-sixties; with religious approaches such as the Christian Damascus Pentecostal Church in the Bronx, Teen Challenge and the Black Muslims; and community-based programs such as the Puerto Rican "Young Lords"—a better understanding evolved of the need for comprehensive, multimodality programming. This approach entailed the creation of a wide range of coordinated services for different clients and even different phases of treatment; or using them concomitantly for selected clients to reinforce treatment. Thus, for methadone patients who cannot function in the community, a combined residential-methadone setting might be used; or for residents in therapeutic communities who have difficulty effecting "reentry" to their local community, methadone maintenance or narcotics antagonists could serve as a supportive bridge back (Brill and Meiselas, 1973).

E.

Interestingly, the modes which today constitute the major modalities for the treatment of heroin addiction and, in some cases, other kinds of drug abuse entail approaches which would not have been too acceptable to therapists in the 50's. They comprise the following:

1. Chemotherapeutic approaches, including methadone maintenance and narcotic antagonists. Methadone maintenance today engages some 90,000 patients in the country and narcotic antagonists only a small number, probably still in the hundreds. These approaches require that patients be stabilized on the supporting drug for a long period of time, if not forever. The objective is not only to offer support and replace the heroin, but to use the medication as a lever to effect changes in life-style. Whether or not the person can eventually get unhooked depends on his stability or fragility (Brill and Lieberman, 1972).

2. Ex-Addict-Directed Therapeutic Communities: These too would not have been too palatable since the model relies almost entirely on using ex-addicts as role models. Most centers use encounter techniques as their primary treatment mode. These communities borrowed from Maxwell Jones in using the therapeutic mileu concept and have also employed Dr. Glaser's reality therapy techniques. They have engaged some thousands of drug users in New York City and are now attempting to develop techniques for augmenting the "reentry" of residents into the community and avoiding relapse.

3. A religious approach such as the former Christian Damascus Church based on Pentacostal tenets was relatively effective with selected Puerto Ricans of the South Bronx in the 60's. "Teen Challenge" in Brooklyn and California also experienced some success, using a residential center approach combined with religious involvement (Brill and Lieberman, 1972).

4. Equally unpalatable to some would be the use of social action as a "viable alternative" for people caught up in drugs. This has been the thrust of the "Young Lords," a Puerto Rican group which engages drug addicts in its social movement as a counter to drug use (Brill and Lieberman, 1972).

5. The use of "rational authority"—This approach would also not be acceptable to many therapists as it involves feelings about the use of authority and coercion in treatment. Thomas Szasz (Szasz, 1976) has, additionally, raised the question of civil liberties and the right of individuals to use drugs as a personal choice as long as it remains in the realm of private behavior. Still others, like Andrew Weil (Weil, 1973) have emphasized the value of achieving "altered states of consciousness"—preferably without drugs, but using drugs if necessary.

The question of "rational authority" is, in any case, a complicated issue that has been misunderstood. In the past, criminal or civil commitment procedures were routinely equated with the Parole or Institutional-aftercare model of treatment. What is needed today is a better understanding of the wide-ranging potential of civil commitment procedures for reinforcing all kinds of treatment services for "recalcitrant" patients at different levels of structuring (Meiselas and Brill, 1974).

6. The role of a central coordinating agency is also still not clearly understood. Because of the wide range of services and modalities required for different kinds of drug users, there is need for a central agency to help all drug-related programs interface effectively. As part of this system, centralized intake units should be available to reach out and engage individuals with drug problems (*Community Crime Prevention,* Chapter 4, 1973). In New York, "Multipurpose Outreach Units" have been set up in all areas of the State and in the criminal justice system to help render this system more viable to the needs of drug-dependent individuals. Hopefully, this intervention could be accomplished early, rather than late, to head off unnecessary stigmatization, labelling and incarceration. New York State's Division of Substance Abuse Services has placed professional staff in Probation offices and courts to accomplish these goals and intervene in the pre-sentence and pre-conviction phases as well.

7. The earlier focus on heroin as the only "bad" drug has given way to a better understanding of the role of other drugs and the need to be equally concerned about them. The former dichotomy between heroin and all other drugs, and between licit and illicit drugs is breaking down. For example, methadone programs have not been able to maintain their focus on heroin alone since, in some 25% of the cases, patients have become dysfunctionally involved with alcoholism or polydrug use. The drug scene has been further confused by the general emergence of polydrug or multiple drug use patterns, with users abusing a variety of drugs, including alcohol, heroin, methadone and other drugs serially or concomitantly. New approaches are being explored to deal creatively with these problems (Brill, 1971). This again highlights the need to center on person rather than substance, with awareness that a person with problems can become dysfunctionally involved with any drug.

8. Dysfunctional alcohol use has emerged more clearly as probably our primary drug problem. As with heroin, there has been a tendency to stereotype in terms of the 5% who are the skid-row personnel. What is clearer today is that the other 95%, including young adolescents and young adults, also need help. The facilities required are probably very similar to those used for other kinds of drug users since their problems may be alike. If we focus again on *person* rather than *drug,* and if we use the understandings derived from individual and group therapy, we can move to mix different kinds of drug users as long as there is a suitable balance in terms of personal and social characteristics, age factors, and needs (Brill, 1977).

9. Though we had, until fairly recently, been dealing almost exclusively with tertiary prevention (to use Gerald Caplan's public health model), we need to be increasingly concerned about primary and secondary prevention. Here too the "state of the art" is incomplete. Newer understandings have appeared which can help us differentiate among education, prevention and intervention and develop more effective programs. Education relates to information-giving and cognitive inputs while prevention involves doing things which can foster individual stability and later head off dysfunctional involvement with drugs. This means starting very early with youngsters—in the early school years and, even before that, in the family itself—to enhance personal stability, generate a better understanding of one's own and others' feelings, and the ability to communicate, relate and develop effective coping and problem-solving skills. The individual would then have "viable alternatives" which could offer him long-standing satisfactions in life without the need to use drugs for non-medical reasons.

There should be recognition that many people are using drugs today for experimental and social-recreational as well as "adaptive" reasons. This is not cause for arrest, stigmatization or even concern in many cases. The task of prevention is not to obviate experimentation since this has proven impossible over the years. It is rather to head off the great leap forward from experimental or social-recreational to dysfunctional use.

From a longer perspective, prevention entails modifying our social institutions, helping render schools and other agencies better related to human needs, family life and the nurturance of children.

These are some of the things learned over the years. While there are still many gaps in the "state of the art," a rational perspective does prevail based on a better awareness of the issues and what remains to be done. This perspective must not again be reduced to the simple stereotypes formerly held. It should instead be expanded to encompass a multifaceted and rational outlook which embodies our best understanding of etiology, epidemiology, treatment and prevention. We need, in brief, to "hang loose" and maintain an open-ended stance so that we can continue to grow. Above all, we must avoid the temptation to succumb to simplistic solutions and regressive retreats.

Summary

This paper has undertaken to outline the development of our thinking about drug abuse treatment since the early 50's. As described, much of the earlier professional thinking emanated from a psycho-analytical framework in terms of etiology and treatment approach. Our thinking today about personality organization derives in great part from this framework and has served to augment and support the various treatment strategies developed.

In the 50's, this thinking tended to stereotype the addict and his family in attributing uniform and unvarying characteristics to them, and in prescribing a uniform treatment approach—namely, the institutional aftercare or parole model of care. The field has moved since then, to a better understanding of the central issue of *diversity*—the fact that drug-dependent individuals comprise a very wide range of individuals with different degrees of involvement with drugs. There is, consequently, a need for a wide variety of treatment responses to meet these different needs. A typology of drug use was described in this paper, specifying a range of use, including also individuals who are functioning stably though involved with drugs—on an experimental or social-recreational level—who do not require treatment at all. Others use drugs adaptively and function better because of them. Still others are dysfunctionally involved with some drug and have a problem which requires treatment. This thinking has led to the multimodality or comprehensive approach to treatment which draws upon such varied responses as chemotherapeutic thrusts, ex-addict-directed therapeutic communities, religious approaches, community action programs, and a host of ancillary methods and services.

Our emphasis on the multimodality approach to treatment was not meant to imply that the different modalities do not also have commonalities of strategy and technique. We take it for granted, for example, that a relationship must exist at the core of treatment—whether in chemotherapeutic programs, ex-addict-directed therapeutic communities, religious approaches, or others. How this actually occurs will vary from program to program since treatment may lean more heavily on individual therapy in some cases, on group or forms of group in other cases—such as the encounters in ex-addict communities.

The concept of diversity and the need for multifaceted treatment responses have been the leitmotifs for the thinking outlined in this paper. Along with the different treatment views described, it assumes a differentiated approach to other areas such as vocational rehabilitation so that a variety of vocational pathways can be defined as well for different kinds of drug users. It also comprises a multiform use of civil certification procedures: while civil commitment was equated with the institutional-aftercare or parole model in the past, it must now be better understood as a varied use of coercion to structure services for different kinds of drug-dependent individuals to the extent necessary, in ambulatory as well as residential programs of all types. Above all, because the "state of the art" is still incomplete, we need to avoid "finalizing" our thinking; and instead, use our understanding of personality organization as a framework for relating to prevailing as well as emerging problems of use so that we can be truly responsive to them.

Bibliography

1. Brill, Leon—"Drug Addiction"—*The Encyclopedia of Social Work,* 17th Edition, National Association of Social Workers, 1977.
2. Brill, Leon—"Historical Evolution of the Current Drug Treatment Perspective" in *Rehabilitation Aspects of Drug Dependence,* Arnold Schechter Editor, CRC Press, Inc., Cleveland, Ohio, 1977.
3. Brill, L.: *The De-Addiction Process.* Springfield, Ill., Charles C. Thomas, 1972.
4. Brill, L.: Drug abuse problems: Implications for treatment. *Abstracts for Social Workers,* NASW, 7 (3): 3–8, Fall 1971.
5. Brill, L.: Drug addiction. *Encyclopedia of Social Work,* NASW, N.Y., 1971.
6. Brill, L. and Lieberman, L.: *Authority and Addiction,* Boston, Little Brown and Co., 1969.
7. Brill, L. and Lieberman, L.: *Major Modalities in Treatment of Drug Abuse,* New York, Behavioral Publications, 1972.
8. Brill, L. et. al.—*Rehabilitation in Drug Addiction,* A Report on a Five Year Community Experiment of the New York Demonstration Center—Mental Health Monograph 3, May 1963, PHS-NIMH.
9. Brill, L. and Meiselas, H.: The treatment of drug abuse: Experiences and issues. Yearbook of Drug Abuse, Brill, L. and Harmes, E., Eds., New York, Behavioral Publications, 1973.
10. Drug Abuse. Chapter 4—of *Community Crime Prevention.* Washington, D.C. One of a series of volumes by the Advisory Commission on Criminal Justice Standards and Goals, January 23, 1973.
11. Duvall, H.J.; Lock, B.Z.; and Brill, L.: Follow-Up study of narcotic drug addicts, Five-years after hospitalization. *Public Health Reports, 73* (3): 185–191, 1963.
12. Fenichel, Otto: *The Psychoanalytic Theory of Neurosis.* New York, W.W. Norton and Co., Inc., 1945.
13. Hollingshead, A.B. and Redlich, F.C.—*Social Class and Mental Illness: A Community Study,* New York: Wiley, 1958.
14. Keniston, K.: *The Uncommitted: Alienated Youth in American Society,* New York, Dell Publishing Co., 1967.
15. Meiselas, H. and Brill, L.: The role of civil commitment in multimodality programming. *Drugs and the Criminal Justice System,* Inciardi, J.A. and Chambers, C.U., Eds. Beverly Hills, Sage Publications, 1974.
16. Nyswander, M., Winick, C., Bernstein, A., Brill, L. and Kaufer, G.: The treatment of drug addicts as voluntary outpatients: A progress report. *Amer. J. Orthopsychiat., 28*: 714, 1958.
17. *Psychodynamics of Drug Dependence,* Jack D. Blaine and Demetrios A. Julius Editors, NIDA Research Monograph 12, USDHEW May, 1977.
18. Rado, Sandor: The Psychoanalysis of Pharmacothymia. *Psychoanalytic Quarterly, 2*: (1), 1–23, 1933.
19. Robins, L.N.—A Follow-Up Study of Vietnam Veterans Drug Use. *Journal of Drug Issues,* Vol. 4, No. 1, Winter, 1974.
20. Sheppard, C.W.; Smith, D.E.; and Gay, S.R.: The changing faces of heroin addiction in the Haight Ashbury. *Intl. J. Addict., 7*: 109–122, 1972.
21. Simmel, E.: Alcoholism and addiction. *Psychoanalytic Quarterly, 17*: (1) 6–31, 1948. Reprinted in *Yearbook of Psychoanalysts, 4*: 1949.

22. Szasz, T.: The Ethics of Addiction. In Uppers and Downers. Smith, D.E., and Wesson, D.R., Eds., Englewood Cliffs, N.J., Prentice Hall, p. 131, 1976.
23. Weil, A.: *The Natural Mind*. Boston, Houghton Mifflin Co., 1973.
24. The New York State Drug Abuse Program—Current Activities and Plans (State Plan), New York State Drug Abuse Control Commission, 1973–1974.
25. Wikler, A.—Conditioning Factors in Opiate Addiction and Relapse in Narcotics—Wilner, D.M. and Kassebaum, G.G.—Blakiston Division—McGraw-Hill Book Co., N.Y., 1965.

Chapter 14

AN ENVIRONMENTAL AND THERAPEUTIC APPROACH TO BREAKING THE SMOKING HABIT

George Stricker, Ph.D., George D. Goldman, Ph.D. and William J. Nemon, M.D.

George Stricker, Ph.D.

George D. Goldman, Ph.D.

Dr. Stricker is Professor of Psychology and Assistant Dean in the Institute of Advanced Psychological Studies at Adelphi University, is a Consulting Psychologist in the Queen-Nassau Mental Health Service of H.I.P., and is in private practice.

Dr. Goldman is Director of Clinical Services of the Postdoctoral Psychotherapy Center of the Institute of Advanced Psychological Studies, Adelphi University where he is also a Clinical Professor of Psychology and Supervisor of Psychotherapy in the Postdoctoral Program in Psychotherapy at Adelphi University and is in private practice.

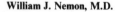

William J. Nemon, M.D.

Dr. Nemon is a member of the American Psychiatric Association, a Member of the Society for Clinical and Experimental Hypnosis, and is in private practice.

188

This paper actually consists of two separate but related presentations. The first is a description of a project that we were involved in a number of years ago, and what some of the effects were on the smokers who took part in it. The second part of the paper will consist of some attempt to understand why the program had the effect it did. The first part is specific to a very particular program, while the second part may apply not only to this project, and not only to smoking, but to a whole range of addictive processes or, more nearly, symptomatic processes. It will present a hypothesis about why the treatment of symptoms can be effective, and what takes place when we attempt to treat a symptom.

In recent years cigarette smoking has become recognized as a major public health problem. Many methods have been developed to help smokers who wish to stop. No method has become accepted as the method of choice, and the rate of success is usually about 20 per cent when there is a long term follow up that is done carefully and with proper scrutiny. There are no programs which consistently produce more than a 20 per cent rate of stopping smoking without recidivism.

The Stop Smoking cruise, which is the particular project that I am going to describe, was a comprehensive plan for helping people to stop smoking. It took place on board the Prudential Grace Lines SS Santa Paula, a luxury cruise liner. The ship sailed from New York City on November 20, 1970 for a thirteen day cruise which included stops at six Caribbean ports. The therapeutic program of the Stop Smoking cruise was multi-faceted. A broad comprehensive approach was employed, utilizing many techniques which previously have been of some benefit in helping some people to stop smoking. The major therapeutic forces that were included were the environment, social identity, social sanctions, group process, hypnosis, breathing therapy, educational lectures, discussions and recreation. Each of these has been used alone in different programs, and each of them has been used with some success with some people. We provided all of them, and the passengers elected, from among the therapeutic alternatives that were offered, those which seemed most appropriate and most helpful for them.

One alternative that was constant for all passengers, and that was inescapable, was the environment. The shipboard environment was considered to be one of the most critical aspects of the cruise. It was designed to be tobacco free, and one advantage a boat provides that is not obtainable in many other settings is that once people are on board and you arrange the environment, it is not easy to escape from it. The environment, then, was an inescapable part of the entire program. All ash trays and matches were removed, the passengers pledged not to bring any cigarettes on board with them and, surprisingly, most of them kept to that pledge. The ship's crew promised not to smoke in the vicinity of the passengers, and they did not, and also promised not to supply any cigarettes, which they adhered to with only some minor exceptions. There was a black market for cigarettes aboard ship, but the great majority of the passengers were quite serious about being involved in the program, and did not participate in it, so that the majority of the participants did not have cigarettes available to them over the thirteen days that they spent on the ship. Being on a ship that was isolated from cigarettes and smokers helped to maintain a smoke free atmosphere and facilitated the acceptance of the idea that passengers must adjust to not smoking. Given this kind of environment, there was a very strong social reinforcement for abstinence which rapidly developed and was maintained. Anybody who did smoke in public drew a very strong negative response from other passengers who also would have liked to smoke but were abstaining successfully, and did not take kindly to a transgressor who not only was violating the rule, but was also tempting them to break their own resolve. Meals and parties were pleasurable social experiences despite the absence of smoking, and provided a striking experience for many passengers. For most of the people who were on board, it was their first experience with going to a party or having a meal when there were not people in their company who smoked, when they did not follow a meal with a cigarette, when cigarettes were not an essential component of the party atmosphere. To support these environmental effects, there were pamphlets, buttons, insignias, a Kick the Habit flag, and a number of other symbols which served to promote the identity of the passengers with the project and which made abstinence a salient and reinforced behavior for the participants.

Normally a vacation cruise is very heavily scheduled with activities for the passengers. The Stop Smoking program was integrated with the shipboard activities so that passengers would be able to choose among therapeutic and social activities, so that the character of each passenger's therapeutic regimen was self-determined. Thus, it would be impossible for us, in a research sense, to say which component of the program was the critical aspect of what was done. Other than the environment, everything else varied from person to person, and from day to day, and the variations were determined by self selection rather than the random assignment that would be necessary if this was a formal research project.

The passengers were divided into four groups, each of which was led by an experienced group therapist. On the first evening of the cruise, the passengers met with their group leader for an orientation meeting. On each following day the group met for an hour and a half session during the day and were offered an optional meeting during the evening, which most passengers attended. The four group therapists used quite different techniques with their patients. Two of the leaders were didactic and theme centered in their approach. They lectured and centered the group process about smoking. A third was theme centered and interpersonal, so that the discussion was about smoking, but also about how it feels to smoke, when people choose to smoke, and what needs it serves. The fourth leader was more oriented towards a sensitivity group approach, with focus on feelings in general and not specifically those feelings that are concerned with smoking. These groups provided the group therapy aspect of the therapeutic regimen.

Hypnosis was conducted in group sessions and this was also available to those passengers who chose to associate themselves with it. A number of sessions were conducted for groups that ranged in size between 20 and 50. The participants were hypnotized as a group, and they were given suggestions that emphasized self-mastery and the positive values of not smoking. They were also taught a self-hypnosis exercise which would reinforce these attitudes. Negative or aversive techniques were not used with the hypnosis, so that the focus was not on the disagreeable consequences of smoking. The focus was on how good it would feel not to smoke rather than on how bad it would feel to smoke.

Participants also had an opportunity to attend scheduled sessions with a breathing therapist. Group meetings were held at regular intervals in which various breathing techniques and exercises were taught. These sessions gained an enthusiastic popularity with a segment of the participants. As with most of the techniques employed, a natural selection process developed in which those motivated for, and responsive to, this approach availed themselves of this method.

Despite the widespread dissemination of information, many people are ignorant of many details relating to smoking and health. Educational lectures were made available to cruise participants through a series of audio-visual talks. However, a majority of the participants did not take advantage of this aspect, preferring to participate in recreational activities. On this cruise, as in other experiences with approaches to help people to stop smoking, the least popular and least effective method was education. People either know and don't care about, or don't care to know, what the effects are, and if they are going to be approached in a meaningful way, teaching them the consequences of smoking is a highly ineffective approach.

In order to deal with any emotional problems that might arise, and we expected the construction of this kind of environment to produce a number of psychological and physical withdrawal problems, a schedule was employed so that a responsible professional would be available throughout the entire cruise, twenty-four hours a day. During the day passengers could contact their group leaders. At night, and while the ship was in port, a doctor on call was designated to deal with any problems that arose. There were only a few such problems on the entire voyage, and these were minor. The number of consequences were much less than we feared and had anticipated in advance.

On the land excursions at the six ports we visited, passengers had the opportunity to test their progress in a less artificial setting, since one could easily obtain cigarettes in the port. Each port was conceptualized as a test stop in which people would leave the protected environment and smoke free atmosphere of the ship and go into an area where people behaved in a much more typical and unregulated manner. They would see the natives smoking and there were many tobacco shops where cigarettes and good Cuban cigars were available. Often participants would go on shore with their group so that they could give and receive support from each other, as though they didn't trust themselves to be alone and preferred to draw mutual support from each other. After a day in port, the evening group then focused on the day's experiences and each passenger's progress. This helped to foster a sense of mastery and provide the passengers with confidence that they could function without cigarettes and without being in an artificial environment.

It should be noted that a good many radio and TV personnel were on board and made the passengers very aware that there was considerable press coverage on this cruise. This probably added to their identity with the program and encouraged the motivation for abstinence.

There were 85 passengers on board ship who qualified as smokers interested in kicking the habit. In a follow-up conducted by mail and telephone one week after the cruise returned, we found that 75 per cent of that group had discontinued smoking. Seventy-five per cent of people who stop smoking after one week following the termination of a project is good, but it is not unusual. The finding with most smoking programs is that there is a very high initial rate of response, followed by a precipitous rate of return to smoking. The literature seems to indicate that an asymptote is reached within a four to six month period, and that most of those people who are going to return to smoking will have done so within that period. For this reason there was also a long-term follow-up that was conducted six months after the cruise, when there was a second mail and telephone survey. At this time, we found that 32 people had stopped smoking, 39 had resumed smoking and 14 were unable to be contacted. If we assume that all 14 of these had resumed smoking, which is the most conservative procedure, and the only procedure that can be recommended from a research standpoint, we still are left with a total of 38 per cent who were able to stop smoking. This figure exceeds what has been typically offered as long-term follow-up data concerning smoking, as the usual results are in the neighborhood of 20 per cent.

When we related the success in stopping smoking to the particular group leader with whom the passenger worked, we found that three of the leaders were highly comparable in their effect, with the rates ranging from 23 to 30 per cent. However, the leader who used the theme centered interpersonal approach was successful with 60 per cent of his group. That is the approach in which the focus was on smoking and the feelings which surround smoking, rather than on more didactic aspects of the effects of smoking. Other analyses of possible differences between those passengers who stopped smoking and those who resumed were relatively unproductive. Out of the large number of analyses that were performed, less than a half-dozen reached statistical significance, and this number is approximately what could have been expected by chance.

With this highly motivated group, then, we find that it is possible, using the procedures that we developed, to help people to stop smoking. There does not seem to be any effective way of predicting who will or who will not be affected by the procedure, but the over-all results were very encouraging.

There are some important considerations before we contemplate generalizing this procedure for a widespread application. Although the project, as a technique for helping smokers, was quite promising, it was never again attempted, nor would anybody hearing the figures involved even consider attempting it. The cost of renting a luxury liner for two weeks is enormous, and 85 passengers did not begin to meet the basic overhead that was involved. Any repetition of the program could not depend upon private funding, and would have to be adopted as a public health venture funded by appropriate governmental or foundation sources. Undoubtedly this would reduce the luxury emphasis of the original cruise and lead to the adaptation of the method to a more modest setting. The use of an isolated facility such as a private hotel might be feasible. However, in making such a modification, some of the factors contributing to the initial success of the project might be ameliorated. For example, the motivation of the participants undoubtedly was higher when they were voluntarily incurring an expenditure of over $1,000 than if they had been treated to a two week vacation by a foundation. The operation of cognitive dissonance would suggest that people who make a great sacrifice are then more likely to make a change consistent with that sacrifice than are people who are only casually committed to a program. Participation in an established treatment program does not have the same motivational impact as participation in an innovative program does, and any Hawthorne effect which may have occurred in our program was accentuated by the widespread media coverage. When the program was highlighted as an innovation and there were television cameras and reporters from *Life* and *Time* and a number of daily newspapers on board, the people were extremely conscious of the project and super-motivated to do what they had originally said they were signing up to do. This particular condition would be difficult to replicate in any extended use of the method. For these reasons, even if the program was transferred intact to another setting, there are some questions about whether the results could be replicated. Nevertheless, the striking success of the original program would make such an attempt worthwhile, and this seems like a reasonable recommendation to be made to a group interested in public health matters.

If the program were to be extended non-commercially, one change can be recommended which might add to the potential success of the effort. Our cruise, for reasons based partly on the international geographic dispersion of the passengers, and also partly on financial considerations, did not provide for any post-cruise follow-up contact other than the two brief research inquiries about their smoking behavior. At the very least the camaraderie, mutual support and reinforcement, and highlighted interest in smoking that was provided by the environment on board ship could have been extended to the land. Periodic meetings of the passengers which would keep smoking and its cessation salient for them would provide for them the same kind of mutual help that is provided by organizations such as Alcoholics Anonymous, and would in all probability have added to the success of the program. It is remarkable that so many people were able to retain their personal resolve in the absence of programmatic support, and likely that more would have been able to do so had the support been provided. If the periodic meetings included professional personnel, so that the therapeutic benefits could continue and the dynamic ramifications of giving up smoking could be worked through, the gains might have been even greater. The determination of the relative benefits of having no follow-up, a follow-up with peer support, and a follow-up with continued group therapy is a matter that would be readily open to research solution.

We have presented a description of the program as it was conducted, the effects that it had, and some suggestions about how it might be generalized. The question that we are left with is, "Why did it happen?" Why should it be that a symptom which is as prevalent as smoking, and which we know to be as difficult to change as smoking, should have been responsive to what seems to be a relatively superficial environmental attempt to change it, and why should it be that over the long run the change was able to be maintained as well and as harmlessly as it was? In trying to understand this event, we can view smoking from two different perspectives, that of psychoanalytic theory and also that of learning theory. For psychoanalytic theory, smoking would be considered a symptom, and smoking, like any other symptom, would represent an expression of both an instinct and a defense against that instinct. Both the instinct and the defense would be coalesced in the symptom that was developed. One simple view regarding smoking is that it represents the expression of oral erotic impulses which are defended against through displacement in the choice of objects. The cigarette is a displaced object, and the impulse is being gratified. There are many more complicated explanations that are also available which invoke concepts such as the masochism present when one symptomatically adopts a habit that is known to be harmful. It does not matter which dynamic explanation is chosen at this point. For the sake of the presentation, we will use the oral-erotic dynamism because it is probably the most widespread and the most simple, but the explanation offered will remain the same no matter what the dynamic meaning of the symptom might be and, in fact, no matter what the symptom might be, so that we might address the same argument not only to smoking, but to eating, drinking or a number of other symptoms.

The alternative approach that learning theory would offer is that smoking is not a symptom, for within the language of learning theory there is no such thing as a symptom, but instead that smoking is a habit. A habit is a repetitive link between a stimulus and a response which is generated by and maintained through reinforcement. Smoking, then, is a habit that would be developed in response to particular circumstances and which would provide the smoker with reinforcement. The reinforcement may consist of the attaining of something positive, such as the pleasure in taste that would come from cigarettes, or the reinforcement may come from the elimination of something which the smoker finds negative, such as anxiety, and it is clearly known that people often will take a cigarette to relax when they are feeling tense. People are seen as smoking either for what they get or what they escape from.

Whether we see smoking as a symptom or as a habit would have quite an implication for what we then expect to happen if we are going to change it. If smoking is considered to be a symptom, and if the symptom is removed without altering the instinct which gave rise to it, then we would expect a symptom substitution to occur because the instinct would then seek alternative expression. If symptom substitution did not occur, then we would expect the rate of recurrence of smoking to be quite high because the instinct is being unsatisfied. On the other hand, if smoking is considered a habit, the habit would be changed by altering the patterns of reinforcement. If the patterns of reinforcement are altered, then there should be no further consequences because there is no instinct that is being unsatisfied, and the person is now getting reinforcement from different sources. As long as the new reinforcement pattern is being maintained, there is little danger of recurrence, and there is no symptom substitution because there is no original symptom.

At this point, we will examine some of the evidence that would enable us to choose between the symptom interpretation and the habit interpretation. The first bit of evidence, which is quite clear, is that smoking, whether we call it symptom or habit, is a very difficult behavior to change. A learning theorist might say that this is evidence for how entrenched reinforcement patterns can become. It appears to us, though, that this indicates that a concept like habit is not a sufficient explanation, and that we must look to an enduring state of the individual in order to explain why a behavior which seems so peripheral should be so entrenched.

A second well established piece of evidence is that there is a very high rate of recurrence. In our project, for example, we went from 75 per cent after one week to 38 per cent after six months, which was just about a halving of the number of people who were able to stop smoking. This suggests that the needs that are being met are not merely reinforcement patterns, or else that the new reinforcement patterns are really not satisfying, in which case we would have to ask why not. A process is occurring that is creating a tremendous pressure in the individual to go back to the initial behavior.

The difficulty in changing smoking patterns and in maintaining this change are arguments that would favor the symptom interpretation rather than the habit interpretation. However, there is also the complexity in the question of symptom substitution, which is a very critical one to the argument. When we look at the short term, symptom substitution is almost universal. When people stop smoking, they almost immediately adopt a variety of clearly identifiable oral erotic habits. They may eat more, drink more, or start chewing gum. There will be a whole variety of new and obvious substitutes that will be adopted. Not only will there be substitutes in these transparent oral behaviors, but there will also be an increase in anxiety which, apart from whatever the physical withdrawal might create, also suggests that there is an unsuccessful attempt to deal with an impulse that is occurring, a process which also is consistent with a symptom interpretation.

However, if we look at the long-term effect there seems to be almost no symptom substitution that occurs. The new oral habits disappear, the weight gain and increase in drinking that occurs is just temporary, and anxiety seems to be reduced over time and no longer is as critical a factor. All of these suggest that the concept of symptom substitution as a long-term effect of giving up smoking is not what a symptom interpretation would predict, but is much more in line with the habit interpretation.

The question that remains is where do we go from here? How can we reconcile a belief in symptoms as being dynamically developed and having an explanation that is rooted in the intrapsychic functioning of the individual with the evidence that a short-term change in the symptom is very easy to accomplish with relatively superficial approaches, and that long-term symptom substitution is very rare.

There are three different ways in which the concept of symptoms can be reconciled with the absence of symptom substitution, and it is necessary to do this in order to maintain a psychoanalytic approach to smoking. The first explanation is that we have, in part, created a straw man, in that a symptom and a habit are not synonymous terms. Of the two terms habit is the superordinate construct and refers to any recurrent behavior pattern. Some habits are symptomatic in origin and expression, while others are not. Some of these recurrent behaviors may have originated as symptoms, but they no longer serve symptomatic purposes for the individual and instead are maintained because they satisfy more superficial needs. These are habits that Allport has described as being functionally autonomous, and persist in the absence of the original motivation which gave rise to them. There are also cases in which a habit may be consistent with, but not expressive of, the needs of the patient. A person who generally has an oral orientation may do a number of oral things because they are comfortable and consistent with character structure, but they may not be direct symptomatic expressions of the instinct that is being experienced. These classes of habit, the ones that are functionally autonomous or the ones that are just consistent with, rather than direct expressions of, need should be the ones that are most available to change and there should not be any danger of substitution for them because they are no longer maintained by active impulse pressures. Thus, one type of explanation for the absence of symptom substitution is the concept we broadly refer to as functional autonomy.

There is a second explanation which also is probably familiar even if we take those behaviors which clearly are symptoms. All symptoms are not equally central in maintaining the psychic equilibrium of the person. Some symptoms are critical to the functioning of the individual and any attempt to alter those symptoms without dealing with underlying issues is likely to be met with either failure or with rapid symptom substitution. Freud's unsuccessful experiments with hypnosis, which initially gave rise to the concept of symptom substitution, undoubtedly were attempts to alter symptoms which were central to the functioning of his patient. However, some symptoms are relatively trivial in the psychic economy and changes in these symptoms will have very little ramification for the individual. In fact, in some cases, the positive gratification that is produced by abandoning a symptom will far outweigh whatever is given up with the symptom. For smoking, as an example, the oral erotic gratification that some patients receive is trivial when compared with the sense of active mastery that accompanies abstinence. There are also a number of events that will occur in a chain. Leaving the model of smoking to consider a different symptom, the elimination of enuresis not only provides a child with more of a sense of self, it also opens up activities that were never before available, like sleeping over at a friend's house, going to camp, or other acts that will provide sources of growth and gratification that will outweigh whatever little is given up by abandoning a symptom that has trivial function. In these cases, where we are dealing with what might be termed minor symptoms, we would expect change to be maintained with no significant substitution.

Finally, there is a third explanation which is much less likely to be familiar, and it not only might explain why symptom substitution does not occur, but may also explain how what appears to be relatively superficial approaches to change can be effective in changing a symptom even if it is a more important symptom for the functioning of an individual. This explanation suggests why you might be able to change central symptoms like obesity or drug addiction as well as smoking. This point is that abstinence itself may function as a symptom, and if this is the case, abstinence can become the symptom which substitutes for the symptom of smoking. The patient begins with a spontaneous symptom which expresses a need directly, and then substitutes for this spontaneous neurotic behavior an artificial neurotic behavior. This artificial symptom which the person now adopts can serve the same function, but perhaps in a more healthy manner. We are all familiar with the almost religious fervor that sometimes is associated with abstinence. In such cases, the intensity of the abstinence suggests that it may be serving some psychic needs. We can look upon the injunction not to smoke as being equivalent to the creation of an artificial phobia, or of an artificial compulsion. In either case, it is a symptom which equally expresses the needs of the person and defends against those needs by avoidance or control rather than by displacement. The existence and the success of this type of change will depend upon the character structure of the patient and whether avoidance, control or displacement is a more comfortable defense to be adopted and maintained, since the impulse being expressed has not been altered in either quality or intensity.

If we recognize that smoking may be changed without symptom substitution if it is functionally autonomous, or if it expresses a trivial need in the overall psychic structure, and we also recognize that abstinence itself may represent a symptom, then a new direction is indicated both in the treatment of smoking and in research on the success of various treatment patterns. In our study we were unsuccessful in distinguishing in advance between those smokers who were able to give up the habit and those who were not. Characteristic of the field, our attention was focused on historic and demographic features of the individual. We compared them as to their sex, their age, their general health, their reasons for smoking, their reasons for not smoking, their prior attempts to give up smoking, and all of the other traditional variables that have been adopted in the literature. What we did not do, and what we might have been more successful in doing, is to study the dynamic role that smoking played for each individual. Those patients whose smoking expressed an important need and who would not be comfortable with either phobic or compulsive defenses are not likely to change their smoking behavior without some type of therapeutic intervention that would deal with these needs. On the other hand, patients whose smoking has become functionally autonomous, or expresses a relatively trivial need, or who could shift from displacement to avoidance or to control as a defense, would probably be responsive to a more superficial intervention based upon environmental manipulation. A determination of the number of patients in each category and, therefore, what the most appropriate treatment for each would be, would be very helpful in deciding how to allocate resources in the service of reducing the public health problem of excessive smoking.

Bibliography

1. Bernstein, D.A. Modification of smoking behavior: an evaluative review. *Psychological Bulletin*, 1969, *71*, 418–440.
2. Bozzetti, L.P. Group psychotherapy with addicted smokers. *Psychotherapy and Psychosomatics*, 1972, *20*, 172–175.
3. Bradshaw, P.W. The problem of cigarette smoking and its control. *The International Journal of the Addictions*, 1973, *8*, 353–371.
4. Guilford, J.S. *Factors Related to Successful Abstinence from Smoking*, Los Angeles: American Institutes for Research, 1966.
5. Hall, J.A. and Crasilneck, H.B. Development of a hypnotic technique for treating chronic cigarette smoking. *International Journal of Clinical and Experimental Hypnosis*, 1970, *18*, 283–289.
6. Hunt, W.A. and Bespalec, D.A. An evaluation of current methods of modifying smoking behavior. *Journal of Clinical Psychology*, 1974, *30*, 431–438.
7. Keutzer, C.S. Behavior modification of smoking: the experimental investigation of diverse techniques. *Behavior Research and Therapy*, 1968, *6*, 137–157.
8. Keutzer, C.S., Lichtenstein, E., and Mees, H.L. Modification of smoking behavior: a review. *Psychological Bulletin*, 1968, *70*, 520–533.
9. Kline, M.V. The use of extended group hypnotherapy sessions in controlling cigarette habituation. *International Journal of Clinical and Experimental Hypnosis*, 1970, *18*, 270–282.
10. Koenig, K.P. and Masters, J. Experimental treatment of habitual smoking. *Behavior Research and Therapy*, 1965, *3*, 235–243.
11. Mausner, B. Report on a smoking clinic. *American Psychologist*, 1966, *21*, 251–255.
12. McFall, R.M., Smoking-cessation research. *Journal of Consulting and Clinical Psychology*, 1978, *46*, 703–712.
13. McFall, R.M. and Hammen, C.L. Motivation, structure, and self-monitoring: role of non-specific factors in smoking reduction, *Journal of Consulting and Clinical Psychology*, 1971, *37*, 80–86.
14. Schwartz, J.L. A critical review and evaluation of smoking control methods. *Public Health Reports*, 1969, *84*, 483–506.
15. Schwartz, J.L. and Dubitzky, M. Requisites for success in smoking withdrawal. In Borgatta, E.F. and Evans, R.R. (Eds.), *Smoking, Health, and Behavior*, Chicago: Aldine, 1968.

Chapter 15

ADDICTION AS A HOMEODYNAMIC PROCESS IN THE FAMILY SYSTEM

Gerald Berenson, Ph.D.

Gerald Berenson, Ph.D.

Dr. Berenson was initially trained as an individual psychoanalyst at our Postdoctoral Program in Psychotherapy. He got further training at the Nathan W. Ackerman Family Institute where he was on the faculty of the training program. He recently helped found the American Family Therapy Association. His current work is in the integration of psychoanalytic theory and family theory.

The title of this paper indicates a perspective central to its theme, that is, in the effort to understand the addictive process we need to broaden the context in which it has been generally considered. The interapsychic definitions of addiction in Fenichel (10) are quite partial and allow little understanding in a larger social context. Sexual longing, a need for security and the maintenance of self-esteem are frequently mentioned. The pre-genital character structure of persons who are involved in the addictive process is universally described. The mind is strained by the ingenuity of psychoanalytic interpretations, for not only is the sexual a representation of the pre-genital but the pre-genital can also be a representation of the genital so that food can be symbolic of the penis in a so-called food addiction. Interestingly enough, in writing about alcoholism, Fenichel asserts the essence of a larger contexual approach when he states that ". . . therapy in such cases will be of no avail as long as these external conditions persist (namely, the situation in which the alcoholic lives) and would become unnecessary if they are changed." To replace external conditions with the family is the start of the approach taken in this paper.

The application of the general systems theory to the psychotherapeutic field is most recent. Murray Bowen, one of the pioneers in the field of family therapy, has discussed systems analysis as a means of understanding the family and shaping therapeutic interventions. The family is viewed as a system which follows the laws of natural systems. A fundamental property of systems is that they must function as wholes. The main objective in family therapy today is to understand "relationship systems." In order to discern the pattern within the seeming choas of the informational and emotional system we call the family. To see how a family system operates we need only to look at our own families.

Change in one member often affects the previously established means of relating within the family. The scapegoating process is exemplary of how systems operate. Families often designate certain members to be the good ones and others to be the bad ones. In terms of the them of addiction, let us consider the case of an addict of any kind. Once the addict is in some form of treatment and supposedly "off the family's back," more problems will continue to emerge unless we appreciate the role of the addict in the family system. One of the causes of the addictive behavior is clearly in response to the need for a scapegoat. There may be a multi-generational transmission process that is a source of the addiction, but this is not of such immediate significance. The members of a family have to deal with each other without the convenience of a scapegoat, as the addict becomes healthier. Other people may come to take the scapegoat's place or he may resume his role when he gets back into the family. The patterns are so well learned that if the family system is not dealt with directly the addict will resume his role even after detoxification, and even if he does not physically live with the family. Other clear instances of families' operating as a system can be noted by the role of children who become disturbed and are supposedly in need of help. They serve an important role in the homeodynamics of the family in maintaining its fixed methods of response, and so perpetuating these problems that are perceived by the family members as originating in the children. The children usually help the parents avoid focusing on themselves or the role of their own nuclear families in the transmission down the generational line. There are many examples of this kind of "sacrifice" and family loyalty on the part of children.

Some of the basic concepts of general systems theory need to be understood before proceeding further. My own evaluation of the human condition has to do with the integration of attachment theory in an object relations context, in a general systems framework. But first I will expound upon the ideas of general systems theory, the basic frame on which the other theories are developed. The idea that one person carries the symptom is negated by the concept that integration is a key process, and that even a psychological dysfunction is a response to the need for integration, in a system that tends toward disintegration. As the parts of a whole work together to achieve this integration, an analyzation of the whole is necessitated to determine the functions of its parts. In order to more effectively make meaningful interventions, to alter an imbalance that has been maintained within a particular family system recognizing the totality of the system must be a goal. Of course, we never know the totality but this must be our direction. We need to choose the areas of greatest payoff, those in which change will affect more change within the total system.

The concept that initial constructs are not the only means by which personality develops is relevant to the organization of a method to intercede in such a system. Bertalanffy extends this in understanding as he theorizes living systems, i.e., the family, as open systems which achieve a steady state by the dynamic balance of input and output. The open system may attain a state independent of initial conditions and determined only by the system parameters. A closed system cannot attain this level of integration. What has plagued traditional psychoanalysis is that it treats people as closed systems, not regarding the primary importance of the constant input and feedback from their environment. Indeed, it does not even consider crucial, real elements of the system. This has enormously important implications for treatment as we will see later. I am not only talking about family therapy, individual therapy can profit as well if it is family-oriented. So we see the principal of equifinality suggests that intervention in a current system issue need not always be dependent on in-depth exploration of the past.

Another principle of general systems theory is one of progressive mechanization. This means that certain leading parts develop which dominate the system. Input from these parts have a greater effect throughout the system than from other parts. Not every area pays off in treatment as we well know. To get back to Murray Bowen again, he will choose to work with the most differentiated person in the family because he feels that this person's change will have the greatest change effect in the system. Another example is to work only with the parents when we get a referral for child therapy. Centralization is the name given to the formation of leading components of the system. It is an aspect of differentiation. Only by the process of progressive mechanization of lower functions can the higher ones emerge in the process of centralization. There are many other aspects of general systems theory, of course, but to explore them all here would go far beyond the scope of this paper. Again, it is the frame on which further theoretical considerations follow.

My interest in attachment theory, as proposed by John Bowlby (7,8) comes from striking clinical evidence in the families I work with that ideas such as attachment, separation and loss touch people profoundly. They touch them in their current situations as well as in memories of times past. Real attachments, separations and losses as well as mythic ones are encountered and can be dealt with on that basis. Myths are most often used to avoid growth concepts and continue the replication of stereotypic behavior in the process of multi-generational transmission. I think of attachment theory and object relations theory (to be gone into later) as processes of centralization in the frame of general systems theory. If I had to think of where to gain entree into a system so as to make the greatest change I would definitely feel it is with the concepts of attachment theory.

For Bowlby attachment behavior is observable and primary. Babies are quieted by socialization processes and can cling at birth. In Harlow's (12) studies of monkeys he demonstrated that clinging took precedence over food. A core tenet of attachment theory is that it is a theory of primary drive, again a critical issue in terms of centralization processes. The child's tie to the mother is most important. The role of actual experience then is the focus and family contributions are enormous. Intrapsychic tension reducing needs, as in the secondary drive theory of Freud, are unnecessary and intestable constructs. What most effectively reduces the fear of the infant is the sight and sounds of the mother. Many studies now report that attachment behavior has a biologically specific function, namely, species survival. Ainsworth (Ainsworth, 1973) talks about the reciprocal feedback system at birth that ensures the infants' closeness and contact with others. The development of attachment consists of the following. There is an undiscriminating social responsiveness for about two or three months. At about six months the process becomes more sophisticated as the ability to discriminate develops. A goal corrected partnership develops at about three years. The critical stages in attachment theory occur much earlier than in Freudian psychology. The idea of object permanence must also, of course, be at a point of development where it can be utilized. Both person permanence and mother discrimination are necessary. Attachment behavior persists throughout life according to Bowlby and this fits into the general systems theory notion of equifinality. We can intervene at any point in the system using whatever parameters we find.

Separation and separation anxiety are critical for Bowlby. We are all attached at birth and separate and lose. This is obvious. But how we reattach and grow with the pain of loss is not so obvious. For Bowlby the notion of separation anxiety is a primary response which is ineducable and is in response to separation from the mother. Freud (Freud, 1959) reached the same conclusion later in his thinking that separation anxiety is primary; Fairbairn's object-relations theory likewise places separation anxiety in the focal position. Freud described internalized objects in his last formulation of separation anxiety in response to object loss. Bowlby considers this too but, in the initial stages of growth and development, early relationships between mother and infant is easily observable. An example of how primary and secondary drive theories work can be seen in the example of a child sucking or overeating when deprived of the mother. For Bowlby the primary drive concept would mean that the child is responding to the deprivation of the maternal relationship. A secondary drive analysis, as in Freudian psychology, would talk about the tension-reducing function of the behavior so that the behavior is secondary. Thus we are deprived of understanding except in a very devious "vissicitudes" analysis of drive and associated behavior.

Fairbairn's (9) work is essentially an interpersonal or object theory. Libido is object-seeking, not pleasure-seeking. The central issue is infantile dependence, and the root of pathology is the inability of the infant to feel loved for its own sake in the context of mother-child interaction. One can easily extend this to include a family system. The object seeking aims of a central and unitary ego are primary. There is no split in psychic structure as in Freud. These are profound changes in psychoanalytic thought and have far reaching implications. It is not within the scope of this paper to give a critique of attachment theory and object relations theory. The reader is advised to go to the sources.

One further word about primary drive theory. Tension reduction and need gratification are insufficient in explaining exploratory and/or creative behavior. Tension reduction is a classical explanation in secondary drive theory. Using Bowlby's approach we can understand this behavior as the normal developmental growth of the individual in a humanistic sense, not out of some tortured sexual instinct which finds its way through the psyche and out into behavior. This second explanation is totally unnecessary and hardly subject to demonstrable observation. We need to be able to talk in primary drive terms if we are to understand at all how we develop. Current infant research does support a great many of Bowlby's ideas.

Now how does this rather complex material make coherent sense so that we can develop a means of intervening therapeutically? I mean to illustrate what I say by using a case history involving a family where the mother was addicted. I will explore each session in some detail so as to demonstrate how the use of attachment theory and object-relations theory can be worked with in a general systems framework.

Theories of addiction abound in the literature. Explanations vary according to the study but up to now there is no one consistent theory which explains this phenomenon. Many different individual character structures are seen in addictive personalities. The etiologies are likewise varied. This is most probably no accident, for addiction is a system phenomenon and can be understood in those terms. Whether we are talking about a low socio-economic level or affluence we need to see it in a broader context than individual dynamics. In individual terms, addiction makes little sense for it stems out of a larger frame. Family theorists have struggled with the notion that certain family structures are seen in addiction. However, nothing reliable has come out of this. Richard Blum (Blum, 1972) in a very interesting study in California has attempted to deal with the problem of the family structure of addicts. The findings are inconclusive and are not specific to drug users. For example, he observes that there was greater disagreement and distance reported between drug users and their parents than between non drug users and their parents. Any number of people other than addicts can say this. In so-called high risk families each person was considered an individual and we do not see the cohesiveness that is present in low risk families. Lack of discipline in families was also said to be a contributing factor in drug use. Blum quotes some British studies indicating a greater number of separations prior to age sixteen in families with drug use. This last part fits into the pattern of attachment and loss which we will discuss more fully. Blum's study is quite useful in discriminating between drug use families and non-drug use families; however these are all after the fact. This explanation leaves us devoid of any etiological understanding. I believe this is so because there is no etiological understanding, only one which employs the construct of equifinality in response to current system parameters in conjunction with attachment concepts.

The L family was seen for ten sessions over a period of eight months. The family currently consists of Mel, a 65 year old physician, his 57 year old wife Ann and their eleven year old daughter, Joan. This is her second marriage and his third. Both have two children from their first marriage. Mel has a son who is an engineer, working in Michigan whom he sees every two years or so. The son is married to a medical student; they have no children. Right now and for the next few years they are living apart, she in school in one city and he working in another. His daughter is a medical student who is married to a resident in medicine in a large New York Hospital. They have no children either and do not visit with the L family at all. Contact is made through the telephone. Ann's family also consists of an older daughter and younger son. The daughter lives in the New York area and is married to a physician. They have two small children, a four year old son and two year old daughter. There is very little contact with the daughter or her family on Ann's part. Though she can get to their home in a short time she sees her daughter about once a year. Again, the telephone is the main means of communication and they speak to each other about twice a month. Ann's son is married to a college student, they have no children. He does visit the L family about every other week, but without his wife. Mel has a sister who is seven years older than he with whom he has no contact. His mother died when he was eight and he lived with his father and sister for one year before being "shunted" out to various family members. His father died three years later and he had minimal contact with him. Mel lived with an aunt and uncle for about seven years, until he was about twenty. He had wirtten a letter to his sister who was living with another family member telling her how difficult his life had been. His uncle intercepted the letter and gave it to his aunt. Upon returning home, he found his clothes packed. He left, never to return or have contact with them again. Ann has two older sisters and a younger brother who was killed during the Second World War. Her oldest sister lives in North Carolina, is married and has what sounds like a psychotic twenty-eight year old son who lives with the family. The next oldest sister is married and lives in Albany. They have no children. Ann has not seen either sister in years though she occasionally gets a telephone call from the sister who lives in North Carolina, Mary, who has spent part of each summer for the past sixteen years in Vermont. There has been no contact with her other sister, Alice. Ann's mother died in 1963 and her father died in 1966. She was first married when she was nineteen years old and quite overprotected. Her parents were friendly with her first husband's parents and arranged the marriage. Her first husband, Fred, was quite cruel to her and they divorced. Her father had married Fred's mother after her mother died. When her father died he left everything to his wife, Fred's mother. She left everything to Fred, her only child, when she died. Fred is now living in New Jersey in a house bought in part by his inheritance of over one hundred thousand dollars which Ann feels really belonged to her since it was essentially left by her parents. She dates the onset of her drug taking as being in 1966, the date her stepmother died and left her former husband all of her family's money.

At the point of starting family therapy with me, Mrs. L was in a drug treatment program but they were having no success. Detoxification would be completed and she would again become addicted to demeral. Her husband was her supplier, writing prescriptions when he supposedly could no longer tolerate her frantic phone calls or banging the walls of her bedroom. His office was in the house and her noises could be heard. I knew nothing about the family when I started treatment except that it was a referral from the drug unit. My personal philosophy was that I would treat it as a system dysfunction so that the initial approach would be to see the interaction and fit it into the systems of origin. From there we would go wherever paydirt was to be found. The first session started with Ann feeling exposed and Mel saying it would be educational. All of my sessions were observed and videotaped. Mel began at once with talk about drugs, saying that he had to give them to her during the week because she was so upset and insistent on getting them. My initial statement about drugs was just about my last. I said I didn't want to talk about drugs because I didn't want to get addicted to them myself. Ann laughed and started to talk about her family, something she was used to doing in the drug program. She talked about being treated as a non-person by her oldest sister and her mother. Mel also began to talk about his family and gave the history of what happened to him after his mother died to when he left his aunt's house. When they were talking it became obvious to me that entree into both individual family systems and the one they created together could easily be through concepts of attachment and loss. I would have done so in some form anyway but here it was staring me in the face. I knew I would have to get to what the addiction meant for the two of them since he was so much a part of it, but I felt that could wait for later. My comment that neither one of them had been in a family yet was seconded by both of them. In direct response to my following statement that perhaps they would die without ever having a family, Mel talked about his struggles to work and get through school. It took him five years to get all the necessary prerequisites for college. He spoke of seeing his father's head bandaged and resolving to become a physician. When he finally got a letter of admittance to medical school, one of the first things he said to himself was that he wished his father could have seen it. He reminisced about his early life with his father and called his own like a "tragedy." The attachment concepts are clear as is the pain of separation. I told Ann that she had done a good job keeping Mel from dealing with his pain and suggested that she take three bottles of demeral a day so as to continue doing him a favor. Her response was nervous laughter. I felt I could gain entrance into the system by dealing with the current dynamic balance and utilize the early deprivations to cement current awareness. This would short circuit an in-depth analysis of early attachments which would likely lead nowhere as it had in the past. My next statement was one that pointed out the necessity for understanding the part drugs played in their mutual avoidance pattern. In order to broaden this to include other aspects of their lives I commented that they needed to know what besides drugs kept them together. Ann said she would like Mel to feel as bad as she did when he was so rotten to her in the beginning of their relationship. Mel's proposal consisted of him telling her that he had gotten a blood test; this was the signal. The tentativeness of their early attachment matched the early ones in their own family. The attachment to me, though it was an initial session, seemed strong. It was wish of course but also there was a reservoir of unfulfilled need which could be tapped and used to bind them together into a more trusting pattern of relating so that they could understand who they were for each other and deal with the introjects. Mel spoke freely of marrying his second wife for money. Ann accepted this and even encouraged him in that process. Part of the arrangement in his marriage to Ann was that she would sell her house and pay his sister an enormous debt. His sister was furious at having lost this hold over Mel. I pointed out that I would have to see the nuclear families of each of them. Both of them were looking for the same thing and could not get it from each other. When I said, "I don't know if I have enough food for both of you," Mel said that I was reaching him. He repeated this several times. In working with the parameter of loss, I introduced them to each other as long lost relatives and hoped they didn't stay lost. Their strength to deal with their lives despite considerable handicaps was stressed. When Ann talked about feeling stupid I pointed out that was her role in the family. Her mother and sister had chosen this role with the collusion of the father. This made considerable sense to her. She had been used to exploration of in-depth feelings on this issue but they were to no avail. She talked about recent and distant rejections from her family and I stressed that her role could be different in the current family system. Everything exploded for her when her mother died. This relates to the recrudescence of feelings of separation and loss.

One myth of their relationship was that Mel was the strong one and I exploded this by a simple statement about his posture. He could not straighten his body and could not shake off the effects of his feeling the lack of meaningful attachment. The system was altered in such a way as it could never get back to the original contract. Mel agreed with my statement that he was not living and talked a good deal about enjoying himself when he was in the Army overseas during the Second World War. Ann loosened up considerably and told me that she had been very nervous, expecting the session to be like the ones she had known where severe confrontational techniques were used. Ann and Mel then were able to talk about their feelings about each other's family and were quite supportive to each other. Ann said she wanted to know that Mel loved her. At that point he started to mention drugs as the reason he couldn't. I cut him short by telling him that he was addicted to drugs himself, her drugs. The session ended by my telling them they hadn't decided to live yet and that I didn't know whether they wanted to.

I have gone over the first session in such detail because something happened during the ensuing two weeks before the second session which allowed for a remarkable change to occur. It could only be understood as a system change for there was hardly time for a revision of basic character structure.

Mel and Ann again came without Joan for the second session. After some initial hesitation and embarrassed smiling, Ann said she was not taking any more pills. I asked Mel if he thought he could stand this and if he couldn't he should start taking pills. I also suggested to her that she could find another supplier. From my point of view I was testing the system change. Ann talked about things having changed for the better between the two of them. I tried to seize the moment to expand the family system and asked about Ann's older daughter coming to a session with her. This drew a blank; it was still too early. A great deal had happened and remained unassimilated. We started to talk about what I felt was a committment on their part to start living. Ann said that she did not feel Mel needed her; he was capable of doing everything hinself. They talked of their loneliness, of never going any place together or having a network of friends or family. Her disappointment in her older daughter was clearly stated. She felt used. Ann picked up on her family of origin and the rejection she felt as a child. She began chewing furiously on her tongue and lip, something which occurred frequently. Mel followed up quite naturally with his own loneliness and lack of positive attachment as a child in his family of origin. They were working together, not accusing one another or dragging up past hurts with one another. The idea of generational transmission within a systems concept was taking hold. Their relationship began to be opened up as Ann talked about her unfulfilled attachment needs. Mel listened carefully and did talk about how he saw Ann fitting into his life. This was the first time they had ever done this. Some of Ann's anger started to come out directly instead of via drugs as she did feel Mel's loving and his very real need for her. Their alienation from their own families had prevented them from touching each other. Mel's work addiction was touched on here. Ann's deep seated feeling that she could be replaced was now voiced. Again, I tried to bind the two of them rather than get at the deep rooted origins of the feeling. Mel was asked to try to feel what Ann was saying and he was very tnetatively able to begin to identify her needs as his own as well. They both were struggling with the pain of loss of meaningful attachment. Mel admitted sadly that he had never told anyone in his life how he really felt. There were some teachers with whom he had come close and with whom he still had meaningful if sporadic contact. At the end of this session Mel invited me to his house. I accepted and said that I had planned one of our sessions to be a home visit.

At the start of the third session Ann told me that she could not get her daughter to come in. This is the daughter of her first marriage, Nancy. She felt it was Nancy's husband, Joel, who was to blame. She will try to get her son to come. My focus for a while was on Mel's children and the lack of connection there. They both talked about wanting to get the whole family together but felt the children would simply not be interested. Ann talked about wanting Joan to come in but Mel vetoed it. He said she did not know what was going on. My statement that she knew very well what was going on was seconded by Ann. Mel said he would have Joan present at the next session. She apparently is having difficulty now and appears more fidgety. I interpreted this as a system phenomenon. As they became more responsible to themselves and each other Joan would need to find a new role. She hadn't had much of a chance to be a child. Joel came up in the session at this point in relation to Ann's feeling of loss. Mel talked about being snubbed; Joel would read the paper when he was there and so Mel decided not to go there anymore. Ann was very upset about Joel's mother doing the babysitting. Here was more proof of denial of membership in the family and keeping her as she was in the system. Mel talked of a teacher he had who treated him well, unlike Joe, even though that man was a specialist and Mel was a general practicioner. I connected this to the father Mel never had. Dealing with this internalized image was hard but the point was focused by me. I was convinced that the pain of the loss of family needed to be brought out in the open and an attempt needed to be made to reconnect. Talk about sex followed as Ann said that Mel does not want to come near her. Mel insisted it was pleasant for him. As they talked it was clear that the pain of destructive separation and fear of attachment played a major role here. Again, I reinforced the idea that drugs played a large role for both of them as a legitimate way of avoiding feeling, of avoiding living. Mel deals with his depression by work. He is up at five A.M. with nothing to do but work. His feeling that no one could help him was confronted directly by my asking him about me. He said he thought I could help him. My direction switched to his children again and we explored how he could get them to a session, how he could get reconnected. As the session ended he slapped me on the knee and put his hand on my shoulder.

Session number four was the first one in which Joan took part. She said she was a little nervous as she came in. Her mother told me that Joan was not sleeping well and that she wanted to come in; Joan promptly denied this. This was, in part, a loyalty response to her mother. She is with her mother to the exclusion of other kinds of relationships. Joan cried without apparent reason and Mel was very protective. The reversal of the parenting role was obvious. Ann said that Joan treated her as if she was a baby. My immediate response was that Ann was a baby but for very good reason and Joan had become the parentified child. I told Joan that she would not hurt her mother if she did not take care of her, and then told the entire family that the reason for Joan to be there was to learn to be the child in the family. My job would be to get Joan out from between them but not increase her guilt and fear of hurting her mother. I told Joan that she should help me and commented on her loving. The parents had done a good job with her. Joan smiled when I said this. The home visit was talked about and the appointment was made. We talked about Mel being like Ann's mother. She identified him this way because nobody could do anything for her mother either. This needed to be dealt with in object relations terms. The fear of loss for both of them was the strongest point here. Joan checked out everything with her mother through eye contact. Ann heard from her sister Mary who sent her a card from Vermont. Her husband called to tell them they had found a new way to get back so they didn't go through New York. Ann talked very longingly about wanting to see her sister but never being invited. Mary would not let anyone stay at her house; she always found a motel nearby. Joan had to stay in a motel when she visited them several years ago. It was clear that Joan hungered for family and wanted to see her aunt despite how she had been treated. Her aunt still sends her stuffed animals though Joan is eleven and quite big for her age.

The home visit was most interesting. First, the physical appearance of the house is contradicted by the poor way in which Ann takes care of herself. The house is warm and lovely. Ann makes gorgeous rugs that decorate the rooms and makes drapes and curtains as well. Her son Neal was there without his wife who was in school that evening. Nancy and Joel came also. Joel's coming surprised everyone including Nancy. He was very businesslike, wanting to get on with whatever I had in mind. Mel greeted me very warmly and was all smiles; Ann was much warmer than she could allow herself to be in the observed treatment sessions. She took pride in telling me she had done all the cooking and there was no interference from Mel. The session lasted about three hours and most of it was at the dinner table. As it turned out, Joe was quite supportive of Mel and was angry at Neal for how he treated his stepfather (Mel). Long held in feelings were aired but not in great anger. Ann's use of Mel to avoid her daughter and her grandchildren came out in the open very clearly. An entirely new picture of the extended family system was seen. Joel was very upset that Mel did not attend his father's funeral. Mel had no idea how hurt Joel was. Of course, none of those feelings was there to be seen at the time. The session ended with everyone feeling that better attachments could be made and that they were all part of a functioning unit with their own inputs.

The next family session began with Mel calling me Jer and Svengali. He felt I came in very respectfully and like a close friend. Ann said that Nancy told her she would like to have me at one of her parties. I pointed out the different picture I had of Ann and of Joel. My point about how collusive Ann and Mel are to keep Ann alone was seen and developed by them. My point about Joel was made even stronger by my talking about his affection for Mel. Mel told me he gave up his addiction, smoking. He is feeling better and his cough is gone. I then suggested the two of them might try to get into the same bed together. During the home visit I had seen that Mel slept in the master bedroom and Ann slept in Joan's bed. Joan used the spare room. They told me that they had in fact gotten into the same bed and that Joan had gone back to her room. The bed in the spare room was dismantled. I told them that I felt my task would now be to get out of their bed so they could be there together. Mel told me that I shouldn't do it too fast and that I should not go too far. At this session Ann brought up the idea of termination. She wanted to know when we would stop. I said we could consider stopping at the end of June. Mel wanted to be sure I would be available if needed and I said I would; Ann seemed relieved. She said she never thought she would feel better and told me she could never have done it on her own. I said she could never have done it alone but was doing it on her own. It is very difficult for Ann to allow herself to feel competent. Mel talked about seeing his son years ago. This was the last time he saw him. I talked of the longing gnawing at him and the fact that he can do something about being a father to his children now. "Before you die, Mel, you ought to do something with your kids," was the way I put it. He looked sad and then thought he could do something this summer.

Joan was in at the next session. I made a deal with her involving her calling me if she wanted to talk to me about anything. It was difficult because of her attachment to her mother and role in the family. I was attempting to increase the opening I had made in the tight family system. Joan said her parents were closer together. Ann said the two of them now are even talking to each other in the middle of the night. They talked about retiring. Mel felt he could not afford to though Ann talked wistfully about traveling. To my comment that they ought to do some more together before they are dead, Ann replied that Mel tells her he can't buy a ticket for something in the future because he may be dead by then. I talked about the transmission from his father and the internalization of the dictum that he did not deserve to feel good. He said that he was surprised he got married because he enjoys being alone so much. It was clear they were just learning to live together and were indeed establishing a new open family system which would eventually include their children. Ann ended the session by supporting my contention that they could always concoct something to keep them apart.

The next family session corroborated what I had thought was happening. Mel talked about going with Ann to a family get-together at Neal's wife's grandparents' home. Ann had initiated going to Nancy's home and also getting Neal there. Both of them talked about a real change in Joel; everyone agreed something dramatic had happened. Joel even offered Neal a cigar. Symbol or not, this was the first concrete item Joel had ever offered Neal. Mel talked about what I had seen between him and Joel, particularly about Joel's father's funeral. He could see Joel's need. Both Ann and Mel talked about going to New York City for the first time in years. They even took a walk on the deserted boardwalk in Coney Island. They were not able to go alone yet, as Ann said she wanted, for Joan was there; but it was a giant step for them. They were able to risk losing without resorting to being addicted. More talk about how they could get together followed. Ann brought up the fact that Mel's daughter was having a baby yet he could not say anything about it. The longing for a family is so great and he is so frightened. Mel responded by a family ploy, denegrating himself. This was to avoid the possible rejection of telling her that he can't be everything for her. This is a family myth from early times in many families. The parenting one will be there all the time, unconditionally. Mel was able to talk about work as interfering with holidays. This was a revelation for the rest of the family. They have started planning for the summer. It was as long ago as 1960 that they last went away for a weekend. Mel tried using drugs as an excuse in a last ditch effort. When I confronted him directly he caved in and admitted to wanting to be loved, cared for.

Ann was actually bubbling during the next session. She had received a phone call from Mary and made an appointment to have lunch with her. They finally met for the first time in years and Ann could see the reality of her sister. Mary is a woman with a horrible marriage and a psychotic adult son. The two sisters talked about their family of origin a bit, but mostly about how they could plan to get together soon. The entire session was spent talking about Ann's feeling of connectedness.

The last session gave focus to what had happened and where they thought they could go together. They did go on vacation with Joan. Mel did take a book but did not open it. He was able to relax and not concern himself with the office. They plan to go away again the next month. Mel went to see his mentor who told him he felt something was quite different about him. His colleagues at the hospital could not believe he could leave his work and go away. They all perceived him as being different. Ann wrote a letter to her sister in Albany asking to get together and did get a tentative "yes" in a letter she received back rather quickly. I worked hard at focusing the transmission process in both their families of origin. Ann was able to remember for the first time that her mother told her that if she, the mother, left her with her father, Ann would be killed by the father. Ann believed it and remembered being frightened when her father grabbed her by the arm to show her how to use the garage door. The internalized image was discussed. Ann talked about her sister in Albany again. She hasn't seen her in about thirty-five years. Separation from their families and separation from each other was the theme.

Mel now wants to get together with the entire extended family system and I encouraged it. Both of them had plans to do this both horizontally and vertically.

This synopsis of the treatment sessions points out the use of system theory in conjunction with attachment theory. I feel these can be integrated into a consistent theory of family and individual development. We can then treat introjects and projections as part of the system instead of purely intrapsychic which they surely are not, but that is another paper. Further work is needed before the process is complete but it is a way to intervene at a current point in the system so as to connect to the past and the future.

Bibliography

1. Ainsworth, Mary. The Development of Infant-Mother Attachments. In Caldwell, B. and Ricciuti, N. (Eds.), Review of Child Development Research, Vol. III. Chicago. University of Chicago Press, 1973.
2. Arieti, Silvano E. Discussion of Ludwig von Bertalanffy's paper, General Systems Theory and Psychiatry—An Overview. In Gray, William; Duhl, Frederick J.; Rizzo, Nicholas D. (Eds.), General Systems Theory and Psychiatry. Boston. Little, Brown and Co., 1969.
3. Bertalanffy, Ludwig von. General Systems Theory and the Behavioral Sciences. In Tanner, J.M. and Inhelder, Barbara (Eds.), Discussions on Child Development, Vol. IV. London. Tavistock Publications, 1960.
4. Bertalanffy, Ludwig von. General System Theory and Psychiatry. In Arieti, S. (Ed.), American Handbook of Psychiatry. Vol. III. New York. Basic Books, 1966.
5. Blum, Richard N. and Associates. Horatio Alger's Children. San Francisco. Jossey-Bass, Inc., 1972.
6. Bowen, Murray. The Use of Family Theory in Clinical Practice. In Haley, Jay (Ed.) Changing Families. New York. Grune and Stratton, 1973.
7. Bowlby, John. Attachment and Loss, Vol. I: Attachment. New York. Basic Books, 1969.
8. Bowlby, John. Attachment and Loss, Vol. II: Separation. New York, Basic Books, 1973.
9. Fairbairn, W. Ronald. Psychoanalytic Studies of the Personality. London, Routtledge and Kegan, Paul Ltd, 1972.
10. Fenichel, Otto. The Psychoanalytic Theory of Neurosis. New York, W.W. Nortan and Co., Inc., 1945.
11. Freud, Sigmund. Inhibitions, Symptons and Anxiety. Standard Edition, 20. London. Nogarthy, 1959.
12. Harlow, Harry F. The Development of Affectional Patterns in Infant Monkeys. In Foss, B.M. (Ed.), Determinants of Infant Behavior, Vol. I. New York. John Wiley and Sons, 1961.
13. Sonne, John C. Entropy and Family Therapy: Speculations on Psychic Energy, Thermodynamics, and Family Interpsychic Communication. In Zuk, Gerald H. and Boszormenyi-Nagy, Ivan (Eds.), Family Therapy and Disturbed Families. Palo Alto, Calif. Science and Behavior Books, Inc., 1969.

Chapter 16

THE TREATMENT OF SMOKING HABITUATION AND SELECTIVE DRUG DEPENDENCY AND ABUSE WITH HYPNOTHERAPY

Milton V. Kline, Ed.D

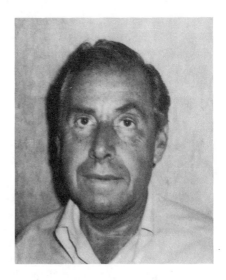

Milton V. Kline, Ed.D.

Dr. Kline is Director of The Institute for Research in Hypnosis and The Morton Prince Center for Hypnotherapy. He is the Chairman of the Council of Professional and Scientific Advisors of The International Graduate School of Behavioral Sciences and is in private practice.

A variety of approaches and methods have been employed in dealing with the problem of smoking habituation. Many individuals are capable of elimi-° nating smoking voluntarily with little apparent difficulty and without withdrawal behavior of any significance. Others require psychological help; this type of help has ranged from educational approaches in smoking clinics to more formalized psychotherapeutic procedures, including the use of hypnosis, either as a motivational or aversive technique. Individual hypnotherapy, ranging from one to four or five sessions, has generally indicated whether this modality would be effective for a patient with this problem. Crasilneck and Hall (1968) have presented a well-documented and controlled investigation of the use of hypnosis in the treatment of smoking habituation, and their statistical results generally coincide with those that have been clinically observed and reported. Follow-up studies after a period of one year indicated that 64 percent of the individuals acceptable for hypnotherapy in connection with smoking habituation were still not smoking.

On the other hand, *the drop-outs,* the recidivists, those who are unable to profit from any educational or therapeutic approach, have continued to constitute a significant hard-core group of smokers. For this group, smoking may frequently be not only undesirable in terms of its general implications, but also actually contraindicated in terms of presenting physiological evidence of emergent pathological medical conditions.

Part of the patient population described in this paper consisted of a group of individuals who had made serious attempts to stop smoking, first on their own, and then with professional help. Many had attended smoking clinics, psychotherapy sessions, and a significant number had received hypnotherapy in an attempt to deal with this problem. All had failed.

All participants in the 12-hour group hypnotherapy session, beginning at 10 A.M. and terminating at 10 P.M., were required to refrain from smoking for 24 hours prior to appearing in the group.[1] The effectiveness of hypnosis in altering the characteristics of dysphoria was noted almost immediately in a large number of participants. Polygraph recordings taken during an initial interview prior to the group session while the participants were still smoking were compared with recordings, taken upon first entering the group situation and then again some time later, following the use of hypnosis as a prolonged relaxation and desensitizing procedure.

The polygraph was utilized to record upper thoracic breathing and midthoracic breathing as well as GSR and blood pressure variations. For the purposes of this study, the upper thoracic respiratory tracings are presented. Previous studies have shown that tension states are readily recognized through breathing patterns and that the influence of hypnosis on respiratory patterning is both distinct and reliable (Kline, 1967). The tracings reported here are typical and representative of most of the patients in this treatment group.

Although the recording for each patient represents approximately a 2-minute interval, in each instance the segments reported were of the same pattern consistency for as long as 15 to 20 minutes in tension states, and for as long as 40 to 50 minutes in relaxed states. Although in a therapeutic situation, subjective reports do have clinical validity, utilization of respiratory tracings gives a more objective indication of the presence of tension, regardless of verbal reports by the patient, and of the effectiveness of hypnosis in establishing relaxation and homeostasis. Showing patients their respiratory tracings recorded during tension states and using hypnotically induced relaxation states has also proven valuable as a feedback device.

During the 12-hour period, patients were required to have visual, tactile, and olfactory contact with cigarettes of their own choosing, but no oral involvement. Periods of hypnosis were used to intensify the need to smoke, and these were followed by relaxation and hypnotically induced sensory gratification of a tactile, oral and olefactory nature.

While in the group situation hypnotic desensitization might be directed in a rotational manner toward one member of the group at a time, our findings indicate that the effects rapidly become somewhat generalized and are often transmitted to the others. Some members of the group also observed that although they had experienced hypnosis previously (usually with minimal response to induction and certainly with minimal response to alterations in their smoking behavior), the hypnotic experience within the group significantly potentiated their own involvement in hypnosis and the degree to which they could experience a reduction in smoking deprivation behavior.

The rationale for both the intensification of tension associated with deprivation and the capability of reducing this tension, initially through therapeutic approaches and eventually through self-hypnosis, is consistent with the concept of desensitization. Desensitization permits the individual to experience, within a therapeutic framework, variables in his own behavior which are discomforting. This process allows for an increasing reduction in discomfort and an allaying of the anxiety associated with its uncontrollable characteristics. Although the concept of reciprocal inhibition may be applied in this context in a broader approach, the use of a desensitizing hypnotherapeutic approach enables the patient to gain a sense of self-mastery in being able to anticipate tension states without the anxiety that is associated with an uncontrollable experience, and to acquire a readiness to manage his own tension in an effective and readily available manner. Within this framework, the earlier emphasis on the ability to create and maintain a state of psychophysiological homeostasis had been reflective and indicative of positive and lasting therapeutic gains with the use of hypnotherapy (Kline, 1969).

Each patient was seen for a brief initial interview of 30 minutes. During discussion with the patient, an assessment of motivating factors for eliminating smoking was made. Hypnotic productivity was evaluated clinically, and a polygraph record of respiration and GSR patterns was obtained. A brief orientation was given to each patient, describing the nature of the treatment process: A group of 10 patients would meet together at 10 A.M. and remain together until 10 P.M.

In addition, patients were instructed that, for 24 hours before the group session, they were to eliminate all smoking. All patients agreed to this condition, and it was further understood that if they could not follow the request, they would notify the therapist, and a date for another group session would be set when they could comply with this requirement. The importance of this criterion was stressed as an essential ingredient of the therapeutic process.

Each patient was instructed to bring an unopened pack of his favorite cigarettes. When the group assembled, the general orientation which had been presented in the initial individual sessions was amplified. The group was told that during the 12 hours they would be together, the focal topic of discussion would be the desire to eliminate smoking and the recognition of those feelings which made the elimination of smoking difficult. Each member of the group was then instructed to open his pack of cigarettes and place them on a small table near his chair. Hypnosis, which had been induced individually in the initial sessions, was again induced individually in a rotational manner, and when the entire group was in a state of hypnosis, relaxation was produced for the entire group for a period of 15 minutes. Following this period, there was no formal termination of hypnosis, but simply instructions to open the eyes. There was no indication that there would be an alteration of the hypnotic state, but the suggestion was given that increased relaxation would be available when needed. Patients were instructed to recognize the onset of tension throughout the entire course of the therapy session and to bring it to the attention of both the group and the therapist as soon as recognized. At this time additional direct hypnosis or self-hypnosis was used to reestablish relaxation and, at times, if indicated, to permit discussion for clarification of the nature of the tension; this discussion, in itself, would frequently have a relaxing effect without further recourse to hypnosis.

Discussion was initiate about how the group members were reacting to the period of smoking deprivation from the day before. The various expressions of this deprivation were contrasted and evaluated within the group setting. Most members indicated a strong desire to smoke, a feeling of some tension in not being able to smoke, and considerable anxiety that they would not able to give up this habit. Deprivation behavior as experienced and expressed by the group was discussed and interpreted by the therapist. The significance of deprivation as a psychological reaction was singled out as the more important consideration in the treatment of smoking habituation.

Techniques to Intensify Smoking Deprivation

Following the period of relaxation, the group was told that it would undertake a series of procedures designed to intensify the feelings of smoking deprivation. A discussion of the various characteristics and patterns of smoking for each member of the group was undertaken in order to indicate in which context each individual experienced the strongest desire to smoke and obtained the greatest pleasure from smoking. For example, many patients indicated that they greatly enjoyed a cigarette with a cup of coffee or following eating. Others indicated they enjoyed smoking when involved in discussions with others, either on a social or business basis, and that intensive interpersonal experiences tended to make them reach for cigarettes.

An evaluation of some of the sensory factors involved in smoking gratification for the various members of the group was presented by the therapist: Many group members liked the feel of a cigarette in their hands. They liked the sensation of holding the cigarette and frequently they held cigarettes more than they actually puffed them. Others revealed the tremendous satisfaction gained from the inhalation of smoke and the respiratory sensations that accompanied inhalation. It became clear that a variety of sensory experiences were involved for each group of smokers, with some individuals finding satisfaction closely related to sensory experiences in the throat and the respiratory apparatus, and others finding tactile and kinesthetic sensations of equal, if not greater, significance.

Techniques to intensify deprivation were undertaken through the use of hypnosis. After each individual had described those characteristics which gave him the greatest pleasure, hypnosis was used to intensify the sensations of touching, holding, and inhaling, emphasizing specifically those qualities the patient himself had described as being most stimulating and satisfying. Along with this, vivid imagery of the smoking process was suggested. During this phase of therapy with each individual patient, the other members of the group were requested to pick up their cigarettes, to hold them, to smell them, but not under any conditions to place them in their mouths. They were instructed that they were free to touch, to hold, and to smell the cigarettes whenever they wished. They were also told that when they were requested to do this as part of the group process, it was mandatory that they participate in the group experience. At times, the entire group was asked to hold cigarettes, to smell them, and, along with these actions, to visualize themselves smoking through hypnotic visual imagery. At no time were they permitted to place cigarettes in their mouths.

Oral stimulation was produced in a variety of ways. The use of the tongue to lice the lips as a form of erotic stimulation was requested on a group and individual basis along with imagery of smoking. Coffee was available and was of a decaffeinated nature so that the element of caffeine, itself, would not be unduly stressed. Minimal amounts of food and other beverages were also available.

Following each intensification of smoking deprivation, hypnosis was used in a systematic manner to produce complete relaxation. Hypnotically induced gratification similar to that which had been reported following smoking was induced first by the therapist and then by each patient using self-hypnosis.

All hypnotic relaxation procedures immediately followed the intensification of deprivation behavior and visual imagery of smoking. During a typical hour, some 10 to 15 minutes would be spent in the intensification of smoking deprivation and the remaining time devoted to discussion and interpretation of these feelings along with the induction of relaxation. Approximate imagery selected and constructed by each patient was incorporated into the stress reduction phase (Kline, 1965). As part of the exposure to deprivation situations to which the patient must adapt in effective smoking control, an assistant was present who smoked cigarettes frequently. The therapist himself did not smoke.

Patients were encouraged to report their continuous subjective feelings and, in addition, certain objective evaluations and observations were made. These included periodic recordings of polygraph responses measuring respiration and GSR. Blood pressure and pulse rates were also obtained for each member of the group at various times throughout the sessions. Measurements were taken during intensification of deprivation and following periods of stress reduction and hypnotic relaxation. A room adjoining the group therapy room was equipped with a polygraph and apparatus for measuring blood pressure and pulse rate; these measurements were taken by the research assistant.

Follow-up studies indicate that the use of a group therapy situation of a time-extended nature in which hypnosis is used first to intensify deprivation behavior and then, within the same setting, to reduce psychophysiological manifestations of deprivation reactions (Kline, 1969; Kline, Wick, and Sigman, in press), has produced, for the group of patients studied here, significantly better results in the control of smoking than have been produced through individual hypnotherapy.

Previous studies have indicated that smoking withdrawal may affect brain functions. Hauser, Schwartz, Ross, and Bickford (1964), reported study by Ulett and Itil (1969), have demonstrated that a significant increase in slow-wave EEG activity following smoking deprivation is a typical sign of decreased vigilance. This finding is consistent with the view of cigarette smoking as a complex psychosomatic phenomenon similar to other habituation disorders. These studies indicated that the electrocortical changes were in the direction of what is usually classified as EEG abnormality.

The effectiveness of hypnosis in altering the characteristics of dysphoria, reducing stress states, and, in general, controlling the behavioral concomitants of smoking deprivation, tends to be associated with the capacity of individual patients to eliminate cigarette smoking. This relationship is consistent with a concept of desensitization and homeostasis associated with the treatment of a wide range of emotional disorders and psychophysiological disturbances (Kline, 1968, 1969; Kline and Linder, 1967). The effectiveness of this form of hypnotherapy would seem to be related to the capacity to obtain relief from the discomfort of deprivation behavior. Although, as Bernstein (1969) pointed out, it is difficult to evaluate which factors in the total treatment of smoking habituation are responsible for change, this evaluation is not essentially different from the problem of determining which variables play the critical role in any type of therapeutic change, particularly when a number of different therapeutic contexts are involved.

The specific influence of hypnosis in creating freedom from deprivation behavior and from the psychophysiological mechanisms which are associated with dysphoria is consistent with the work reported by Kline and Linder (1967), indicating that in the face of intensified emotional stress, particularly involving abreactive components, the hypnotic experience tends to create a state of homeostasis. The maintenance or the reinduction and reinforcement of homeostasis would seem to be essential ingredients for increasing the degree of voluntary behavior which individuals are capable of exercising in conflict situations; they constitute important factors in the therapeutic results obtained through hypnotherapy. Relaxation of the sort that is obtained within the hypnotherapeutic context would seem to be a significantly more complex phenomenon than simple muscular or skeletal relaxation (Kline, 1969; Kline and Linder, 1967).

Clinical Cases in Related Instances of Drug Dependency, Habituation and Abuse

Although our clinical-experimental studies of the use of hypnotherapeutic approaches in the treatment of cigarette habituation and of feeding disorders in relation to dependency factors have not extended into experimental investigations with drug addiction from other sources, there has been considerable use of hypnotherapy based upon techniques similar to those related to smoking behavior which, on a clinical basis has been used in treating a variety of such presenting problems.

Case 1. Methodone Addiction

The literature on Methodone is extensive, contrasting and at times conflicting, but definitive positions have been taken with regard to its uses as a therapeutic alternative for heroin addiction. It is clearly recognized that Methodone produces a subjective change parallel to those produced by heroine and is about as potent as morphine when both are given subcutaneously. Methodone certainly produces a physical dependence by morphine except that the onset of the abstenance syndrome is slower. Difficulties in detoxifying patients on Methodone are well known and in a number of instances where patients were strongly motivated to do so, they have been treated on hypnotic levels.

A twenty-seven year old married woman who had been on a Methodone program for three years with a gradual reduction of the Methodone from 100 mg to 25 mg was seen when in the course of trying to reduce below the 25 mg level, withdrawal symptoms had become unmanageable. She was very anxious to be free of Methodone and had achieved good results in slowly moving down to the 25 mg level, but once going below that, she would experience some degree of depersonalization, extreme anxiety and an inability to function in terms of dealing with her work assignments which up to that time she had managed quite well. She also complained of severe physical pains throughout the whole body, incapacitating nausea, and a general sense of being "sick."

Hypnosis was used for producing at first a generalized state of relaxation and alteration in pain and other signs of discomfort and at the same time a recollection visually and on a sensory basis of the experience of well being which could be recalled very accurately and with strong subjective feeling during hypnosis.

This patient was taught to use self hypnosis with an occular fixation technique and then to use a tape recording for induction at times when she, herself, did not feel capable of beginning the process herself. Over a period of six weeks, she gradually reached the point where all Methodone was withdrawn. During the intense period of withdrawal symptoms daily use of hypnotherapy and self hypnosis was employed for those 6 weeks. At the end of that time, she was able to use the self hypnosis several times a day and was seen on an office visit basis once a week. These visits were finally cut to once a month, although the self hypnosis continued on a daily basis of two to three times. The patient always had the option of using greater amounts of self hypnosis or diminishing it, based upon the demands of her own personal situation. Six months after being first seen, this patient no longer required hypnotherapy, although she continued to use the self hypnosis once or twice a week for generalized relaxation. She no longer had any withdrawal symptoms, was functioning well, and returned to graduate school which she had left a number of years before.

Case 2

A fifty-five year old woman was seen at the request of her internist because of a barbiturate dependency to alleviate insomnia, that had extended for a period of twenty-five years. The amount of Seconol that was consumed was excessive and the patient could not sleep without it. Hypnosis was, at first, difficult to induce, but after approximately ten or twelve hours, the patient began to experience increasingly deeper states of hypnosis and ultimately entered a medium state within which she could experience complete relaxation, sensory and motor alterations and respond to simple post hypnotic suggestion. Self hypnosis was taught by the use of tape and gradually, Seconol consumption was reduced from her presenting level to complete withdrawal within a period of three weeks. During this time, withdrawal symptoms were negligible although in the past when she had attempted to stop Seconol on her own, apart from the insomnia, she would become severely depressed and irritable.

During the period of hypnotherapy which extended over some four months, the patient was able gradually to learn to sleep by the use of self hypnosis and within two weeks of withdrawal from Seconol, had no significant subjective withdrawal symptoms. A one year follow-up indicated the patient still using self-hypnosis, and sleeping quite normally for a period of seven to nine hours each night.

Case 3. Methadrine Habituation

A twenty-eight year old unmarried woman was seen for habituation to Methadrine. She originally had been given Methadrine in order to suppress her appetite and deal with a weight problem that reflected a variety of personality difficulties for which she had received psychotherapy over a period of several years.

Her initial motivation for help was prompted by the fact that her source of Methadrine had been cut off by the death of the physician who had been supplying her with weekly amounts and at the time she was first seen, she had up to that period been taking an average of ten to fifteen tablets of Methadrine daily.

Withdrawal symptoms included agitation, depression, insomnia, a variety of somatic complaints and the expression suicidal thoughts. Hypnosis was readily induced in this patient and almost from the beginning, all withdrawal symptoms could be reversed and eliminated both during hypnosis and post hypnotically, for a period of five to six hours. The patient was taught to use self hypnosis and also to employ tape recording for reinforcement. Supportive psychotherapy along with the hypnosis was maintained for a period of three and one-half months, during which time virtually no withdrawal symptoms were present. The patient was discharged with the recommendation that self hypnosis continue to be used. Follow-up study one year later indicated that the patient was married, pregnant, leading a normal life, with relatively little use of the self hypnosis except at times of some stress and in no way seeking alternative drug involvement. She was seen following the birth of a normal healthy male child and again was given some help in relation to the recurrent feeding disturbance which now seemed to be quite manageable on a hypnotic level.

In similar manner, a number of patients dependent upon drugs such as Quaalude, Valium, Meprobinil, Biphetamine and Ritalin have been seen for essentially drug abuse problems. For the greater part, when there has been positive motivation and a reasonably high degree of hypnotic susceptibility, the results have been positive and achievable within one or two months, at times with only supportive therapy, and at other times with more intensive psychotherapy.

These results are consistent with the report by Martin (1974) on the reduction of adolescent drug abuse through the use of post hypnotic cue associations in which all patients treated by him were involved in a total number of sessions ranging from six to fifteen and follow up study of six months indicated that in all cases, drug abuse had virtually stopped and no serious substituted behavior was reported subjectively by the patients, their family or school.

In taking a somewhat generalized view of the area of addiction, Wikler (1973) reports on the dynamics of drug dependence and submits a conditioning theory for research and treatment. He believes that drug dependence is largely a consequence of certain rather subtle pharmalogic actions of drugs of abuse coupled with equally subtle conditioning processes and concludes that control of drug availability however possible is essential for prevention. In this connection the World Health Organization has stressed that the term "psychic dependence" is a feature common to all types of drug dependence. There is a feeling of satisfaction and a psychic drive requiring periodic or continuous drug administration to produce pleasure or avoid discomfort. This concept has strong common sense appeal. In the tolerant and physically dependent drug uses, each dose is said merely to stave off or suppress the "pain" associated with abstinence phenomena. Relapse is due to the craving aroused by the memory of the "pleasures" experienced before in the state of psychic dependence. A conditioning hypothesis can be used as a model here with drug dependency defined as habitual drug using behavior that is contingent for its maintenance on pharmacologic and, usually, social reinforcement. Social reinforcement of drugs and of drug use is the function not only of mythologies about drug effects but also cultural, political and economic conditions and, obviously, requires an overall perspective for its complete management.

Drug abuse is, perhaps, a vaster problem than is generally recognized since it is not always reportable, and statistics regarding it are essentially inaccurate. Much drug abuse is the result of self medication by patients with access to prescriptions or, at times, the purchasing of such prescription drugs illegally. In the instances of abuse that occur within the framework of patients seen for psychotherapy, this being an increasingly prevalent issue, management of such problems with the use of the hypnotherapy utilizing techniques that have been described in relation to the treatment and management of cigarette habituation have been, for the greater part, gratifyingly successful.

In attempting to develop an adequate frame of reference to understand the manner in which hypnosis, as a treatment modality, contributes to the essentially psychotherapeutic management of habituation behavior, addictive or addictive-like behavior and drug abuse behavior, it is necessary to examine some of the observable phenomena that occur with the use of hypnosis in such treatment context. In essence, the role of hypnosis both through its induction, maintenance and reinforcement of hypnotically induced reactions via self hypnosis, is designed to maintain freedom from the withdrawal behavior which is presented in each individual instance and, at the same time, to prevent the emergence of alternative signs of stress and symptomatology.

To summarize the present clinical position with regard to the therapeutic gain derived from hypnotherapy in the instances described in this paper, one might say that such therapeutic gain is the result of desensitization and homeostasis achieved both through the hypnotic experience, the post hypnotic alteration in behavioral functions and the maintenance of this newly achieved state through self hypnotic reinforcement.

In this connection, a study by O'Connell and Orne (1968) has suggested that the kind of central relaxation that is involved with hypnosis is not simply muscular since electrodermal activity which is not muscular in origin but rather autonomic, is reported in experimental investigations.

This is supported by our polygraphic observations over a period of a number of years. Patients during prolonged hypnotic relaxation reveal a persistence of relaxation and a reduction in stress and sensory disturbances that seem to be different from that produced by simple muscular relaxation. Blood glucose levels of diabetic and normal subjects show that hypnosis brings about homeostatic mechanisms of a very consistent nature and can produce a sense of well being.

Maiolo, Porro and Granone (1969) found that the hypnotic state, while not different from the normal in hemodynamics and metabolism, did show significantly lower standard deviations in the distribution of response for patients in hypnotic states as opposed to waking states. They concluded that homeostatic factors appeared to be significantly greater for patients in hypnosis than in non hypnotic states, using themselves as their own controls.

Black and Friedman (1968) found that hypnotic anesthesia produced a significant effect on the pituitary-adrenal access to pain. Black and Wigan (1961) found increased heart rate as the conditioned response can be abolished in hypnotic deafness. To Black and Walter (1965), these findings suggest that possible cerebral levels where hypnotic blocking takes place at least with regard to hearing are probably at some point below the frontal cortex but above heart and regulating centers in the medula, and at the level of the hypothalamus.

Our own clinical investigations have demonstrated that hypnosis can initiate abreaction to sensory intensification with imagery which are related to significant alterations in polygraphic functions.

It would appear that through the use at times, of the intensification of sensory and motor functions with silent, if not overt abreaction, there is followed a period of lessened cortico-hypothalamic-cortical relations. There, thus, emerges a relaxed state which upon clinical observation, polygraph assessment resembles a state of complete quiescence. This quiescence produces relaxation which frequently is so great as to have not only momentary but persistent therapeutic value for a very considerable period of time, and leads to the maintenance of newly acquired behavioral reactions.

Hypnosis and Conditionability[2]

In the main, contemporary work with hypnosis has emphasized the emerging distinction between the hypnotic state and the hypnotic relationship. This distinctiveness permits a clarified awareness of the process of hypnotic response and the alterations in behavior organizing mechanisms which may accompany this response formation. It would seem invalid to consider hypnosis as a singular phenomenon, but more realistically as a process of adaption within which there are varied and selective shifts in receptor and effector mechanisms (Kline 1961, 1963, 1965, 1967).

Within such a process, one concept which emerges in present-day thinking about hypnosis is that the multiphasic aspects of the hypnotic process and of hypnotic behavior which result from a fundamentally central process take on the form of the behavioral structure within which the experience of hypnosis is organized. There can be as sharp a differential in response formation within the hypnotic process as outside it, thus obviating the recognition of the nature of hypnosis via the expression of simplistic or one dimensional responses. The nature of hypnosis is inherently bound up with the meaning or the function of the experience. Experiential involvement in the hypnotic process must be studied from both the intrapsychic and interpersonal levels of involvement. It is not unlikely that, at the present time, different theories of hypnosis represent operational examples of different mechanisms of function within the hypnotic process.

Ultimately, all who use hypnosis must face a basic problem: the relationship of hypnosis to other dimensions of behavior. For example, what is the relationship of hypnosis to conditioning? Clinical observations suggest that when one deals with human conditioning and examines the effects of human conditioning it is not infrequent that one may be observing the results of a hypnotic experience and of a hypnotic process underlying this aspect of behavior. The basic process of conditioning and of the induction of a conditioned response is by its repetitiousness and reinforcement similar to and suggestive of hypnotic procedure. On the other hand, the conditioned response which is acquired in a laboratory situation may show sharply different characteristics.

A conditioned response of a nonhypnotic type shows a pattern of extinction, tends to go into somewhat more rapid extinction, whereas the "conditioned" response which appears to be the result of hypnosis frequently displays much greater strength and tenacity.

In an earlier study during the investigation of reactions of amputees to prosthetic adjustment, the writer (1959) became concerned with the problem of conditioning and found that it was difficult to produce relatively simple conditioned responses in human subjects, but when the same approach was utilized within a hypnotic situation, conditioning appeared to be achieved rapidly and, in a number of instances, could not be extinguished quickly even though this was the experimental objective (Kline 1952). There has not been a great deal of systematic work dealing with the effect of hypnosis upon conditionability either in experimental settings or in relation to therapeutic applications. Russian investigators have, drawing upon Pavlovian theory, extended concepts of conditioning and conditionability in relation to hypnotherapy in a wide range of applications, but due to differences in definition of terms and interpretation of theoretical constructs, the data is not readily applicable to the manner in which hypnosis may be viewed and utilized in behavioral science studies in countries outside the Soviet sphere (Kline 1959).

Nevertheless, Edmonston (1972) has reviewed and presented the most distinct and comprehensive data on the effects of neutral hypnosis on conditioned responses which bears some relation to the main issue under discussion now. Edmonston, in reviewing his data (1972) essentially presents an experimental analysis of Pavlov's cortical inhibition theory of hypnosis. This theory indicates that as hypnosis deepens, there is interference with the voluntary but not with the involuntary components of conditioned responses, due to a progressive spread of cortical inhibition. Edmonston clearly points out that earlier experimental work on this prediction has been sparce and inconclusive. On his own part, in a series of carefully and methodically converging studies, he analyzes and interprets the complexities, the experimental flaws and the inaccurate interpretations inherent in the research that has centered on the Pavlov position.

In the main, he has concluded that hypnotic studies have been concerned primarily with the effects of complex hypnotic phenomena such as amnesia and age regression on conditioned responses or the effect of hypnotic induction on complex motor and verbal learning. Conditioned responses and their relation to hypnosis have been of primary concern to the Russian investigators. Pavlov (1927) in his early work concluded that hypnosis brought about a prolonged, monotonous and environmental stimulation, created in the cells of the cortex a state of radiated inhibition. In this respect, he was quite clear that the portion of the central nervous system involved in hypnosis, the cortex, was such that he said, "We are dealing with a complete inhibition confined exclusively to the cortex, without a concurrent dissent of the inhibition that centers regularly in the equilibrium and maintenance of posture." He further added, "Thus, in the form of sleep (hypnosis) the plane of demarcation between inhibited regions of the brain and the regions which are free from inhibitions seem to pass just beneath the cerebral cortex."

Edmonston concluded from a survey of the scanty experimental data that there is "no clear cut conclusion as to the fate of previously established conditioned responses following the induction of hypnosis." (Plapp and Edmonston, 1965).

Based on his own work, Edmonston (1972) further concluded that voluntary motor functions are inhibited by hypnotic induction just as Pavlov indicated that they would be and that nonvoluntary functions appear not to be. Clinical experience utilizing a variety of sensory-motor techniques in hypnotherapy (Kline, 1971) have indicated that a wide range of symptomatic responses which are on an involuntary level and function in many respects like conditioned responses can be readily altered, modified and removed without alteration in the homeostatic equilibrium of the patient. Likewise, in a number of situations, it has been observed that hypnotically induced responses and modifications or alterations in behavior can be induced directly and through self-hypnotic reinforcement maintained over a long period of time and assume many of the characteristics of an acquired conditioned response.

Thus, to all intents and purposes, without going into some of the involved and overly determined methodological issues relative to conditioning and its role in both neurotic behavior and psychotherapy, there is strong evidence that the process of conditionability is one which can be influenced by hypnosis and one which hypnosis has an inherent relationship to, and can be incorporated within the therapeutic process. As such, the entire sphere of communication theory within psychotherapy must be considered as an aspect of the conditionability process.

While the Soviet work, were it to be reviewed and analyzed in detail, would constitute a study of its own, it is nevertheless interesting to make references to various aspects of what they refer to as cortical dynamics, particularly the coactivity and interactivity of the first and second signaling systems during hypnosis which have been studied to a limited degree, but nevertheless present provocative observations which are pertinent to therapeutic theory and concept. R.M. Pen and M.P. Dzhagarov (1936) carried out research into the formation of conditioned responses during hypnosis and concluded that the establishment of a new conditioned response was not readily obtained in deep hypnotic states but was very possible during light hypnotic states although characterized by some difficulties. The conditioned response which was established was in their observations, characterized by a certain amount of frailty. At the same time, these investigators succeeded in observing a state of hypnosis within which a disappearance of conditioned reactions to verbal stimuli occurred while the direct stimuli were maintained. The details of the hypnotic procedures and aspects of the hypnotic relationship are unfortunately lacking and, though obscured by semantics and different therapeutic orientations, nevertheless seem to be consistent with out clinical observations. Symptom formation which becomes autonomous, like a conditioned response, can be altered relatively permanently by hypnotic procedures and newly acquired conditioned responses involving involuntary behavior can be brought about more readily, when at all possible, in lighter hypnotic states rather than in deeper ones. This is of considerable interest and warrants further investigation in relation to therapeutic application.

In connection with the differences noted between the levels of hypnosis and conditionability, Soviet investigators (Smolenskii-Ivanov, 1955) reported that the latent period of the conditioned motor reactions during light stages of hypnosis varied within normal limits or else somewhat exceeded them, and amounted to 0.8–1.8 seconds. In the deeper stages of hypnosis, it fluctuated from 4 to 10 seconds. This differential is of considerable significance and should be confirmed by more detailed studies and observations. Nevertheless, it has clear implications for therapeutic techniques as well as theory. The writers also reported that in the hypnotic condition, where with the aid of verbal reinforcement, they were able to form conditioned reactions in the form of one autonomic reaction or another, that even such a complex autonomic reaction as the act of vomiting could be elucidated. Thus, with hypnosis, they had the feeling that they could create new conditioned responses with various stimuli and autonomic reactions. One specific observation in this connection was that they felt it was necessary for the patient in hypnosis to know the verbal designation of this autonomic reaction. This is consistent with our own clinical experience in which in eliminating symptoms of pain, organ system dysfunction and the creation or maintenance of states of well being, it is very important for the patient in hypnotherapy to have a clearly defined designation of what the organ system response is expected to be like and to be able to conceive of it. In instances of treating patients with functional bladder disturbances and in a number of cases of functional disorders of the uterus and urethral tract, rapid and permanent relief could be afforded when the patient was able to visualize the designated organs and the response that was being suggested during the hypnotic session. The Soviet authors (1955) concluded in their observations that automatic conditioned reactions formed and consolidated upon verbal reinforcement during hypnosis were found to be maintained from one and one-half to four years.

More in relation to technique, although obviously related to interacting process, these investigators found that the manner in which verbal suggestions were given, particularly the loudness of the voice of the therapist, played a significant role in the effectiveness of establishing conditioned responses. They felt that on the basis of their investigations with a large number of patients that it was essential to revise what they considered to be obsolescent conceptions existing in the field of hypnotherapy and that it was necessary to adopt a more viable method of conducting verbal suggestions, almost always in a low voice. Based on extensive studies, they concluded that the elaborations and consolidation during hypnosis of new conditioned responses can be carried out in light stages of hypnosis. They also observed that these conditioned responses are preserved in the waking state. The latent period of conditioned responses considerably increased during hypnosis in the majority of subjects. They felt that in hypnosis the formation and consolidation of autonomic conditioned reactions was very effective and relatively easily produced when the subject knew the verbal designation of the reactions. In effect, he was able to form new conditioned responses between any given stimulus and autonomic reaction with the sole aid of verbal reinforcement.

In considering the importance of hypnosis on conditionablity, we are obviously dealing with one of the important variables in the modification of behavior disorders. In keeping with Wolpe's (1971) consideration of the use of hypnosis and behavior therapy, wherein he considers behavior therapy to be clearly defined as the application of experimentally established principles of learning to the purpose of changing unadaptive habits, it is clear that the ability to influence conditionability is a prime element in developing a viable system of behavior therapy. Wolpe states that, "Where neurotic responses are conditioned to situations involving direct interpersonal relations, the essence of reciprocal inhibition therapy has been to inhibit anxiety by the instigation of patterns of behavior that express other feelings that are relevant." While the mention of conditionability and the conditioning process have to be redefined and expanded somewhat within the framework of human neurosis and the behavioral modification of such neurosis, it is clear that the ability to alter involuntary mechanisms as well as to bring about new responses which have the strength of a conditioned response, is an integral part of the therapeutic procedure. In this respect, hypnosis would appear under the circumstances which now remain to be delineated as well as defined, a potent and readily available condition for undertaking therapy.

In attempting to synthesize the available data on the effects of hypnosis on conditioning, as well as the limited work that has been done on hypnosis and conditionability, it would appear that the degree to which hypnosis can be utilized in relation to the conditioning process must be based on the nature of the hypnotic or the hypnotherapeutic experience, the means for achieving this, and from both a dynamic and theoretical point of view, the function which hypnosis assumes in that connection. Insufficient attention has been paid in contemporary work with hypnosis as to the function of hypnosis. It has been noted from clinical experience that the function of hypnosis varies according to the role involvement (Kline, 1953), or as Orne (1969) has so clearly stated, the "demand characteristics of the hypnotic situation." In being able to bring about functional alterations in the role that hypnosis plays for the individual, different therapeutic potentialities and outcomes become possible. Without sufficient recognition and structuring of this functional role of hypnosis, such therapeutic outcomes may not be at all possible.

It is difficult, but nevertheless, important, to distinguish between behavior which results from the hypnotic experience and the essential nature of the hypnotic state itself, both subjectively and objectively. Also, there are obvious paradoxes which exist under these conditions. For example, we know that many subjects will act very critically. Not all of their functions are uncritical. The uncriticalness is highly selective. The return to prelogical levels of thinking, to prelogical levels of affective response which may have a dissociated characteristic and lack the ideational integration which we associate with normal consciousness is not a constant phenomena; it is a selective one.

In a report (Kline, 1952) describing primate-like behavior in a hypnotic subject, it was noted that apparent "unlearned" responses could be elucidated in such a state. This led, in later publications (Kline, 1960; 1963), to the theoretical position that studies of the learning and adaptive mechanisms in subjects in deeply regressed hypnotic states reflect a shift in response formation from chronological levels to levels composed of elements of ontogenic regression (Kline 1960).

For example, in a deeply regressed state, the presentation of a dental click will produce in many subjects, erotic arousal which may result in frenzy, resulting in spontaneous orgasm or may lead to involuntary sexual acting out. This is a reaction which has been observed in infraprimates as well.

Hypnotic alterations of consciousness may be considered to fall into two major categories: (1) that which is produced by the particular level of hypnosis achieved by the subject and, (2) that which is produced by the hypnotic instrumentation being employed, and this relates to the function of the hypnosis and particularly to the function of the hypnotic relationship. Hypnosis is clearly neither a simple nor singular reaction, but rather a compactly agglutinated state within which stimulus function may become radically altered and reality mechanisms become more flexible and capable of multifunctional transformation. Perceptual constancy may be replaced by a multiplicity of perceptual organizing devices. For this reason, present day finding and observation with hypnosis may contain seemingly paradoxical and conflicting results.

The often expressed idea that everything observed or produced on a hypnotic level can be observed or produced on a nonhypnotic level is both true and meaningless, unless one can establish definitive criteria for what constitutes hypnotic and nonhypnotic. We can differentiate between the deliberate induction of the hypnotic state and the state in which no deliberate induction has been made. But, this does not rule out the presence of a hypnotic process, either spontaneously or indirectly.

The acceptance of hypnotically induced behavior would appear dynamically to be consistent with the implication that hypnosis involves a degree of self exclusion and the capacity to accept subjective responses without the necessity for critical evaluation by the self. This may permit the structuring of hypnotic perception and behavior on a pre-logical level which would be consistent with greater interaction with the process of conditionability.

In considering the total dynamics that may be involved in creating the hypnotic basis for altering both the existence of certain involuntary or conditioned responses and allowing for accessibility to newly acquired conditioned responses it is essential to consider the fact that the form or level of hypnotic interaction that is created in the treatment situation follows the function that has been designated in the interpersonal relationship. Thus, form follows function but that function must be one of the most clearly designated goals in the process of therapeutic communication. Without this basis, the form of hypnosis which evolves can vary from one which permits only relatively simplistic enhancement of suggestibility to one that provides less accessibility than may be present in the waking state.

From the point of view of psychological activity, the basis for the appearance of a functional level of hypnosis that permits accessibility to the conditioning process may be considered as the construction of invariance or the concepts of the self through conservation.[3] (Piaget, 1954.)

Conservation may be equated on a behavioral level as the activating element behind reality appraisal, structuring body image and awareness of self in relation to externalized symbols. In this respect, conservation is the process of logical organization even though it may deal with illogical components. It may well be that much of what happens within the reconstruction-conservation process in hypnosis is very similar to what goes on in the condensation-reconstruction process in dreaming. The process of conservation might therefore be considered as the result of operational reversability. Operational reversability is based upon Piaget's (1957) genetic model of the development of logical structures in the mental development of children and relates to the capacity to manipulate observations through the logical associations of externalized connections as compared with the capacity to deal with observations linked to internalized associations. Response mechanisms relate to modality functions of tension, awareness and the gradations of consciousness as they may be viewed in terms of criticalness and vigilence. Operational reversability in this sense, is a structural process within which congitive and perceptual mechanisms develop and emerge.

Based upon these underlying observations, concepts and implications, the writer has during the past number of years utilized hypnosis in relation to symptom modification approaches in psychotherapy in which the goal has been the direct alteration of focal symptoms in brief hypnotherapeutic contacts, reinforced through the use of self hypnosis and the utilization of audio tape recordings (Kline, 1970; 1972).

For the greater part, patients who have been seen in such treatment sessions are seen only for two or three times with the average time of the treatment session being two hours. The emphasis has been upon the utilization of dissociative and conditioning techniques along with specific training in the utilization of self hypnosis, which as taught, incorporates vivid recall and revivification of the hypnotherapy experience through the use of audio tape recordings. In each instance, specific tape recordings are made for each patient, and are made during the sessions. They are designed to reinforce therapeutic goals and at the same time, to facilitate the use of self hypnosis spontaneously at designated times without having to rely on self induction or formalized induction at all.

A variety of therapeutic techniques have been employed which, for the greater part are based on the use of some degree of dissociation, time distortion and the development of imagery which becomes linked with the therapeutic goal. Each tape recording has been specifically prepared in keeping with the individual needs of the patient and the circumstances surrounding the history and difficulties presented for treatment.

In some instances, a series of tapes are prepared and the proper sequence of utilization is outlined and discussed with the patient. In a number of instances, patients have been seen on only one occasion, but in the majority, three sessions have been more typical. Case illustrations have included problems of insomnia, smoking habituation, a broad range of psychosomatic and psychophysiological disorders, frigidity, impotence, pain and anxiety problems relating to forthcoming surgery and special adaptation requirements in relation to specific organic disorders. Particularly responsive have been problems of obesity and drug dependence.

Brief Clinical Illustrations

A number of patients presenting long histories of psoriasis have been significantly helped and in a number of instances, the psoriasis was completely eliminated by inducing under hypnosis various sensations in each and every area of the body where the lesions of psoriasis have been present (Kline, 1954). The more intense the experience, the more likely the therapeutic outcome. In several instances, following two or three sessions, and with daily use of audio tape recordings, patients have reported that for six to eight months later, sensations of warmth have appeared spontaneously ten to fifteen times a day in each effected area of the body. Frequently, rapid improvement is noted and is continuous and progressive.

In cases of migraine, patients have been taught by touching the painful area of the head to experience a sense of ease and a feeling of lightness and at times, a sensation designated and created by the patient's own description of what to them is the "most normal, comfortable feeling about the head." Frequently, this is tied in with the ability to visualize the self, pain free, and again reinforced through visual imagery and audio tape recordings.

A number of patients with functional disorders of the urethra which had required continuous dilation with minimal therapeutic results were helped within two or three hypnotherapy sessions, by being able to experience the feeling or sensation of dilation which they then could bring about merely by thinking about it in the waking state. Symptomatic improvement occurred within three or four days and in ten such cases that have been followed for a year, there has been no return of the symptom. The sensations of dilation continue to occur spontaneously so long as the patient uses the self hypnosis via audio tape as a reinforcement at least once a day for an average period of four to five minutes.

The function of hypnosis and the incorporation of sensory motor and imagery activity appears to assume the characteristics of "new learning" which effects the conditionability of the acquired symptomatic behavior and leads to rapid and effective improvement through a process which may be linked to or connected with conditioning. The dynamics and mechanisms of this type of hypnotherapeutic procedure and its relationship to conditioning theory demands a great deal more experimental research for a fuller understanding of its substance. On the clinical level, it is quite clear that a viable and rapid means of dealing with a broad range of functional disorders within a brief period of treatment is both possible and, in terms of the durability of the results, justified.

Notes

1. In more recent modifications of this approach, group sessions have been reduced to six with comparable therapeutic results.
2. A modified version of this section entitled, *The Effect of Hypnosis on Condition-ability* is a chapter in "Hypnosis and Behavior Therapy" Dengrove, E. (Ed.), Charles C. Thomas, 1978, Springfield, Illinois.
3. Conservation as a congitive perceptual process is here used in the way Piaget utilized it in his concept of the development of logical structures.

References

1. Barkley, Russell A., Hastings, James E. and Jackson, Jr., Thomas L. Effects of rapid smoking and hypnosis in the treatment of smoking behavior, *Int'l J. Clin. and Exp'l Hypnosis,* 1977, vol 25, #1, 7–17.
2. Bernstein, D.A. Modification of smoking behavior: An evaluative review. *Psychol. Bull.,* 1969, 71, 418–440.
3. Black, S. and Friedman, M. Effects of emotion and pain on adrenocortical function investigated by hypnosis. *British Medical Journal,* 1968, 1, 477–481.
4. Black, S. and Walter, W.G. Effects on anterior brain responses of variation in the probability of association between stimuli. *Journal of Psychosomatic Research,* 1965, 9, 33–43.
5. Black, S. and Wigan, E.R. An investigation of selective deafness produced by direct suggestion under hypnosis. *British Medical Journal,* 1961, 2, 736–741.
6. Crasilneck, H.B. and Hall, J.A. The use of hypnosis in controlling cigarette smoking. *Sth. med. J.,* 1968, 61, 999–1002.
7. Edmonston, W.E., Jr. The effects of neutral hypnosis on conditioned responses in hypnosis. In, Fromm, E. and Shor, R. (Eds.) *Responses in Hypnosis: Research Developments and Perspectives.* New York/Chicago: Aldine-Atherton, 1972.
8. Glad, Wayne R., Tyre, Timothy E. and Adesso, Vincent J. A multi-dimensional model of cigarette smoking, *Amer. J. Clin. Hypnosis,* vol. 19, #2, Oct. 1976, 82–90.
9. Hauser, H., Schwartz, B.E., Ross, G. and Bickford, R.G. Electroencephology. *Clin. Neurophysiol.,* 1964, 17, 454. Cited by Judith A. Ulett and T.M. Itil, Quantitative electroencephalogram in smoking and smoking deprivation. *Science,* 1969, 164, 969–970.
10. Kline, M.V. A note on primate-like behavior induced through hypnosis: A case report. *Journal of Genetic Psychology,* 1952, 81, 125–131.
11. Kline, M.V. Hypnotic retrogression: A neuropsychological theory of age regression and progression. *J. Clin. and Exp'l Hypnosis,* 1953, 1, 21–28.
12. Kline, M.V. Psoriasis and hypnotherapy: A case report. *Journal of Clinical and Experimental Hypnosis,* 1954, 2, (4), 318–322.
13. Kline, M.V. Soviet and western trends in hypnosis research. *International Journal of Parapsychology,* 1959, 1, 89–105.
14. Kline, M.V. Hypnotic age regression and psychotherapy: Clinical and theoretical observations. *International Journal of Clinical and Experimental Hypnosis,* 1960, 8, (1), 17–35.
15. Kline, M.V. (Ed.) *The Nature of Hypnosis: Contemporary Theoretical Approaches.* New York: The Institute for Research in Hypnosis and the Postgraduate Center for Psychotherapy, 1961.

16. Kline, M.V. (Ed.) *Clinical Correlations of Experimental Hypnosis*. Springfield, Ill.: Charles C. Thomas, 1963.
17. Kline, M.V. Hypnotherapy. In Wolman, B. (Ed.) *The Handbook of Clinical Psychology*. McGraw-Hill, 1965.
18. Kline, M.V. (Ed.) *Psychodynamics and Hypnosis: New Contributions to the Practice and Theory of Hypnotherapy*. Springfield, Ill.: Charles C. Thomas, 1967.
19. Kline, M.V. Sensory hypnoanalysis. *Int. J. Clin. Exp. Hypnosis*, 1968, 16, 85–100.
20. Kline, M.V. The role of desensitization and homeostasis in relation to the therapeutic gain derived from hypnotherapy. Paper read at Amer. Psychol. Assn., Washington, D.C., August 1, 1969.
21. Kline, M.V. The use of extended group hypnotherapy sessions in controlling cigarette habituation. *International Journal of Clin. Exp. Hypnosis*, 1970, 18, (4), 270–282.
22. Kline, M.V. Research in Hypnotherapy: Studies in Behavior Organization, In Bliz, R. and Petrilowitsch, N. (Eds.) *Akt. Fragen Psychiat, Neurol*. Vol. 11. Basel: Karger, 1971.
23. Kline, M.V. Hypnosis and Therapeutic Education in the Treatment of Obesity: The Control of Visceral Responses through Cognitive Motivation and Operant Conditioning. In Langen, Z. (Ed.) *Hypnose and Psychosomatische Medizin*. Stuttgart: Hippokrates Verlag, 1972.
24. Kline, M.V. and Linder, M. Psychodynamic factors in the experimental investigation of hypnotically induced emotions with particular reference to blood glucose measurements. *Proc. 7th European Conf. Psychosom. Res.*, Rome, September, 1967.
25. Kline, M.V., Wick E. and Sigman, R. Hypnotherapy and therapeutic education in the treatment of obesity. Psychiat. Quart.
26. Maiolo, A.T., Porro, G.B. and Granone, F. Cerebral haemodynamics and metabolism in hypnosis. *Brit. Med. J.*, 1969, 1, 314.
27. Martin, R.D. Reduction of adolescent drug abuse through post-hypnotic cue association. Conseiller Canadien, Vol. 8, number 3, 1974, 211–216.
28. O'Connell, D. and Orne, M.T. Endosomatic electrodermal correlates of hypnotic depth and susceptibility. *Journal of Psychiatric Research*, 1968, 6, 1–12.
29. Orne, M.T. Demand Characteristics and the Concept of Quasi-controls. In Rosenthal, R. and Rosnow, R.L. (Eds.) *Artifact in Behavioral Research*. New York: Academic Press, 1969.
30. Pavlov, I.P. *Conditioned Reflexes*. London: Oxford University Press, 1927.
31. Pen, R.M. and Dzhagarov, M.P. The formation of conditioned connections during hypnotic sleep. *Arkh. Biol. Nauk*. 1936, 9, (1–2).
32. Piaget, J. *The Construction of Reality in the Child*. New York: Basic Books, 1954.
33. Piaget, J. *Logic and Psychology*. New York: Basic Books, 1957.
34. Plapp, J.M. and Edmonston, W.E., Jr. Extinction of a conditioned motor response following hypnosis. *Journal of Abnor. and Social Psychology*, 1965, 70, 378–382.
35. Sanders, Shirley. Mutual group in smoking, *Amer. J. Clin. Hypnosis*, vol. 20, #2, Oct. 1977, 131–135.
36. Smolenskii-Ivanov, A.G. *Works of the Institute of Higher Nervous Activity*. Pathophysiological series, Vol. 1. Moscow: The Academy of Sciences of the U.S.S.R., 1955.

37. Stanton, H.E. A one session hypnotherapy approach to modifying smoking behavior, *Intern'l J. of Clin. and Experimental Hypnosis,* 1978, vol. 26, #1, 22–29.
38. Ulett, J.A. and Itil, T.M. Quantitative electroencephalogram in smoking and smoking deprivation. *Science,* 1969, 164, 969–970.
39. Wikler, A. Dynamics of drug dependence: Implications of a conditioning theory for research and treatment. *Arch. Gen. Psychiat.,* 28:611–616, May 1973.
40. Wolpe, J. The use of hypnosis in behavior therapy. Paper presented at the 1971 meeting of the American Psychological Association, Washington, D.C.

Chapter 17

THE TRANSCENDENTAL MEDITATION (T.M.) PROGRAM: SELF ACTUALIZATION AS TREATMENT FOR DRUG ABUSE

Margaretta K. Bowers, M.D. and Michael Grossman, M.D.

Margaretta K. Bowers, M.D.

Michael Grossman, M.D.

Dr. Bowers is Clinical Professor of Psychology and Supervisory of Psychotherapy in the Post-doctoral Program in Psychotherapy at Adelphi University. She is a member of Task Force on Meditation, Council of Research and Development of the American Psychiatric Association and is in private practice.

Dr. Grossman is in the private practice of Family Practice and Preventive Medicine in El Toro, California. He has lectured extensively on Transcendental Meditation and preventive medicine and has been a teacher of the Transcendental Meditation Program.

It is paradoxical in modern living that there is increasing technological physical advancement and no parallel increase in personal psychological fulfillment. Anxiety, psychosomatic illness and drug abuse have become more prevalent. The rapid pace of our technological society seems to be directly related to the increase in anxiety. Contemporary society is exposed to more information and overstimulation. The book, *Future Shock* (Toffler, 1970) explains that man must now assimilate information in one month that has taken decades or centuries to accumulate. Stress resulting from the overload of our nervous system causes a disruption of the physical functioning of the body and a mental and emotional instability.

Stress was defined as a specific syndrome by Hans Selye in 1935 (Selye, H., 1956) as "the nonspecific response of the body to any demand made upon it." Selye's term for the stress response, the general adaption syndrome, consists of three stages: the alarm reaction, the stage of resistance and the stage of exhaustion. In the alarm reaction the sympathetic nervous system stimulates the body into the stage of hyperresistance. This situation of hyperresistance to danger or disease is maintained in the second stage until the stress situation is resolved, or else one succumbs to a state of exhaustion, the third stage.

We are bombarded by stressing factors every day. The stresses of modern life are refined and subtle. No longer are tigers and lions running after us; now, our sympathetic nervous system is stimulated in traffic jams, by noise, sarcastic remarks, daily pressures at work or school, and family life. Although the so-called fight or flight reaction still occurs, we cannot act on our impulses.

We suppress the fight or flight reaction, but chemical, physiological and psychological consequences are not avoided. How many of us carry pills in our pockets—sleeping pills, tranquilizers or stimulants? How many of us can't wait to go for a coffee break? In 1970, the United States drug companies produced 5 billion doses of barbiturates, five billion doses of tranquilizers and 3 billion doses of amphetamines. Two hundred million prescriptions for these drugs were written in 1970 (Bloomfield, H., Cain, M., Jaffe, D. 1975.) How many of us have escaped the consequences of the accumulation of stress in our bodies? Hypertension today is a fact of life, as one third of all adult males in the United States suffer from it. One half of all deaths in the United States are related to heart disease and circulatory problems. The prevalence of other psychosomatic illness in our society is widespread; i.e.,: ulcers, headaches, asthma, migraine, insomnia, and allergies (Bloomfield, et al. 1975).

The major cause of drug abuse, drug misuse and drug addiction is the increasing tension and stress which people try to avoid and eliminate by using tranquilizers, sleeping pills, amphetamines, etc. However, alcoholism is America's most used, abused, and the most destructive drug problem. No other drug has led to more health problems, both psychological and physical.

Second to alcoholism, cigarette smoking is our greatest drug addiction problem. We all know about the detrimental effects of cigarette smoking to our health. Recently younger people are turning to other drugs, such as marijuana, hashish and other hallucinogens, while others are turning to opiates, such as heroin and cocaine in their desperate search for fulfillment (Marcus, J., in Press). This lack in self-fulfillment is evidenced as well by the current statistics of crime and divorce.

Typical medical approaches have not been successful in alleviating the condition of stress and tension that is reactive to the pace demanded by contemporary life-styles.

The Transcendental Meditation (T.M.) program was introduced in Western society as an alternative method to cope with this wide-spreading problem. The T.M. technique is a simple, natural, mental procedure, first taught in the United States in 1959, by Maharishi Mahesh Yogi (Maharishi Mahesh Yogi, 1966, 1969, 1972, 1973, 1975). This technique was first innovated in the most ancient written records known, The Vedas of India. Maharishi Mahesh Yogi taught T.M. to thousands of people each year and as the demand and interest in it grew, he began to train Westerners as teachers of the program. Implementation progressed geometrically since. The first U.S. teachers training program was in 1965; the number of people meditating has increased in 1965 to over a million by 1975.

T.M.'s appeal and success is related to the simplicity of the procedure. It is not a belief system, a system of dieting or postures. It is a simple mental technique which makes use of the natural tendency of the mind to allow for the experience of a most profound quietness of mental functioning. Subjectively one experiences a thought at progressively more and more refined levels of thinking, until thinking becomes so quiet, that one experiences being awake without having any thoughts, without thinking anything in particular, an experience of consciousness itself. By contacting this inner area of quietness, many profound physiological and psychological changes are effected. People practice T.M. not solely for the pleasantness of the experience itself, which is practiced 20 minutes, twice a day, but especially because of the considerable effects which linger even while they are active. Studies show that the T.M. technique improves perceptual activity, learning ability, memory, and job performance (Orme-Johnson, D.W., Donash, L., Farrow, J. 1974) (Kane Hakos, D., Lukas, J. 1974). This technique is suited to people who are striving to be dynamic and actively involved, as opposed to those who withdraw from the world to avoid dealing with problems.

The practice of the technique allows for the experience of progressively quieter levels of thinking, until all thought is transcended, and one experiences awareness without any content. Because of the intimate connection between the mind and body, we can correlate anxiety states, calm states, dreaming states, sleeping states with physiological measurements. Therefore, we would expect to see some corresponding physical changes reflecting this most profound quieting of the mental functioning.

The first scientific studies published on the T.M. technique were in Science in 1970 by Wallace (Wallace, R.K. 1970). They were exciting because they clarified the basic physiology of meditation. Previously only a small number of Indian Yogis or Japanese Zen monks were available for studies. But now, large numbers of easily accessible Americans were eager to further scientific understanding of meditation. (Kanellakos, D., Lukas, J., 1974.) The physiological state produced during T.M. can best be described as a state of restful alertness. The most dramatic physical change is the drop in metabolic rate of about 17%, as compared to the metabolic rate while sitting in a chair with eyes closed. This is a much more profound drop than the slow decrease in metabolic rate during sleep, which usually reaches a maximum 8 or 10%. In T.M., breath rate slows down considerably, cardiac output decreases about 25%, skin resistance increases as spontaneous galvanic skin responses decrease, indicating deep relaxation and a decrease in anxiety levels. Chemical changes in the blood have been noted. Most interesting is that there is a 3-to-5-times-faster decrease in blood lactate during T.M. than occurs during sleep. Lactate has been associated in a number of studies with anxiety states, and individuals who are prone to have anxiety attacks have increased lactate in their blood. Anxiety-prone individuals will respond to an injection of lactate with an anxiety attack. The exact mechanism of this is undetermined, but this observation suggests that during T.M. there are chemical changes in the blood that effectively cause a decrease in anxiety.

While the body is in a very profound resting and relaxed state, the mind (the brain as seen in the electroencephalogram) seems to be in a unique state of restful alertness, unlike the sleeping, dreaming or normal waking state. A sophisticated investigation of the EEG patterns during practice of T.M. was conducted by Banquet. (Banquet, J.P., 1972 and 1973). He used computer spectroanalysis to identify component frequencies in the EEG recording and compare readings taken simultaneously from different areas of the brain. He found that during the first minutes of meditation, alpha waves increase in frequency and amplitude, spreading synchronously from the back to the front of the brain. After about 5 minutes of meditation, synchrony between the dominant and silent hemispheres occurs. Following there is a shift to the slower frequencies (mainly theta patterns) which are totally unlike the theta and delta patterns of drowsiness. Many meditators also show a subsequent stage consisting of synchronous beta waves of nearly constant frequency and amplitude over the entire scalp. In ordinary waking consciousness, brain waves are random in pattern. During T.M. they become coherent in phase and frequency in both hemispheres, with equalization of energy output and amplitude in the right and left hemispheres. Certainly further research is necessary to establish the significance of the brain wave synchrony during T.M., to understand more specifically the physiological and psychological changes that people experience gradually with the practice of the T.M. technique.

A study by Orme-Johnson (Orme-Johnson, D.W., 1973) showed the changes in the galvanic skin response (GSR) to stressful stimuli. Orme-Johnson exposed 8 T.M. practitioners to loud noises while he monitored their GSR, then compared their response to a control group. The meditators displayed rapid GSR habituation. They stopped responding after 11 repetitions whereas non-meditators needed about twice as many trials before they achieved habituation. Also Orme-Johnson found that the T.M. practitioners' GSR came back more quickly to normal with less fluctuations after the stressful stimuli, both indicating a more stable functioning of the autonomic nervous system to stressful stimuli and greater adaptability and resistance to stress.

In the second part of the study Orme-Johnson measured spontaneous fluctuations in the GSR, independent of any apparent external stimuli and found that non-meditators produced about 34 spontaneous GSRs at more than 100 ohm amplitude in about 10 minutes, which is about average for the normal American adult. Meditators produced less than 10 GSR fluctuations in a similar 10 minute time, suggesting that meditators have significantly less anxiety than non-meditators. Then Orme-Johnson taught the controls T.M. and within two weeks after instruction, the fluctuations were down to less than 15 per 10 minute rest period, indicating that the resting level of the sympathetic nervous system activity is decreased within a very short time after starting T.M.

Autonomic stability is most important to medical health. People with a stable autonomic nervous system show less motor impulsivity, more resistance to noise and demonstrate better measures of mental health and less susceptibility to conditioning than the labile person. Autonomic instability may be a predisposing factor to psychosomatic and mental illness. Thus, this study suggests that the T.M. technique allows people to be more adaptive and stable in handling the tremendous amounts of stressful stimuli that are in the environment.

There are several studies of the effectiveness of T.M. in alleviating various psychosomatic illnesses. A study by Drs. Benson and Wallace (Benson, H., Wallace, R.K., 1972) of hypertensive patients who started T.M., noted a decrease in the systolic blood pressure by 10 and one-half points, and diastolic by 5 points after 20 weeks of starting T.M. They expected these changes to increase after longer periods of practicing T.M.

Honsberger and Wilson (Honsberger, R., Wilson, A.F., 1973) studied asthmatic patients who started the T.M. technique and found that 94% showed improvement by air way resistance determination, while 61% of the patients reported improvements subjectively, which were confirmed by their physicians. Other studies are being done, using the T.M. technique as treatment for various psychosomatic illnesses.

Many psychological studies have been performed on practitioners of T.M., concluding that the practice of the technique leads to an easing of psychological disturbance, the development of a mental clarity that is conducive to a natural, gradual growth process. A discussion of these studies is the subject of a recent book by psychiatrists, H. Bloomfield, M. Cain and D. Jaffe entitled, *T.M.: Discovering Inner Energy and Overcoming Stress,* referred to in this paper.

Psychologist Maynard Shelly (Shelly, M.W., 1973) has hypothesized a correlation between man's search for happiness and autonomic arousal. He suggests that happiness and psychological well-being depend on a person's ability to maintain an optimum level of arousal. Hyperarousal motivates the experience of tension; insufficient arousal, the experience of boredom. Shelly describes two kinds of pleasure: quiet enjoyment and exciting pleasure, correlated with increasing arousal. Stress which raises the optimum level of arousal and repeated exposure to stress systematically denies the enjoyment in activity by constantly raising the level of arousal. Deprived of satisfaction in the daily quiet routine, a person seeks increasing excitement which becomes a feedback cycle necessitating an addiction to increasingly fleeting highs, which only leads to further exhaustion, tension and depression. By reducing stress and restoring a balance in the autonomic nervous system, T.M. provides the physiological stability necessary to break this addiction. Shelly had predicted that T.M. allows for increased enjoyment in daily quiet activities by normalizing the brain's optimum of arousal, stabilizing it at a more low, normal level. Shelly tested his theory (Shelly, M.W., 1972) by questioning 150 T.M. meditators and a control group of 150, of the same age and background. Results comparing the average scores of meditators to non-meditators showed meditators to be happier individuals, more relaxed, less sad, experiencing enjoyment more often, seeking arousal as much as non-meditators but avoiding extreme forms of arousal, seeking social contacts as often as non-meditators but spending more time alone, developing deeper personal relationships, and depending more upon their personal resources and less on external surroundings for happiness.

Further evidence that T.M. promotes psychological health has been reported in a variety of studies (Kanellakos, D., Lukas, J., 1974). The studies in different populations using different measurement scales all show similar results.

Seeman (Seeman, W., Nidich, S., Banta, T., 1972) at the University of Cincinnati tested the hypothesis that T.M. promotes self-actualization. Self-actualization as defined by Maslow (Maslow, A.H., 1968) can be described as relatively spontaneous behavior (far more spontaneous than for non-self-actualizing people) in one's life, one's thought, one's impulses, etc. Maslow feels that self-actualized persons tend to live in terms of their own wants, likes, dislikes and values, and are more self-sufficient, assertive and affirming. In Seaman's study they used the Shostiam's Personality Orientation Inventory for measuring the characteristics of self-actualization along with the capacity for intimate contact. The results in just two months of practicing T.M. showed that the meditators improved their mental outlook in comparison with people not practicing T.M. and the increasing, persistent long-range effects have been reported in a later publication (Nidlich, S., Seeman, W., Dreskin, T., 1973).

Orme-Johnson (Orme-Johnson, D.W., 1974) studied 13 members in a drug abuse program at a Texas army base. Seven members learned T.M. and 6 did not. At the study's inception he administered the MMPI (Minnesota Multiphasic Personality Inventory) to all participants. Ten weeks later after one group had learned T.M., he readministered the MMPI to all participants. He found that meditators showed significant decreases in measures of manifesting anxiety, hypochondria, personality disorders, while the non-meditators showed no change during the period.

Doucette (Doucette, L.C., 1972) at McMasters University in Canada noticed that university students practicing T.M. significantly decreased their tension and anxiety when compared to control groups.

Ferguson and Gowan (Ferguson, P.D., Gowan, J., 1974) used two different measures of anxiety as well as the Northridge Developmental scale to measure anxiety, depression, neuroticism and self-actualization. They tested three groups: 31 students prior to beginning T.M., a control group, and a group of 16 long-term meditators who had been meditating about three and a half years. After they tested all the groups, the first group then learned T.M. and they found that after six weeks the new meditators significantly decreased their anxiety scales as well as their depression and neuroticism and increased their self-actualization. The longer-term meditators scored higher positive ratings on each of the scales than the beginning meditators, very suggestive of the fact that T.M. has an accumulative effect which increases as the years of practicing T.M. continue.

In a study by Sheeter (Sheeter, H., 1975) of 80 students at a public high school in Canada, students after 14 weeks of practicing T.M. showed changes measured by the Jackson Personality Inventory, of decreased anxiety, conformity, and increased self-esteem, innovation, energy level, tolerance and creativity. The control groups showed that changes were due primarily to the effect of the T.M. technique itself and not to the intellectual involvement with the theory.

Perhaps the most complete study yet undertaken in the psychological changes of T.M. is under the direction of Bernard Glueck (Glueck, B.D., 1973; Glueck, B.C., 1972; Glueck, B.C. and Stroebel, C.S., 1974, 1975), the director of research at the Institute of Living in Hartford, Connecticut. The Institute has a computerized system to analyze brain waves and has computerized storage records of the daily behavior and treatment progress of all patients. The patients, matched for age, sex and personality, were paired into 1 of 2 experimental groups, one learning T.M., the other learning alphabiofeedback. All the patients received the usual hospital treatment which consisted of intensive psychoanalytically-oriented psychotherapy, group therapy, psychoactive drugs, and a regular schedule of ward activities, including a high school program for younger patients. The T.M. or biofeedback was added as additional treatment for the patient. As of May 1974, 142 patients had started T.M. with a small number starting the biofeedback training. The study is based on the long-term follow-up, and the results are to be published soon in a major psychiatric journal. Most of the patients learned T.M. very easily. The few patients who stopped seemed to reveal that they experienced a loss of their usual symptoms too quickly and the shock of losing their familiar defenses was too frightening, so they stopped. Most of the patients and their therapists reported very positive effects. However, many of the patients involved in the biofeedback eventually stopped the alpha training because they were not able to carry over the alpha control to the normal situation outside the laboratory. The T.M. practitioners found it very easy to practice on their own, once the carefully controlled original learning sessions were over. The alpha-biofeedback was difficult to teach many of the patients. Many needed 30 laboratory sessions before they could learn to control their alpha waves, whereas over 90% of the people practicing T.M. learned to adapt from the beginning of the practice.

The 132 patients who continued to meditate represented a broad cross section of the hospital population, ranging from ages 15 to 55 over a broad range of diagnostic categories. The researchers have not been able to comment upon one category's improvement as compared to another. Rather, it seems to be an across-the-board improvement, which is something that we would expect to find from the earlier physiological changes that have been reported. T.M. is not a specific technique for any particular problem, but a natural deep resting response whereby the body and nervous system eliminate stress and tension.

Sleep is the usual mechanism of eliminating stress and tension, and we do not yet know the exact chemical and psychological mechanisms whereby sleeping rejuvenates us and relieves the fatigue and anxiety of the previous day. Sleep deprivation studies (Freeman, F.R., 1972) show sleep to be necessary for normal functioning. Sleep deprivation causes irritability and irascibility, slurred rambling speech, a drunken-like behavior, and eventually mild psychotic or paranoid symptoms. Sleep is characterized by four stages which indicate a deepening relaxation and unconsciousness. REM sleep, which we know to be the subjective correlate of the dreaming stage, is seen after the deepest stage of sleep. After sleep deprivation there is a compensatory increase in REM sleep in the next night of undisturbed sleep. Also, depriving one of REM sleep, but not of non-REM sleep, produces irritability and emotional instability. Thus it seems that dreaming is a necessary mechanism to release the accumulated psychic and psychologic tensions. During sleep, the decreased metabolic rate which gradually levels off at about 8% corresponds to longer periods of dreaming. This suggests that the deeper the rest, the more normalization of stress occurs. Dreaming may be the mental artifact of this process of stress release.

During transcendental meditation a similar process may be at work. The first thing to happen is the ease with which one begins to think of the mantra, the meaningless sound which is used for its sound or vibrational quality. The deep quiet state of T.M. which is subjectively experienced as a quiet experience of the mantra is repeatedly interrupted by thoughts. The thoughts are variable in intensity and anxiety content. One is taught to allow thoughts to come and go freely. However, often repressed feelings will come into consciousness without overshadowing the quietude of the overall experience.

The partial lifting of the repression barrier may occur during T.M. for several reasons. One theory is that the ideational content of dreams is related to increasing access to the non-dominant hemisphere where repressed memories may be stored. Since T.M. equalizes the energy output and amplitude of brain waves in both hemispheres and also creates a synchronization of the brain waves in both hemispheres, it may allow for the lifting of the repression barrier. The spread of alpha and theta waves from the occipital area to the frontal area may allow the frontal area, which is known to be associated with the faculty of memory, to lift its repression barrier. The hypersynchrony produced by T.M. may result in the inactivation of the higher cortical centers with a concomitant imposition of the basic lessening or idling rhythm from the quiet limbic system. Quieting the limbic system would quiet that basic behavior (the rage, anger, and intense emotional behavior) which would not only explain the autonomic nervous system responses to T.M., but would also explain why intense anxiety, fear and anger is not usually produced by the anxiety-producing repressed thoughts which may come into consciousness during T.M. Also, immense anxiety is not produced because the repressed thoughts come through somaticised and symbolised so the painful content is often not conscious. For example, crying with profuse tears during the 20 minutes of T.M. is not uncommon, yet the meditator usually will not even know why he is crying.

T.M. allows one to easily accept the content of thought, and to learn a detachment which allows the natural processes to dissipate the anxiety of past traumatic experiences. Therefore, the release of stress and psychological anxiety proceeds effortlessly without dwelling on content or analyzing it. This natural process of release of anxiety and tension can be compared to the dreaming process. The quietude of deep sleep seems to be interrupted by the activity of dreams, but as shown in dream deprivation studies, one does not have to analyze dreams in order to have a release of psychic tension. Rather, the act of dreaming seems to be an actual release of psychic tension.

The aforementioned possibilities show that there is good suggestive evidence that the T.M. program is a natural process by which people may become healthier. Just as sleep is necessary for effective functioning, T.M. contributes to increased creativity, self-fulfillment, self-actualization and happiness.

The vast majority of people who start T.M. do not start because they are sick, but rather to experience a fuller life. T.M. is very successful in treating the healthy normal person as seen in studies on creativity (MacCallum, M., 1975), athletic performance (Reddy, M., Bai, J.L., Rao, V.R., 1975), job productivity (Frew, D.R., 1974), perceptual motor performance (Show, R., Kolb, D., 1975) (Pivot, M., 1975) (Blasdell, K.S., 1975) and as shown in the studies measuring self-actualization.

There are, however, a large number of studies showing T.M. to be successful in treating psychologically ill (Glueck, B.D., 1973; Glueck, B.C., 1972; Glueck, B.C. and Stroebel, C.S., 1974, 1975) persons in correctional institutions and drug abusers.

One of the first studies on T.M. in a prison environment was conducted by Orme-Johnson using hard-core addicts (Orme-Johnson, D.W., Kiehlbauch, Moore, Bristol, 1975) at a program in a federal correctional institution at La Tuna, Texas. The frequency of the spontaneous GSR of 12 addicted prisoners was measured. They were given the MMP test before beginning T.M. and two months later their spontaneous GSR was compared with a control group of 7 prisoners. Over the two-month period the spontaneous GSR was significantly less in the regular meditators than in the irregular meditators, and significantly less than the non-meditators. There was a correlation between the decrease in the spontaneous GSR and decrease in obsessive compulsive behavior, as measured by MMPI.

Another study completed at the maximum security state prison institution at Stillwater, Minnesota (Ballou, D., 1975) using the Spielberger Anxiety Inventory, was administered to an experimental group of 64 prisoners and control groups over a 10 week period. Within a few days the meditating group showed significant reductions in both momentary and general anxiety levels.

Their anxiety level also remained at a low point throughout the 12 month study. A high degree of personality change was reported which corresponded with the regularity of meditation and reduction in anxiety. During the 12 months, the prisoners violated prison rules less and participated more in self-improvement and recreational activities. Similar results were obtained in a study of nearly 50 inmates and several staff members who learned T.M. at the Federal Correctional Institution in Lompoc, California (Cunningham, N., Koch, W., 1975).

There have been many studies testing the success of T.M. in eliminating and preventing drug abuse and drug addiction (Kanellakos, D., Lukas, J., 1974; Marcus, J., in Press). T.M., as I have explained, is not a technique specifically to treat drug abuse or any other specific problem. It is a process by which an individual experiences a pleasurable quietness within himself, restructuring his responses to stressful stimuli, gradually carrying that pleasurable state of restful alertness more profoundly into his activities over a period of weeks, months and years, so that life becomes more fulfilling.

A cause of drug abuse—alcohol, cigarettes, tranquilizers, amphetamines, barbiturates, etc., is the increasing need for the outlet of stress and tension. These drugs serve as coping functions in a variety of ways. Some drugs enhance the self image, producing a feeling of self-confidence, self-esteem, and well-being. T.M. is effective in establishing a feeling of self-esteem and well-being by directly contacting an area of quietness and peace within the self, a feeling which carries over into one's everyday life. This seems to indicate that in T.M. the channels of communication with the wellsprings of inner resources are opened and continue to be available to the self. (Bowers, M.K., in Press.)

Some drugs serve as inhibitors of restraints. Drugs, such as alcohol and marijuana, allow previously controlled suppressed impulses to be released without feeling personal responsibility and guilt. In many instances drugs are used for an easing of psychic pain, alleviating the anguish of frustration, loss, and disappointment. T.M. allows repressed thoughts and impulses to be released effortlessly and easily during those 20 minutes of meditation, without anxiety-laden content in them. Thus, one is able to experience intimacy of contact without anxiety in a more productive way than with the use of alcohol, marijuana or other drugs.

A tired depressed person may take an amphetamine; an insomniac may take a sleeping pill; a bored person may experiment with psychedelics. Each person is using drugs to restore his physiological equilibrium and feeling of well-being. Because T.M. naturally restores this equilibrium by reducing stress and maximizing one's ability to enjoy life, it may offer a realistic solution to the problem of drug abuse. Studies using the T.M. program for drug abusers are described in two articles by Jay Marcus "Transcendental Meditation: a

New Method of Reducing Drug Abuse," and "Transcendental Meditation: Consciousness Expansion as a Rehabilitative Technique." *Psychedelic Drugs* (in Press 1975).

One of the first reports on drug abuse (Winquist, T., 1969) concerned the drug abuse patterns of 525 students who practiced T.M. for at least 3 months. Of 111 subjects who regularly used psychedelic drugs prior to T.M., 86% stopped, 14% decreased their use. Half of the regular drug users stated that their use of drugs changed with T.M. because life became more fulfilling. One-fourth of the drug users said that the drug became less pleasurable. One-tenth stated that they no longer desired the drugs. Typical answers to why they stopped using drugs were: "Every part of my life has greatly improved and now I have extreme contentment." "Life after meditation finally became satisfying. I no longer need drugs." "The drug effects interfered with the good effect of meditation." "Now I think dope makes me frazzled and passive." "Drugs have naturally fallen by. I don't try to stop. After awhile I just found myself not taking them anymore."

The authors are quite aware of the annoyance with which the scientifically trained researcher views such anecdotal testimonials. Yet they have repeatedly found similar statements made to them personally by T.M. meditators. Over the course of the past five years they have had occasion to know personally and to be able to watch the ongoing growth of personality and maturity in young scattered immature "hippies" who had been heavy drug users for years and who had just begun T.M. The process is most marked in the teenage group and is especially outstanding in those who have gone on to become teachers of T.M. This is without doubt due to the fact that in their training to become teachers and their twice a year period of 6 weeks graduate study they are permitted much more intensive meditation under skilled supervision. Yet it is still difficult to realize that they have personally experienced that T.M. meditation is more pleasurable than mainlining heroin. Their only complaint has been the need to relocate their personal relationships to find new friends who are equally finding self-realization in T.M.

Winquist's early findings and anecdotal reports led Benson and Wallace to study the drug habits in 1862 T.M. practitioners (Benson, H., Wallace, R.K., 1971, 1972). Individuals in a T.M. teacher training course were asked to recall their drug use and attitude before learning T.M. The average time they practiced T.M. was 20 months.

The results showed that subjects gradually and progressively decreased their use of illegal drugs as the practice of T.M. continued. After 21 months of meditation most had stopped completely. Before starting T.M. about 80% used marijuana and 28% used it heavily. After 6 months of T.M. only 37% used marijuana and 1% used it heavily. The decrease in LSD was even more striking. Before T.M. 48 used LSD with 14% using it heavily. After 21 months only 8% used LSD. Similar changes were seen in the use of barbiturates, amphetamines and narcotics. Of those who continued to use drugs after starting T.M., over half had been irregular in practicing the T.M. technique. All subjects felt that the T.M. technique had been influential in lessening drug use.

Benson and Wallace (1972) noticed comparable changes in the use of alcohol and cigarettes. In the 6 months preceding T.M. 60% used hard liquor and 4% were heavy drinkers. After 21 months of T.M. only 25% took hard liquor and almost none drank heavily. Forty-eight percent smoked cigarettes before T.M., half of them heavily but after 21 months of T.M. 16% smoked and only 6% heavily. A typical example is a 36-year-old housewife who meditated a year. She said:

> "Before I started meditating I smoked cigarettes fairly heavily. Now I don't smoke at all. I quit very easily without any effort and without realizing I was doing so at first, gradually over a year's time. I also drank alcohol at parties. Now I never do, for through meditation I could feel this was damaging. I knew this before, but could not stop when it was socially expected, but after meditating a year I found I could enjoy myself in any social situation without any such crutches." (Otis, L.S., 1974.)

These two studies are subject to certain criticisms. First, the sample is not representative of meditators in general because it consists only of the highly motivated meditators who had gone on to advanced teacher training. Secondly, there was no control group of drug users who did not learn T.M. Thus there is no indication whether the decrease in drug use might not have occurred in a similar group without meditation. Also, the investigators posed questions worded in such a way as to indicate the answers they hoped to obtain. These studies show that drug abuse does decrease greatly among a certain select group of meditators, but it did not provide conclusive evidence to whether its decrease is widespread among meditators, or whether the drug use and personal characteristics of those who practice T.M. were different from other drug-using populations. Also those who dropped out of T.M. and returned to drugs were not included. The high selectivity of the group's makeup does not justify generalizations of similar results in other groups.

There are more recent studies which eliminate these criticisms. In Sweden a study conducted by Eva Brautigam (Brautigam, E., 1975) suggests that T.M. may be effective for hard core narcotic abusers. Through a hospital hepatitis unit she obtained 29 heroin users. (She felt their need to be urgent and offered them T.M. training for treatment of drug abuse.) Upon acceptance they were divided into experimental and control groups. One started T.M. immediately, the other had weekly counseling sessions. The study was initially designed to last six months but there was strong pressure from the control group to begin meditation. After the first 3 months, in view of their request and because the research results from the initial 3 months time were sufficiently clear, all of the subjects were permitted to learn T.M. and members of the control group began to meditate. Prior to the beginning of the study, the average use of hashish was about 20 times a month for both groups. During the 6-month period, the T.M. groups' use of hashish declined to an average of less than once a month in the month following T.M., and gradually increased to about 6 times a month, where it remained stable in the last 3 months. The control group maintained a constant average hashish use of 18 times a month during the initial 3 months of nonmeditating. After they started T.M. they followed the same pattern as the experimental group. With hard drugs the experimental group again declined significantly while the control group increased in drug use. Although not an extensive study, there is indication of a substantial reduction in drug abuse following T.M. The reduction was most substantial among the regular practitioners of T.M. At the end of the 6 months, 6 of the 10 members of the original T.M. group were classified as regular meditators. Their use of hashish averaged 3 times a month, whereas the irregular meditators used the drug about 10 times a month.

The author of the study pointed out that Meditators felt better subjectively within one week of starting the practice. Also Meditators felt the effects of T.M. as integrative and long lasting compared to the fleeting "highs" of drugs.

Shafii, Lavely and Jaffe of the University of Michigan School of Medicine conducted a study (Shafii, M., Lavely, R.A., Jaffee, R.D., 1974) of marijuana use and T.M. in which 187 of 525 meditators in the University of Michigan area were contacted. Of those contacted, 30% reported they were not currently meditating, and were disqualified from the study. Those who answered the initial questionnaire were asked to name people who were similar to them in personal characteristics and circumstances, but did not meditate. Those named served as controls. The final sample consisted of 126 subjects who practiced T.M. from 1 to 39 months, and a control group of 90. The subjects were above average intelligence. Over 98% of the T.M. control group were white, approximately 36% were under the age of 30, and an excess of 67% were college graduates or working for a degree. The meditators and controls were asked whether they had used marijuana during the last 4 years. Of the meditators 69% were users with a mean frequency of marijuana use of 7.6 times per month before T.M. Of the control, 51% were users (average for college students in 1971) and indicated they used marijuana 3.6 times per month. Following T.M. the mean of the meditators fell to 2.8 times per month, while the control group stayed the same. The meditators were classified in groups according to how long they had been meditating. It was found that the longer a person meditated, the more likely he would lower or stop the use of marijuana. In group 1 practicing T.M. from 1 to 3 months, there was a 46% decrease and 23% stoppage compared to 15% stoppage in the controls. In those practicing T.M. from 4 to 24 months there was also a significant decrease in stoppage of marijuana use following T.M. In group 5 practicing T.M. from 25 to 36 months, 69% ceased marijuana use in contrast to 15% cessation in the controls. This group was similar to those subjects in the earlier Benson and Wallace study, and the decrease in marijuana use was comparable.

This research suggests that the difference between the group practicing T.M. from 1 to 6 months and the group practicing T.M. from 13 to 36 months may partly be explained by the fact that the longer term meditating group is composed of more committed meditators. The group of new meditators might experience a dropout rate close to the 30% found in the T.M. initiates who were contacted. Such a dropout rate would probably result in lower drug use for the long term meditators since it might eliminate drug taking meditators.

In addition, the Shafii (Shafii, et al 1974) report indicated a reduction in cigarette smoking in those who had been meditating 13 months or more. Seventy-one percent of those practicing T.M. more than two years smoked significantly less cigarettes, and 57% totally stopped smoking. The control group did not show a change in cigarette use.

Two larger T.M. and drug abuse studies were completed in 1975 and are described below. Of all the drug studies available they are probably the best evidence of T.M.'s value in drug abuse.

In the first study (Katz, D., 1975) a drug history questionnaire was distributed to 269 high school and college students who had decided to learn the T.M. technique, and a control group of 198 matched by age and sex. After T.M. instruction both groups were given questionnaires 3 times in two month intervals. One hundred and fifty of the T.M. subjects and 110 of the control group returned at least one follow-up questionnaire. Drug use was not significantly different in subjects or controls one month prior to the T.M. group learning the technique.

In the first month after learning T.M. the mean use of drugs fell to 3 times per month, while the control group maintained their usual use of marijuana and/or hashish. In the 8 months of the study the T.M. group decreased from 52.7% using marijuana and hashish about 6.5 times per month prior to T.M., to about 30% using marijuana and hashish 3 times per month after T.M. The control group increased from 45% users to 61% at the end of the study.

The results obtained from those using beer, wine and hard liquors prior to T.M. showed reduction in the same direction but less dramatically. However, results indicated the value of regular meditation. At the end of the 8 months study, 20% who were regularly practicing T.M. used liquor once a month. Fifty-one percent of the irregular meditators and 64% of the non-meditators used liquor at least once a month.

The study suggests that students practicing T.M. decreased their use of marijuana, hashish and alcohol; regular meditators decreased their use of these substances more than those practicing T.M. irregularly. Another finding was that those non-users of marijuana who start T.M. are less likely to use marijuana than students who do not start T.M.

A second study was conducted with 76 outpatient drug abusers in the drug rehabilitation center in Germany (Schenkluhn, H., Geislen, M., 1975). T.M. was the primary therapy. The subjects were generally heavy to moderate drug users. Two months prior to beginning T.M. the drug users were as follows: 42 of the subjects used marijuana and hashish; 11 used LSD and other hallucinogens; 10 used amphetamines and barbituates; 5 used opiates. After 12 months of T.M. the number of drug users fell from 89% to 34%. The decrease in the use of cannabis products was 58%, hallucinogens 91%, amphetamines and barbituates 96%, and opiates 78%. The researchers found no significant trends to give up drugs (excluding LSD and other hallucinogens) before starting T.M. The significant but lesser reduction in the use of marijuana was probably due to the fact that its use is accepted and expected in subcultures, just as alcohol and cigarette use are accepted and expected in the dominant culture.

There were definite phases in drug use noted in the above study. At the beginning of instruction in the T.M. technique there was nearly total absence of drug use because of the two-week abstinence period required for proper instruction. In the first four months after T.M. instruction there was a trend towards slightly increased drug abuse. In the fourth to eighth month, drug use lessened and was followed by a constant low level in the 8th to 12th months. This pattern was also found to some extent in the other studies mentioned and may be characteristic of a withdrawal pattern, when the T.M. program is used. Most of the researchers have reported that the more psychologically ill the drug abusers are, the more the drug abusers require extensive follow-up to make sure they are meditating correctly. Also, Dr. Glueck's program (Glueck, B.C., Stroebel, C.S., 1974, 1975) of teaching T.M. to hospitalized psychiatric patients indicates that the patients need more attention from the T.M. teacher. The actual course structure worked very well for normal individuals, normal meaning normal neurotic, anxiety, stress-ridden individuals. But when we have very psychologically sick individuals starting T.M., they still need the basic hand holding that is provided by many therapeutic programs. Thus we see T.M. as an adjunct to all kinds of therapies. One may need psychotherapy, one may need counseling, one may need behavior therapy, etc., etc. One can add T.M. to these therapies and allow T.M. to provide the integrated natural growth of the personality while we hold the patient's hand and help him to function.

The usual course structure to start the T.M. program is as follows:

1. Introductory lecture describes the benefits of T.M. and scientific research.
2. Preparatory lecture describes the mechanisms of T.M. and prepares one to learn T.M.

3. Short personal interview with T.M. teacher.
4. Personal instruction by appointment.

5–7. Three daily group meetings with other new meditators discussing practical aspects of meditating, theory of T.M. and long term changes to look for.

8. Monthly checkups for the first year to insure proper practice continues.
9. Optional advanced lectures—weekly.

Requirements for the course are:

1. Time: One must be able to attend the four consecutive 2-hour sessions in steps 4, 5, 6, 7.

2. Financial: The International Meditation Society is a federally tax-exempt, non-profit educational institution whose purpose is to teach T.M. to as many people as quickly as possible. The organization requires a minimal fee for the T.M. program including the extensive follow-up program; adults $125, college students $65, high school students $55, married couples and children under 14 years $200, junior high school students $35 and children under 10 years, 2 weeks allowance.

3. One is required to abstain from "non-prescription" drugs for 15 days prior to personal instruction since it has been found that these drugs including marijuana and hallucinogens disallow the physiological changes of the "restful alert" state to occur easily and spontaneously and therefore make learning the technique more difficult. Once the practice has been learned there is no regulations about drug use.

The International Meditation Society has set up the Institute for Social Rehabilitation in Fairfield, Iowa, to create a more intensive T.M. course for institutionalized drug abusers and hospitalized psychiatric patients, based on the experience of T.M. teachers in the studies mentioned previously. The programs include: educating the staff about T.M.; frequent contact with the T.M. teacher and frequent checking to verify correctness of the practice; educational tapes to give a thorough appreciation of the personal development which can take place through the T.M. program; contact with the local T.M. center after leaving the institution. The complete T.M. program for institutionalized patients is estimated at $600 per year per client.

Conclusion

The T.M. Program is a method of producing a physiological state of "restful alertness." The regular practice of T.M. leads to permanent changes in physiology and mental health. The scientific research on the T.M. technique only started five years ago, yet in these five years, the research on the T.M.

program has shown more substantial evidence of improving mental health and reducing drug addiction and drug abuse than have most other programs shown in a much longer time period.

Bibliography

1. Ballou, D., "Transcendental Meditation Program at Stillwater State Prison" (University of Kansas, Lawrence, Kansas), *Scientific Research on the Transcendental Meditation Program: Collected Papers*, Vol. 1, Orme-Johnson, D.W., Farrow, J.T. (Eds.), MIU Press, New York 1975.
2. Banquet, J.P., "EEG and meditation," *Electroencephalography and Clinical Neurophysiology*, Vol. 33, pp. 449–458, 1972; Banquet, J.P., "Spectral Analysis of the EEG in Meditation," op. cit., Vol. 35, pp. 143–151, 1973.
3. Benson, H., Wallace, R.K., "Decreased Drug Abuse with Transcendental Meditation: a study of 1862 subjects." *Proceedings of the International Symposium on Drug Abuse*, C.J.D. Zarafonetis (ed.). Philadelphia, Lea and Febiger. pp. 369–376. 1972; Congressional Record, Serial No. 92-I Washington, D.C., U.S. Government Printing Office. 1971.
4. Benson, H., Wallace, R.K., "Decreased Blood Pressure in Hypertensive Subjects who Practised Meditation," Supplement II to *Circulation*, Vol. 45 and 46, October 1971.
5. Blasdell, K.S., "The Effect of Transcendental Meditation Technique upon a Complex Perceptual Motor Task" (University of California at Los Angeles, California), *Scientific Research on the Transcendental Meditation Program: Collected Papers*, Vol. 1, Orme-Johnson, D.W., Farrow, J.T. (Eds.), MIU Press, New York 1975.
6. Bloomfield, H., Cain, M., Jaffe, D., *T.M. Discovering Inner Energy and Overcoming Stress*, Delacorte Press, New York, 1975.
7. Bloomfield, H., and Kory, R., *Happiness: The T.M. Program, Psychiatry; and Enlightenment*, Simon and Schuster, N.Y., 1976.
8. Bowers, Margaretta K., Transcendental Meditation as an Adjunct to Hypnotherapeutic Intervention, *J. Am. Society Clinical Hypnosis*. In Press.
9. Bowers, Margaretta K., Transcendental Meditation as a Therapeutic Modality, a chapter in *Scientific Research on Transcendental Meditation: Collected Papers* ed. by John Farrow. In Press.
10. Brautigam, E., Effect of Transcendental Meditation on Drug Abusers," (University of Lund, Lund, Sweden), *Scientific Research on the Transcendental Meditation Program: Collected Papers*, Vol. 1, Orme-Johnson, D.W., Farrow, J.T. (Eds.), MIU Press, New York 1975.
11. Cunningham, M., Koch, W., "The Transcendental Meditation Program and Rehabilitation: a Pilot Project at the Federal Correctional Institute at Lompoc, California" *Scientific Research on the Transcendental Meditation Program: Collected Papers*, Vol. 1, Orme-Johnson, D.W., Farrow, J.T. (Eds.), MIU Press, New York 1975.
12. Doucette, L.C., "Anxiety and Transcendental Meditation as an Anxiety Reducing Agent," McMaster University, Hamilton, Canada, January 1972.
13. Ferguson, P.D., Gowan, J., "Psychological Findings on Transcendental Meditation," (Paper presented to the California State Psychological Assoc., Fresno, California, 1974).

14. Freemon, F.R., *Sleep Research: A Critical Review,* Springfield, Illinois, Charles C. Thomas Publishers, 1972.
15. Frew, D.R., "Transcendental Meditation and Productivity," *Academy of Management Journal,* Vol. 17, No. 2, pp. 362–368, 1974.
16. Glueck, B.D. March, 1973. Current research on Transcendental Meditation. Rensselear Polytechnic Institute symposium on the Science of Creative Intelligence and Management Science. Hartford, Connecticut.
17. Glueck, B.C. April 12, 1972. A psychodynamic and neurophysiologic assessment of Transcendental Meditation. Presented at the International Symposium on the Science of Creative Intelligence, Fiuggi Fonte, Italy.
18. Glueck, B.C. and C. Stroebel, May 1974. The use of Transcendental Meditation in psychiatric hospitals. Presented at the 127th annual meeting of the American Psychiatric Association, Detroit, Michigan.
19. Glueck, B.C. and C. Stroebel, May, 1975. Biofeedback and meditation in the treatment of psychiatric illness. *Current Psychiatric Therapies.* Vol. 15. ed. J.H. Masserman. New York: Gruner Stratton, Inc., (in press).
20. Honsberger, R., Wilson, A.T., "The Effects of Transcendental Meditation upon Bronchial Asthma," *Clinical Research,* Vol. 22, No. 2, 1973.
21. Honsberger, R., Wilson, A.F., "Transcendental Meditation in Treating Asthma," Respiratory Therapy. *The Journal of Inhalation Technology,* Vol. 3, No. 6, pp. 79–81, November-December, 1973.
22. International Meditation Society, 1015 Gayley Avenue, Los Angeles, California.
23. Kanellakos, D., Lukas, J., *The Psychobiology of Transcendental Meditation, a Literature Review,* W.A. Benjamin, Inc., Menlo Park, California, 1974.
24. Kanellakos, D., et al., *Enlightenment for Ideal Rehabilitation,* Presented at the Third International Conference on Drug Abuse, Liverpool, England, 6 April 1976.
25. Katz, D., "Decreased Drug Use Through the Transcendental Meditation Program" (MIU, Fairfield, Iowa), *Scientific Research on the Transcendental Meditation Program: Collected Papers,* Vol. 1, Orme-Johnson, D.W., Farrow, J.T. (Eds.), MIU Press, New York 1975.
26. MacCallum, M., "Transcendental Meditation and Creativity" (California State University at Long Beach, California), *Scientific Research on the Transcendental Meditation Program: Collected Papers,* Vol. 1, Orme-Johnson, D.W., Farrow, J.T. (Eds.), MIU Press, New York 1975.
27. Marcus, J., *T.M. and Business,* McGraw-Hill Book Co., N.Y., 1977.
28. Marcus, J. "Transcendental Meditation: A New Method of Reducing Drug Abuse," *Drug Forem,* Vol. III, No. 2, winter 1974.
29. Marcus, J., "Transcendental Meditation: Consciousness Expansion as a Rehabilitative Technique," *Journal of Psychedelic Drugs,* (in Press).
30. Maharishi Mahesh Yogi. 1966. *The Science of Being and the Art of Living.* Stuttgart, Germany: Spiritual Regeneration Movement Publications.
31. Maharishi Mahesh Yogi. 1969. On the Bhagavad-Gita: A new translation and commentary. Chapters 1–6. Baltimore, Maryland: Penguin Books, Inc.
32. Maharishi Mahesh Yogi. 1972. Video-taped course on The Science of Creative Intelligence. Tapes available through Maharishi International University, Los Angeles, California.
33. Maharishi Mahesh Yogi. 1970–1973. Video-taped residence course lecture series. Tapes available through Maharishi International University, Los Angeles, California.

34. Maharishi Mahesh Yogi. 1972–1975. International symposia on the Science of Creative Intelligence. Tapes available through Maharishi International University, Los Angeles, California.
35. Maslow, A.H. 1968. *Toward a Psychology of Being.* New York: D. Van Nostrand Co.
36. Nidich, S., Seeman, W. Dreskin, T., "Influence of Transcendental Medication: A replication," *Journal of Counselling Psychology,* Vol. 20, No. 6, pp. 565–566, 1973.
37. Orme-Johnson, D.W., "Autonomic Stability and Transcendental Meditation," *Psychosomatic Medicine,* Vol. 35, No. 4, pp. 341–349, July-August, 1973.
38. Orme-Johnson, Kiehlbauch, Moore, Bristol, "Personality and Autonomic Changes in Meditating Prisoners," (La Tuna Federal Penitentiary, Texas), *Scientific Research on the Transcendental Meditation Program: Collected Papers,* Vol. 1, Orme-Johnson, D.W., Farrow, J.T. (Eds.), MIU Press, New York 1975.
39. Orme-Johnson, D., and Farrow, J., (eds.), *Scientific Research on the Transcendental Meditation Program: Collected Papers,* Vol. I, West Germany, MERU Press, 1976.
40. Orme-Johnson, D., *Individual Life in Accord with the Laws of Nature—A New Paradigm for Social Order,* Presented at the United Nations 5th Congress on the Prevention of Crime and Treatment of offenders, Geneva, Switzerland, September 1975.
41. Orme-Johnson, D.W., "Transcendental Meditation for Drug Abuse Counselors," *Scientific Research on Transcendental Meditation: Collected Papers,* Orme-Johnson, D.W., Donash, L.H., Farrow, J.T. (Eds.), Los Angeles, MIU Press, 1974.
42. Otis, L.S., "If Well-Integrated but Anxious, Try Transcendental Meditation" *Psychology Today,* Vol. 7, No. 11, April, pp. 45–46, 1974.
43. Pivot, M., "The effects of Transcendental Meditation upon Auditory Discrimination" (University of Victoria, Victoria British Columbia, Canada), *Scientific Research on Transcendental Meditation: Collected Papers,* Vol. 1, Orme-Johnson, D.W., Farrow, J.T. (Eds.), MIU Press, New York, 1975.
44. Reddy, M., Bai, J.L., Rao, V.R., "The Effects of the Transcendental Meditation Program on Athletic Performances," (Lal Babadar Stadium, Hyderabad, India), *Scientific Research on the Transcendental Meditation Program: Collected Papers,* Vol. 1, Orme-Johnson, D.W., Farrow, J.T. (Eds.), MIU Press, New York, 1975.
45. Schenkluhn, H., Geislen, M., "A Longitudinal Study on the Influence of the Transcendental Meditation Program on Drug Abuse," *Scientific Research on the Transcendental Meditation Program: Collected Papers,* Vol. 1, Orme-Johnson, D.W., Farrow, J.T. (Eds.), MIU Press, New York 1975.
46. Scientific Research on Transcendental Meditation: *Collected Papers,* Orme-Johnson, D.W., Domash, L., Farrow, J. (Eds.), Vol. 1, Los Angeles, MIU Press, 1974.
47. Seeman, W., Nidich, S., Banta, T., "The Influence of Transcendental Meditation on a Measure of Self-Actualization," *J. of Counseling Psychology,* Vol. 19, No. 3, pp. 184–187, 1972.
48. Selye, H. 1956. *The stress of life.* New York: McGraw-Hill Book Company.
49. Shafii, M., Lavely, R.A., Jaffee, R.D., "Meditation and Marijuana," *American Journal of Psychiatry,* Vol. 131, No. 1, pp. 60–63, 1974.
50. Sheeter, H., "The Transcendental Meditation Program in the Classroom. A Psychological Evaluation of the Science of Creative Intelligence," (York University, North York, Ontario, Canada), *Scientific Research on the Transcendental Meditation Program: Collected Papers,* Vol. 1, Orme-Johnson, D.W., Farrow, J.T. (Eds.), MIU Press, New York 1975.

51. Shelly, M.W., "A Theory of Happiness as it Relates to Transcendental Meditation," Department of Psychology, University of Kansas, Lawrence, Kansas, 1972.
52. Shelly, M.W., *Sources of Satisfaction,* Lawrence, Kansas, University of Kansas Press, 1973.
53. Show, R., Kolb, D., "Improved Reaction Time Following the Transcendental Meditation Technique" (University of Texas, Austin, Texas), *Scientific Research on Transcendental Meditation: Collected Papers,* Vol. 1, Orme-Johnson, D.W., Farrow, J.T. (Eds.), MIU Press, New York, 1975.
54. Toffler, Alvin. *Future Shock.* Random House, New York, 1970. (Paperback edition) Bantam Books, New York.
55. Wallace, R.K., "Physiological Effects of Transcendental Meditation," *Science,* Vol. 167, March 27, 1970, pp. 1751–1754.
56. Winquist, T. "The Effect of the Regular Practice of Transcendental Meditation on Students Involved in the Regular Use of Hallucinogenic and Hard Drugs" (Department of Sociology, University of California at Los Angeles), 1969.

INDEX